Fifth Edition

THE UNITED STATES AND CANADA
A SYSTEMATIC APPROACH

Fifth Edition

THE UNITED STATES AND CANADA
A SYSTEMATIC APPROACH

D. Gordon Bennett
The University of North Carolina – Greensboro

Jeffrey C. Patton
The University of North Carolina – Greensboro

James M. Leonard
Marshall University

For information about this book, contact:
   Sheffield Publishing Company
   P.O. Box 359
   Salem, Wisconsin 53168
   Telephone: (262) 843-2281
   Fax: (262) 843-3683
   E-mail: info@spcbooks.com
   Website: www.spcbooks.com

Copyright © 2011, 2006, 2000, 1996, 1995, by D. Gordon Bennett, Jeffrey C. Patton, and James M. Leonard

ISBN 13: 978-1-879215-52-8
ISBN 10: 1-879215-52-7

All rights reserved. No part of this publication may be reproduced, stored in a retrieval system, or transmitted in any form or by any means, electronic, mechanical, photocopying, recording, or otherwise, without the prior written permission of the publisher.

Printed in the United States of America

7 6 5 4 3 2 1

To Carolyn, Margaret and Jennifer

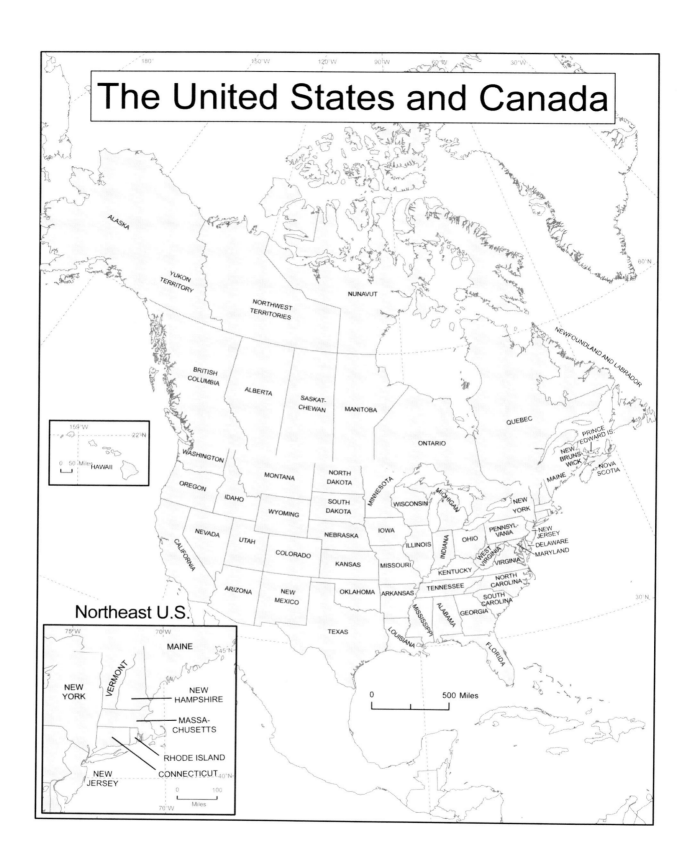

CONTENTS

CHAPTER 1 INTRODUCTION — **3**

    Questions Geographers Ask — 3
    The Study of Geography — 5
    The Use of Maps — 5
    The Region — 7
    The Role of Geography in Everyday Life — 10
    Careers for Geographers — 10
    Review of Introduction — **13**
    Introductory Exercise--Geographic Tools and Techniques — **14**
    Direction, Distance and Location — 14
    Exercise 1 — **17**
        Time Zones — 18

CHAPTER 2 THE PHYSICAL ENVIRONMENT — **21**

    The Making of a Continent — 21
        Plate Tectonics and Mountain Building — 23
    Natural Geologic Hazards — 26
        Earthquakes — 27
        Volcanoes — 30
    Physiography — 32
        The Continental Shelf — 34
        The Coastal Plain — 35
        The Appalachian Highlands — 40
            Karst Formations — 45
    The Interior Lowlands — 46
        Continental Glaciation — 47
        The Great Plains — 48
    The Rocky Mountains — 52
    The Intermontane Plateaus and Basins — 56
    The Pacific Mountains and Lowlands — 58
        The Eastern Series of Mountains — 58
            Mountain Glaciation — 61
        The Western Series of Mountains — 63
            Earthquakes and Transform Faults — 64
        Discontinuous Lowlands Between the Mountains — 65
    The Canadian Shield — 65
    Hawaiian Islands — 67
    Physiography Review — **68**
    Physiography Exercise I — **69**
    Physiography Exercise II — **75**

CHAPTER 3 WEATHER, CLIMATE, VEGETATION AND SOILS — 81

- Weather and Climate — 81
  - Air Masses — 81
  - Atmospheric Hazards — 84
    - Hurricanes — 84
    - Tornadoes — 89
    - Thunderstorms and Hail — 91
    - Droughts — 93
    - Floods — 95
  - Global Climatic Change — 96
  - Climatic Regions — 97
    - Eastern and Northern North America — 97
    - Western North America — 98
- Natural Vegetation and Soil Patterns — 100
  - Major Biomes — 104
    - Forests — 104
    - Tundra — 105
    - Grasslands — 106
    - Deserts — 106
- **Weather, Climate, Vegetation and Soils Review — 107**
- **Weather, Climate, Vegetation and Soils Exercise — 109**

CHAPTER 4 HISTORICAL DEVELOPMENT SETTLEMENT AND EXPANSION — 115

- The Original Inhabitants: The Native Americans — 115
- European Exploration and Settlement — 118
  - Spanish Claims — 118
  - French Settlement — 119
  - English Dominance — 121
- The Birth and Territorial Expansion of the United States — 125
  - African American Life in the Colonial South — 126
  - Migrant Trails West — 130
- The Birth and Territorial Expansion of Canada — 131
- Early Immigration and Population Growth — 132
  - The Trail of Tears — 134
- Population Change in the United States — 135
  - African American Life in the Late 19th Century — 139
- Canadian Regionalism — 142
  - Heartland and Hinterland in Canada — 144
- **Historical Geography Review — 145**
- **Historical Geography Exercise — 146**

CHAPTER 5 POPULATION — 149

- Population Density — 149
- Natural Increase — 152
- Immigration — 154
  - Immigration Policies in the United States and Canada — 158
  - Internal Migration — 159
  - Westward and Sunbelt Migration — 159
- Culture — 166

Language	166
Race and Ethnicity	169
Religion	172
Poverty	174
Where the Poor Live	175
Who the Poor Are	178
Whites/Non-Hispanics	179
African Americans	179
Hispanics	180
Native Americans	181
The Elderly	181
Children	181
The Working Poor	182
Possibilities of Reducing Poverty	182
Population Review	**183**
Population Exercise	**186**

CHAPTER 6 THE ECONOMIC BASE   **191**

Categories of Economic Activities	191
Agriculture	192
International Trade in Agriculture	193
Farmers and Farm Size Ownership	195
Agricultural Regions	197
Manufacturing	205
Manufacturing Employment Since World War II	205
Industrial Location Factors	207
Changes in Manufacturing Employment and Location	212
Services	215
Economic Base	218
Changes in the American Economy	220
Economic Base Review	**226**
Economic Base Exercise	**228**

GLOSSARY   239
INDEX   249

THE UNITED STATES AND CANADA

A Systematic Approach

Figure 1.1 -- Saguaro National Park near Tucson, AZ. These saguaros are one of the defining species of the Sonoran Desert. Capable of reaching heights of 50 to 60 feet they are the largest North American cactus and under ideal conditions they may live for nearly 200 years. (Courtesy United States National Park Service).

CHAPTER ONE

INTRODUCTION

Geography deals with people in different parts of the earth, their activities, and how they interact with the physical environment. Geography could, thus, be defined as the study of the distribution and spatial interrelationships of physical and cultural phenomena on the earth which give a unique character to particular places. There are many other possible definitions of geography, but no matter which one is accepted, they all suggest that the main interest of the geographer is "location." The geographer's central concern, therefore, is **spatial**.

Questions Geographers Ask

A geographer, then, is primarily interested in the question "**where?**". There are two major types of **location**: absolute (specific) and relative. The **absolute (specific) location** of Chicago can be accurately stated as being 41°49' north latitude and 87°31' west longitude (Figure 1.2). Several associations could be inferred from this information alone. For example, the fact that Chicago is located in the north and in the interior of the continent implies that it has a harsh climate. Anyone who has spent much time there would agree.

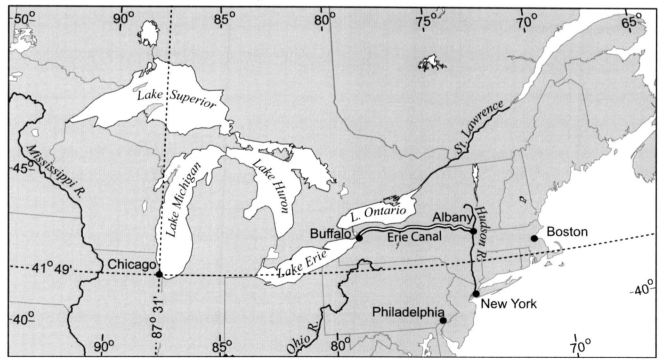

Figure 1.2 -- Finding Locations on Maps

Nevertheless, much more can be inferred from a description of the **relative location** of Chicago. For example, to say that Chicago is located at the southern tip of one of the Great Lakes (with shipping access to the rest of the world), in the heart of the most productive agricultural area of the world, and at the focus of land transportation routes tells us much more about the role of Chicago in the hierarchy of world cities. The relative location, rather than the absolute location, allowed Chicago to become a major manufacturing and transportation center.

Geographers refer to two different types of relative location. These are site and situation. **Site** refers to the physical characteristics of the place. For example, one might describe a city as being built on granite or on alluvial deposits at the confluence of two rivers. New York City's site is a series of peninsulas and islands at the **estuary** of the Hudson, a navigable river emptying into the Atlantic Ocean. This tells us that New York should have a good deep harbor with much coastline, giving it access both to other countries by ocean trade routes and to the interior by way of the Hudson River. But, this site does not differ radically from those of Boston or Philadelphia. New Orleans, on the other hand, has a poor site below the level of the Mississippi River, which surrounds much of it. This proved disastrous when Hurricane Katrina hit in 2005.

Why, then, is New York such a dominant port? The answer has to do with a change in **situation** which permitted New York City to attain primacy. Situation refers to the location of the place in reference to the area surrounding it--its **hinterland**--and with which it interacts in numerous ways. New York at one time was smaller both as a city and as a port than Boston or Philadelphia. The situation changed with the construction of the Erie Canal along the Mohawk Valley which linked the Hudson River and New York City to the Great Lakes, which in turn were a link to the great breadbasket of the Midwest (the Corn Belt). Thus, the potential New York hinterland was enlarged to include the great agricultural area of the Midwest in addition to the surrounding coastal plain and upper New York state. This did not cause New York's primacy; it permitted it. A series of decisions still had to be made to take advantage of the change in situation. Even though transportation is by different means over different routes, the rest of the cities on the east coast have never caught up to New York in either population or shipping. The site of New York City did not change, but its situation did. New Orleans also has an excellent situation with access into the interior of the nation via the Mississippi River and its many tributaries.

Only on rare occasions does the site of a town or business change. A river might change its course to a position farther from a city or a severe earthquake might suddenly shift a place a few feet. While sites typically remain stationary, their situation can, and often does, change, as in the case of New York City.

A change in situation can also affect a much smaller area, such as when a road is upgraded by building a concrete median or fencing off direct access to adjoining land. Either change might limit direct access to businesses along that road and cause a loss of customers and possibly the ruin of a thriving enterprise. Such changes beyond the owners' control which cause a negative impact are referred to as **wipeouts**. On the other hand, if a major retail store were built near an existing business, causing a great increase in customers, this would be called a **windfall**.

Relative location and specific location answer the question "**where?**" Another question geographers ask is "**what?**"; that is "what is where?". To ask "what?" is to ask about identifying and differentiating characteristics. In what way is one thing similar to or different from another?

Geographers also ask the questions "**how?**" and "**why?**". If geographers can answer the question "what is where?", then they want to know how it got to be there, why it is there, and the importance of it being there. When people ask "what is where?", "why is it there?" and "how did it get to be there?", they are asking geographical questions. The answers to these questions might depend on terrain, climate, people, human activity, or even an infestation of the Asian mosquito.

The Study of Geography

The discipline of geography is both broad in its coverage and integrating in its nature. It brings together aspects of both the social and the physical sciences. Traditionally, it has been divided into physical and human geography. Both subfields attempt to answer the fundamental geographic questions "What is where?" and "Why is it there?"

Physical geographers study the natural environment and are concerned with the characteristics, processes, and distribution of such physical elements as climate, landforms, soils, and vegetation. **Human geographers** deal with the location and distribution of people and their activities, including livelihoods, settlements, political systems, recreation, etc. **Regional geography** is the study of all or most of these physical and human characteristics as they affect, or give character to, particular areas. In other words, these factors are studied within the context of a particular part of the world. The **systematic**, approach encompasses specific topics within both human and physical geography, including population, economic activities, physiography, and climate. Geographers also study **geographic techniques**, such as map design, air photo interpretation, computer cartography, sampling and data collection techniques, and remote sensing.

This book will explore the physical and human factors which combine to create the variety of unique landscapes of the United States and Canada. This region will be examined regarding its physical setting, historical development, population trends, and economic activities. Then, selected major issues and problems will be discussed. Finally, a traverse across the continent will be presented to illustrate the changes a traveler would find in the landscape when crossing from one coast to another.

The Use of Maps

Tens of thousands of years ago on some grassy plain or mountain pass someone knelt down and scratched a simple sketch to show the others in his or her group where game or water or shelter could be found beyond the next hill or rocky outcrop. The date when this first map was scratched in the dirt or its author will never be known. However, we do know that the human activity of translating one's perception of his or her world into a graphic form is one that pre-dates virtually all other forms of written communication and that all cultural groups have developed a mapping tradition. There are many candidates for "the oldest map still in existence"--- a 25,000 year old view of the area around the village of Pavlov in the Slovak Republic inscribed on a mammoth tusk, from Germany a 32,500 year old star map of the constellation of Orion inscribed on an ivory tablet, a 12,000 year old inscribed mammoth tusk unearthed in the Ukraine interpreted as depicting a series of dwellings along a river, from what is now Turkey a nine foot long wall painting dated to 6,200

B.C. that appears to be a plan of the town of *Catal Hyük, or* a 5,000 year old Babylonian clay tablet showing land ownership. Which is the oldest map depends on one's definition of a map. Fundamentally, a map is a spatial surrogate, but are all representations of space maps? The discipline of cartography investigates the process of creating maps, including paper maps, computer displays, or maps formed in the mind. Among other things, the science of cartography is concerned with how maps communicate spatial understanding, how they affect a culture's view of the world, and their function as analytic tools.

Geography has long been associated with cartography since almost everything a geographer studies can be, and usually is, mapped. Until the middle of the 19th century, the geographer and the cartographer were one in the same. Advances in cartography were the same as advances in geography--representation of the earth as a sphere, the determination of the size of the earth, and the discovery and delineation of the major land masses of the earth.

By the early 1800s, with the exception of the polar latitudes, most of the remaining "blank areas" of the globe had been filled. At that time scholars increasingly turned to questions of how people in different parts of the globe lived and how they interacted with their physical environment and with each other within the same area and in other parts of the world. Thus, the modern science of geography came into being. Geographers no longer used maps to simply record new discoveries; now, they used them as analytical tools to formulate theories and to explain complex spatial relationships. In addition to showing the location of mountains, cities, and rivers, maps portray the dispersion of ideas, changes in voting patterns from one election to another, and the degree of environmental degradation. These new demands on cartography were met with a series of new techniques, including the dot map, choropleth shading, graduated symbols, and cartograms (Figure 1.2).

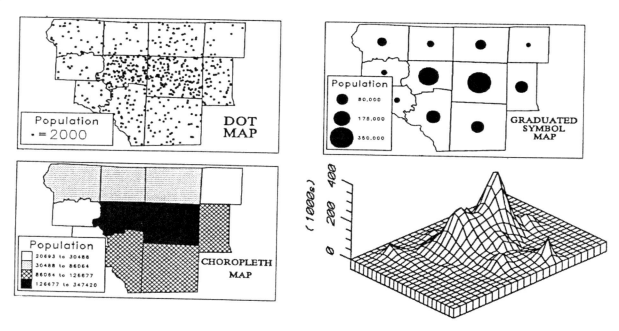

Figure 1.2 -- Four Techniques Displaying the Same Population Data.

Today, with widespread availability of computers, even more powerful techniques are being utilized (Figure 1.3). Geographic information systems, satellite images, global positioning systems, three-dimensional models, animated maps, and virtual reality are the tools geographers utilize for collecting, analyzing and communicating even more complex spatial information. One marvels at the pictures that NASA has provided of Mars or a passing comet, but perhaps the most important images and data that the space missions have provided have been of the earth. In startling detail weather patterns, geologic structures, rain forest depletion, desertification, and the effects of a cruise missile attack are revealed to the geographer and other researchers with the knowledge to use a wide array of satellite and airborne sensors.

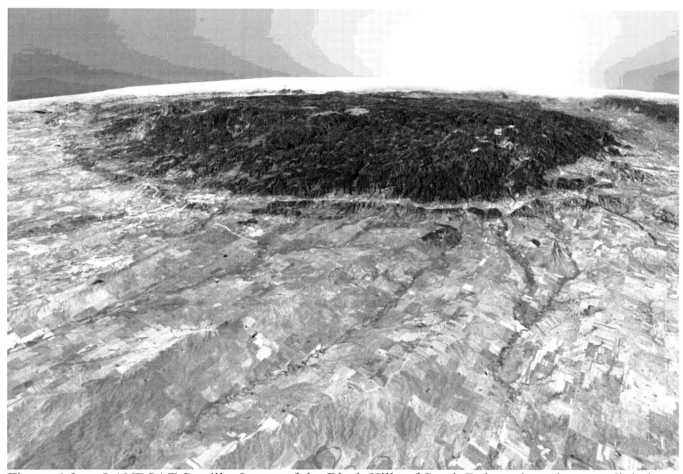

Figure 1.3 -- LANDSAT Satellite Image of the Black Hills of South Dakota draped over a digital elevation model (courtesy the United States Geological Survey).

The Region

Geographers study the location and distribution of many phenomena in the world by asking the questions where, what, how, and why? The purpose of the investigation can be descriptive, analytical, theoretical, or predictive. The means of analysis can be quantitative or descriptive.

Although it is not necessarily the *raison d'etre*, most geographers delineate regions at some point during the course of a geographic study.

There are two main types of regions: formal and functional. Richard Hartshorne defined region as "an area of specific location which is distinctive from other areas and extends as far as that distinction extends." This is what geographers refer to as a **formal region**. It is an area with one or more similar characteristics that can be delineated on a map. A region can be defined by one feature, such as temperature or language, or by many factors in combination; that is, they can be either **single-factor** or **multi-factor** regions. There can be physical regions based on climate, soil, or vegetation or there can be cultural regions based on language, economic activities or other culture traits. Broadly speaking, physical and cultural features can be integrated to determine major culture regions. Two classic attempts at cultural regional delineation were by Wilbur Zelinsky in *The Cultural Geography of the United States* and by Joel Garreau in his book *The Nine Nations of North America*. However, there is a myriad of possibilities, such as on Figure 1.4.

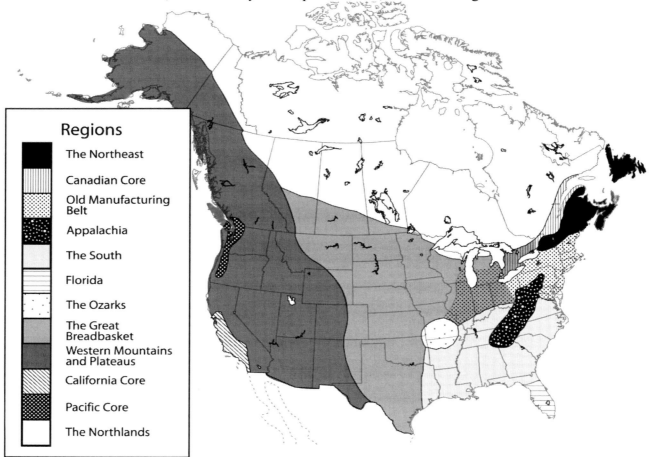

Figure 1.4 -- A Regionalization Scheme for the U.S. and Canada

There is also a kind of region defined by activity or function. It is termed the **functional region**. A functional region is not defined by its internal similarities but rather by an activity or several activities that bind it into an area of functional cohesiveness. For example, a trade area of a city could be delineated by a line enclosing the area from which customers come to shop in the city. This would constitute a single-factor functional region (Figure 1.5).

Many geographers would say that all regions are based on process, and, thus, all regions are functional. They would say it is just that the results of some processes are more durable or static than others, and, thus, such regions seem to be based on similarities rather than on visible processes. In fact, some geographers would say not only that all regions are functional, but that all are based on **nodality**. They would point out that the earth is covered with important **nodes** or points. (A city would be such a node.) Nodes are connected by roads, highways, railroads, power lines, airlines, telephone lines and so forth. People, things, and ideas flow along these connections between nodes.

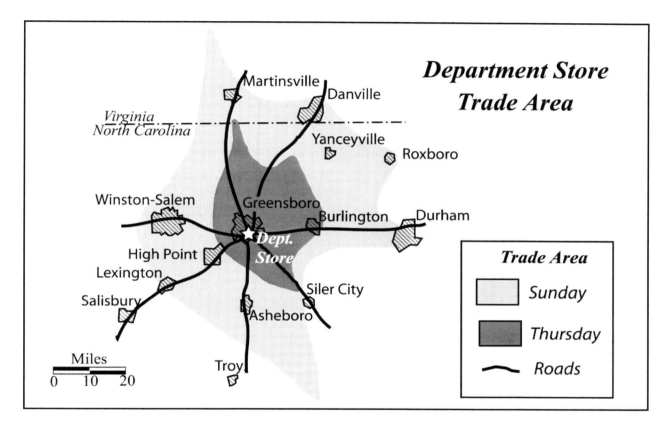

Figure 1.5. Trade Area for a Retail Store

Flows are not random, however, but go up the hierarchy of nodes toward and to the most important, or perhaps the largest, node. These nodes gain at the expense of less important or smaller nodes until the most important become regional capitals. If the pattern and direction of these flows can be discerned, a line can be drawn around the totality of these functions on a map, and a multi-functional (or perhaps multi-nodal) region will have been delineated.

Whether termed formal, functional, or nodal, the delineation of regions is very useful in our comprehension of the world. Regional delineation is not just a theoretical, mental abstraction; it is a concrete means of solving a wide variety of societal and business problems. It is not possible to understand politics, international relations, international trade, sovereignty, sales, marketing, advertising, distribution, and so on without the use of regions.

The Role of Geography in Everyday Life

Anyone who has ever vacationed by car, or tried to find a new store or friend's house in a city, can relate to the necessity of being able to read a map or the utter confusion of not being able to do so. Vacations can be both more enjoyable and more educational when we know how the landforms and cultural features got to be the way they are and why the climate, vegetation and soils are as they are. Maps in news articles and newscasts usually make unfolding events easier to understand and their causes and impacts clearer. The increased use of weather maps in newspapers and on television enable everyone to better comprehend not only what the weather will be, but also why it is going to be that way.

Geography is an integrating discipline which synthesizes information and theory from aspects of both physical and social sciences concerning various parts of the world. Students taking courses in other disciplines often find the linkages among them clarified through geographical inquiry. Even the study of the humanities are frequently enhanced by a geographic foundation in the area conveyed through literature, art, or other means of expression.

Nearly one out of every five Americans moves during any year. When seeking a new place to live, a background in location analysis can result in a more satisfactory residential decision--and usually a more profitable one when selling.

Careers for Geographers

Although geography has gained much attention during the last five to ten years, courses in this discipline in many states have not been adequately integrated into the public school curriculum. The Japanese, Russians, Canadians, Germans and other Europeans generally receive a much more thorough geographic education than is true for most students in the United States. Consequently, not only do U.S. competitors know more about their own country and other lands than most U.S. students and citizens, but they also know more about the United States than do many of its citizens! Hopefully, geographic education will continue to grow in the public schools of the U.S. before its citizenry and its leaders are outfoxed by a better prepared opponent.

Other geographers--particularly those who have specialized in studying other cultures--have found work with the Central Intelligence Agency, the State Department, and intelligence divisions of the armed forces. In an ever increasingly interdependent and competitive world, only those who correctly perceive the thoughts and actions of those who would endanger their nation can make the kinds of decisions that will keep the nation both safe and secure.

During the last two decades, geographers have found jobs in urban and regional planning agencies. As our cities have grown larger, the need to plan for industrial, commercial, and residential development while safeguarding the environment has become crucial. Decisions reconciling the "highest and best use" of the land with the rights of homeowners and the preservation of the environment require planners with broad geographical knowledge. The creation of thoroughfare and comprehensive transportation plans which will move people quickly and efficiently, while minimizing the dislocation of citizens and the damage to natural resources, requires an ability to integrate numerous physical and human factors.

A growing number of persons who combined a geography major with study in communications have been appearing as television weather forecasters. They have learned not only the skills of television presentation but also an understanding of how the weather changes from day to day.

GIScience technology continues to be a growth industry, both locally and nationally. In 2004, the U.S. Department of Labor identified geotechnology as one of the three most important emerging and evolving fields along with nanotechnology and biotechnology. Most government agencies and private organizations that use geographical data either have added or plan to add GIS and related spatial technologies to their operations. Thus, employment opportunities for geographers with expertise in geographic information systems (GIS), remote sensing, and cartography are very strong.

Those geographers who enjoy outside jobs often work as park rangers or surveyors or with hydrologists, foresters, geologists, and so on. Most of these occupations require an in-depth background in physical geography, as well as additional work in an allied natural science.

Geographers interested in population find jobs with the U.S. Bureau of the Census, planning agencies, consulting firms, and commercial and industrial companies. Some combine their demographic expertise with their cartographic or computer skills, while others integrate their knowledge of population geography and related social sciences to study a variety of problems facing this and other nations (Figure 1.6). Others who take additional courses in public health and family planning can work with family planning agencies or the World Health Organization.

Other geographers who have taken courses in economic geography often find lucrative positions in land development companies and other real estate enterprises. Still others apply their study of location analysis and demographic variables to problems of business in identifying future locations of retail stores as well as markets for current establishments. Those with an interest in solving problems in developing countries have taken additional courses in economics. They investigate economic development problems in these lands and suggest possible solutions.

These are just some of the kinds of jobs in which professional geographers are employed. Their key value is their ability to synthesize a wide variety of physical and cultural factors into a meaningful analysis of a particular place or problem.

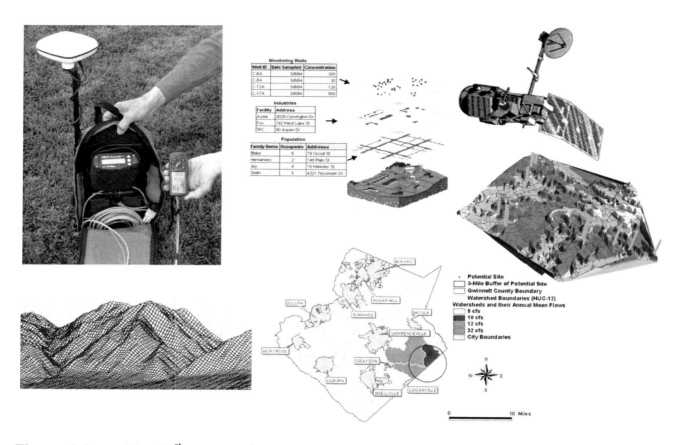

Figure 1.6 -- The 21st century demographer collects data analysis using Global Positioning Systems (GPS) and satellites, analyses data using Geographic Information Systems (GIS)software and uses digital elevation and 3-d models, computer cartography, and animation to display the data. (Images courtesy of the USGS and NASA**).**

Review of Introduction

1. Discuss the main interest and concern of the geographer, including the questions geographers are likely to ask.

2. Discuss the two main types of location in which the geographer is interested.

3. Discuss the main approaches to the study of geography.

4. What is cartography and how has it changed over time?

5. What are the two main types of regions and how are they defined?

6. In what ways can geography be used in everyday life?

7. What types of careers do geographers pursue?

NAME_____

INTRODUCTORY EXERCISE

Geographic Tools and Techniques

The basic tool and technique for solving geographic problems since the time of the Greeks has been the map (including the globe) and mapmaking (cartography). Almost everything a geographer studies can be, and usually is, mapped. In addition to academic geographers, there are millions of other people--probably even you--who use maps frequently.

There are simple maps and complex ones. There are city street, highway, weather, land use, and population distribution maps. In addition, there are maps showing demographic characteristics, agricultural products, minerals, industrial production, housing quality and value, historic sites, and recreational facilities (to name only a few). Some maps are in black and white, while others are in color; some use patterns, while others use symbols. Increasingly, cartographers use computers to more easily display the information that they want to show on a map. One special type of map is the cartogram, which is a map-like representation of a particular idea. Another special kind of map is one of a variety of remote-sensed images transferred to earth from a satellite hundreds of miles above.

Direction, Distance and Location

There are several aspects of maps about which one needs to be aware. The general assumption is that, unless otherwise noted, north is at the top of the map. However, it is still a good idea to indicate north with an arrow unless there are grid lines of latitude and longitude on the map. Since this course involves a discussion of regions and places throughout the United States and Canada, it is important for the reader to be able to determine the specific location of each one before trying to understand the significance of its relative location and the spatial interactions with other places.

Lines of latitude are referred to as parallels. They encircle the earth in an east-west direction parallel to the equator (0°Lat.)--the line drawn around the earth midway between the North Pole (90°N.) and South Pole (90°S.). Parallels measure angular distances north and south of the equator, with the distance between any two being about 69 miles (111 km). (See Figure 1.7.) The equator is the only parallel that divides the earth into two equal parts and, thus, is the only one that is a great circle.

Lines of longitude are known as meridians. They extend from the North Pole to the South Pole, with each one being one-half of a great circle. The one running through Greenwich, England was arbitrarily designated as the Prime Meridian (0°Long.) at an international conference in the mid-1880s when England was the dominant power in the world. The meridians measure angular distances to the east and west of the Prime Meridian. Since they converge at the poles, the distance between any two meridians (degrees of longitude) decreases from about 69 miles (112 km) at the equator to 34.5 miles (56 km) at 60° of latitude to O mile at the poles (Figure 1.7). Movement along any parallel is to the east or west and movement along any meridian is to the north or south.

Estimates of distances between locations with which one is most familiar are often much more accurate than for other places. For instance, St. Louis is approximately equidistant (about 600 miles, or 970 km) from Pittsburgh and New Orleans. Salt Lake City is about that same distance from Los Angeles and Portland, Oregon. On the North America map, draw a circle around your location having a radius equal to the distance from St. Louis to New Orleans (Figure 1.8). Did you realize the distances to these places were equal to one another as well as between the other places shown on the map? Whereas it does not take long to drive between many of these locations, intervening variables, such as mountains, densely settled areas, and the lack of connecting interstate highways, can significantly extend the time it takes to travel. Time is often more important than straight-line distance.

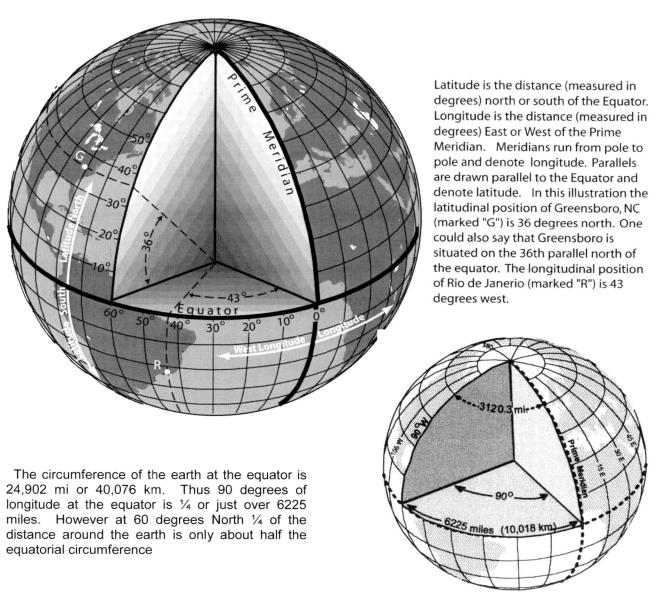

Latitude is the distance (measured in degrees) north or south of the Equator. Longitude is the distance (measured in degrees) East or West of the Prime Meridian. Meridians run from pole to pole and denote longitude. Parallels are drawn parallel to the Equator and denote latitude. In this illustration the latitudinal position of Greensboro, NC (marked "G") is 36 degrees north. One could also say that Greensboro is situated on the 36th parallel north of the equator. The longitudinal position of Rio de Janerio (marked "R") is 43 degrees west.

The circumference of the earth at the equator is 24,902 mi or 40,076 km. Thus 90 degrees of longitude at the equator is ¼ or just over 6225 miles. However at 60 degrees North ¼ of the distance around the earth is only about half the equatorial circumference

Figure 1.7 -- Angles of Latitude and Longitude

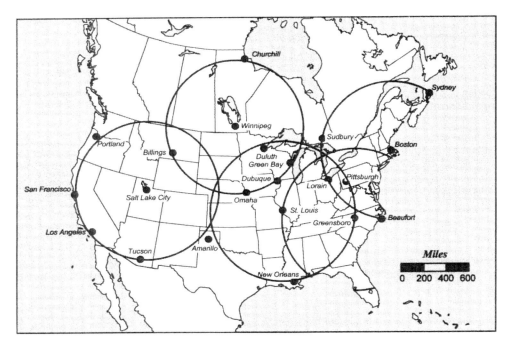

Figure 1.8 -- Lines of Equal Distance

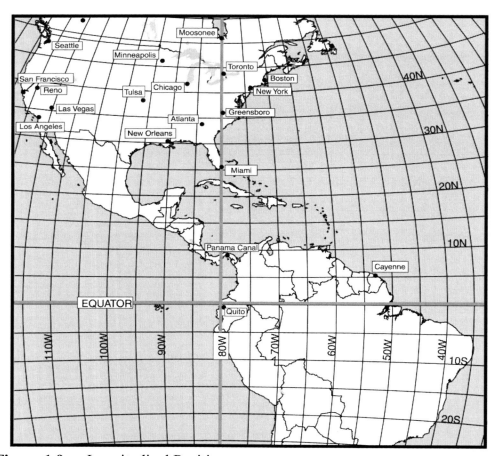

Figure 1.9 -- Longitudinal Position

Exercise Answer Sheet   Name _____

Look at the location of some places in the Western Hemisphere. Compare their latitudinal and longitudinal positions and examine the distances between them (Figure 1.9).

1. Which city is directly north of Miami: Atlanta, Toronto or New York City?

   _____

2. Which is closest to Miami: the Panama Canal, Boston or Minneapolis?

   _____

3. Which is nearest the latitude of Las Vegas: Atlanta, Los Angeles or Greensboro?

   _____

4. The distance between Boston and Tulsa appears to be about the same as from Miami to Quito, Ecuador. How do you know the distance between Boston and Tulsa is less?

   _____

5. Which city lies on nearly the same longitude as Toronto: Atlanta, New Orleans or Quito?

   _____

6. Draw a line east-west and another north-south through Greensboro. About what proportion of the U.S. and Canada is north and south of your latitude and east and west of your longitude?

   _____
   _____

7. Now extend your east-west line to the Eastern Hemisphere (Figure 9). How much of Europe, of Africa, and of western Asia are north of your latitude and how much are south of it?

   _____
   _____

8. If it is 2 a.m. Tuesday in Montreal, what time and day is it in Los Angeles (Figure 10)?

   _____

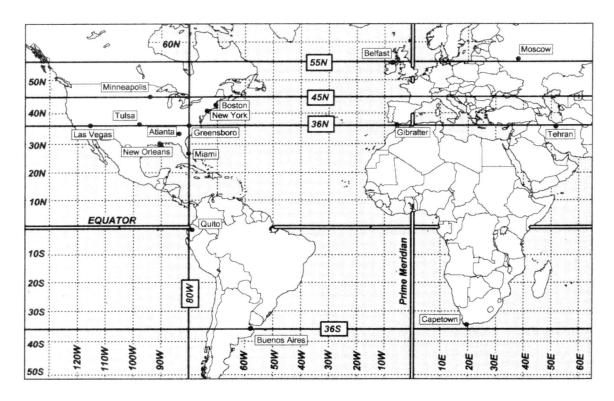

Figure 1.10 -- Latitudinal Position

Any place can be located by using this grid of parallels and meridians. But since the area bounded by any two adjacent parallels and any two adjacent meridians is rather large, more detail is often needed. Therefore, each degree of latitude or longitude is divided into 60 minutes (60') and each minute is divided into 60 seconds (60").

Time Zones

In addition to determining distance and direction, meridians are also useful in determining time zones around the world. Since there are 360 degrees in a sphere and 24 hours in a day, the earth rotates (360/24) 15 degrees every hour. Thus, each 15th meridian from the Prime Meridian is a control meridian for a time zone. (However, not all countries adhere to this scheme.) Eastern Standard Time (EST) in the United States and Canada is controlled by the 75th meridian west, Central Standard Time (CST) by the 90th, etc. When it is 9 p.m. EST, it is 8 p.m. CST; that is, the time zone to the east of where a person is located is an hour later, and the one to the west is an hour earlier (Figure 1.10). In early April, when most of the U.S. changes to Daylight Saving Time, clocks are turned forward one hour as each time zone adopts the control meridian to its east.

In addition to time controls, the day is controlled by the International Date Line, which is approximately the 180th meridian. One of the easiest ways to visualize this is to make a diagram of each 15th meridian with the 0 meridian in the center and the 180th meridian at each end (Figure 1.11).

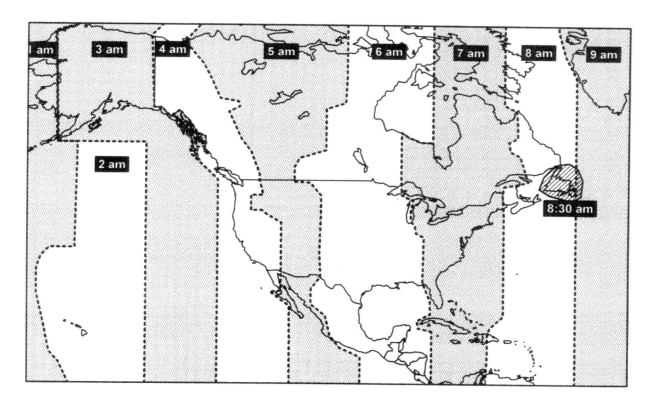

Figure 1.11 -- Time Zones

Figure 2.1 -- Differences in how easily local rock layers can be eroded has resulted in the fantastic "badlands" topography of Bryce Canyon National Park.

CHAPTER TWO

THE PHYSICAL ENVIRONMENT

The Making of a Continent

During the late 1950s and early 1960s, a revolutionary theory was taking form. Known as **plate tectonics**, the theory was based on the concept that the outer shell, or crust, of the earth is broken into a dozen or so large pieces called plates and that these plates are floating upon the partially molten upper level of the mantle known as the **asthenosphere**. Throughout the 1960s and early 1970s, the scientific community argued the validity of the theory. But by the late 1970s, enough evidence had been gathered that all but a handful of scientists had become convinced. The new theory proved to be a powerful tool in reconstructing the geologic history of our planet and the stages of development of the North American continent.

The oldest rock exposed on the surface of North America is near Canada's Great Slave Lake and is nearly four billion years old. That rock is thought to have once comprised part of a large volcanic island, or micro-continent. Beginning around four billion years ago this micro-continent collided with other micro-continents, merging together in a process called **suturing**. By 1.8 billion years ago, virtually all of the earth's land masses were combined into a single supercontinent called **Pangea I**.

After a period of nearly 500 million years, a mass of magma beneath this supercontinent forced it to break apart with the various pieces being carried in separate directions by the molten material. One of these was the ancestral core of North America, called the **craton**. By a billion years ago, however, the various continents had reversed their courses and collided once again forming **Pangea II**. Then, 700 million years ago, this second supercontinent began to break up and move apart.

Less than 500 million years ago, the continents of the Western Hemisphere began to take on the shape as we know them today (Figure 2.2). **Pangea III** formed when the European and African plates collided with the North American plate forming the Appalachians, a mountain chain which would have rivaled today's Himalayas. Then, some 200 million years ago, soon after the rise of the dinosaurs, the super-continent of **Pangea III** began to split apart along the same zones where the pieces had been joined 100 million years earlier, with the various continents moving slowly into the position they are today. This was paralleled by rising sea level and the submergence of all but the highest elevations of North America.

These events were followed by further epochs of ocean raisings and lowerings, mountain building, and numerous erosional processes, including glaciation. Between 80 and 180 million years ago, additional volcanic islands formed and were merged with the main landmass of North America. Then, they were pushed to higher elevations creating the Rockies, then the Sierra Nevada and Cascades, and finally the Coast Ranges. (See BOX 2.1 for a discussion of the relationship between plate tectonics and mountain building.)

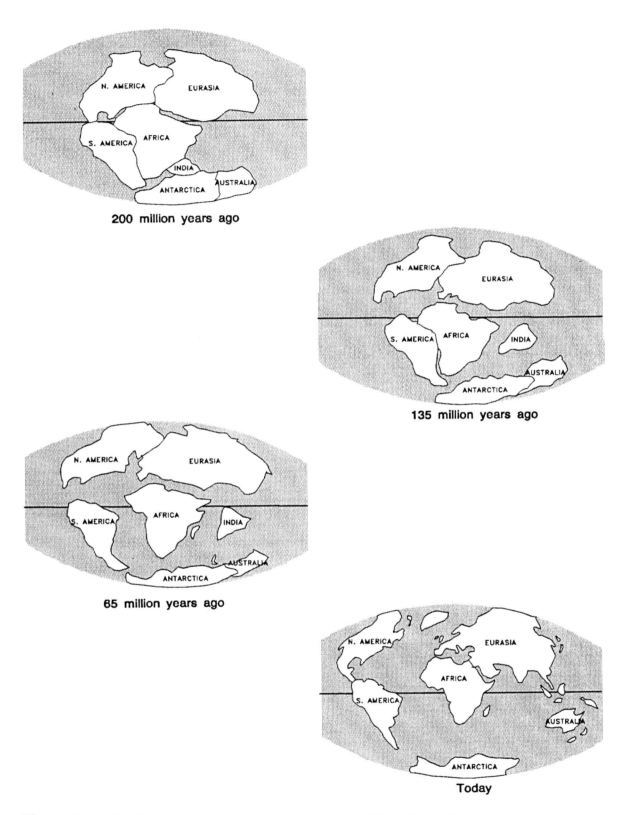

Figure 2.2 -- Continental Movement During the Last 200 Million Years.

BOX 2.1--Plate Tectonics and Mountain Building

The earth is composed of a solid inner core, a molten outer core, the lower mantle, the upper mantle (containing the partially molten **asthenosphere**), and the lithosphere or **crust**. The solid crust encompasses the warmer and more fluid interior layers of the earth like the thin shell of an egg. The earth's shell is broken into 12 or so large fragments and numerous smaller pieces called "plates." On the floor of the world's oceans long linear ridges mark plate boundaries where magma rises from the asthenosphere to form new lithospheric crust. Unequal temperature in the upper mantle is thought to form convection currents in the partially molten magma of the asthenosphere. As the magma moves it carries the overlying lithospheric plates across the earth. Typically the oceanic crust formed at the ridges moves across the earth until it encounters a continental lithospheric plate. The thinner and denser oceanic plate will plunge beneath the thicker, but more buoyant, continental crust in a process called subduction. The down warping oceanic plate will often form a deep trench as the crust slips back into the mantle (Figure 2.3). The friction and the intense pressure from the subduction causes heating, melting and increased buoyancy of the magma so that some of the lightest magma rises to form island arcs in the ocean or mountain systems along the coast on landmasses. The Aleutian Islands of Alaska are a notable example of an island arc formation. Most of the mountains of the Western Unites States and Canada were formed when islands and micro continents were carried from the **Mid Pacific Rise** and pushed up onto the western edge of North America in a process known as **accreted terrane** or **exotic terrane** indicating that the accreted slivers of land were actually formed elsewhere. When two continental plates collide very large mountains can form as the two continents **suture** into one. The Himalaya Mountains are the result India and Asia colliding while the Appalachian Mountains formed from the collision and suturing of North America with Africa and Europe.

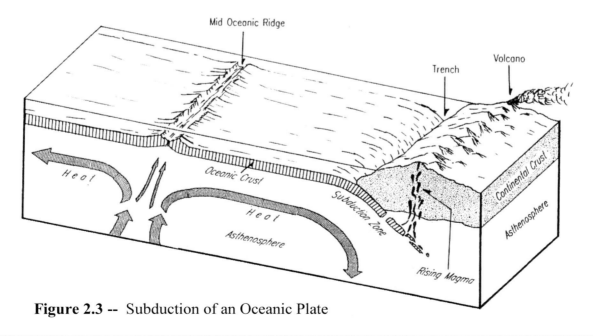

Figure 2.3 -- Subduction of an Oceanic Plate

The movement, collision and destruction of tectonic plates caused the crust to fold and break, volcanoes to rise and jagged rifts to cross the surface while running water, flowing ice and the wind wore the mountains down and filled the valleys with sediment. How these forces played out over millions of years is reflected in the present **physiography** or shape of the earth's surface, in the U.S. and Canada today. The tremendous pressure on previously deposited igneous (rock formed from cooling magma or lava) and sedimentary rocks created a vast metallic mineral wealth (Figures 2.4 and 2.5). Many of the sedimentary deposits left by receding seas have proven to be valuable nutrients for agriculture, while decayed matter from plants and animals under long-term intense pressure has yielded significant deposits of fossil fuels, such as coal and petroleum (Figure 2.6).

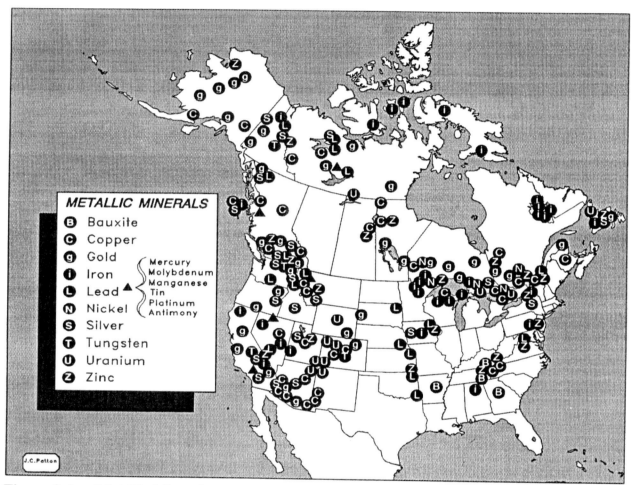

Figure 2.4 -- Metallic Minerals

Figure 2.5 -- The Bingham Canyon Copper Mine in Utah is the largest human-dug hole on the planet, ¾ of a mile deep and over 2 ½ miles wide. Operations began in 1906 and today the mine produces over 300,000 tons of copper a year. Nicknamed "The Richest Hole on Earth," the value of the copper and other minerals extracted from this one mine exceeds that of the Californian and Klondike Gold Rushes combined.

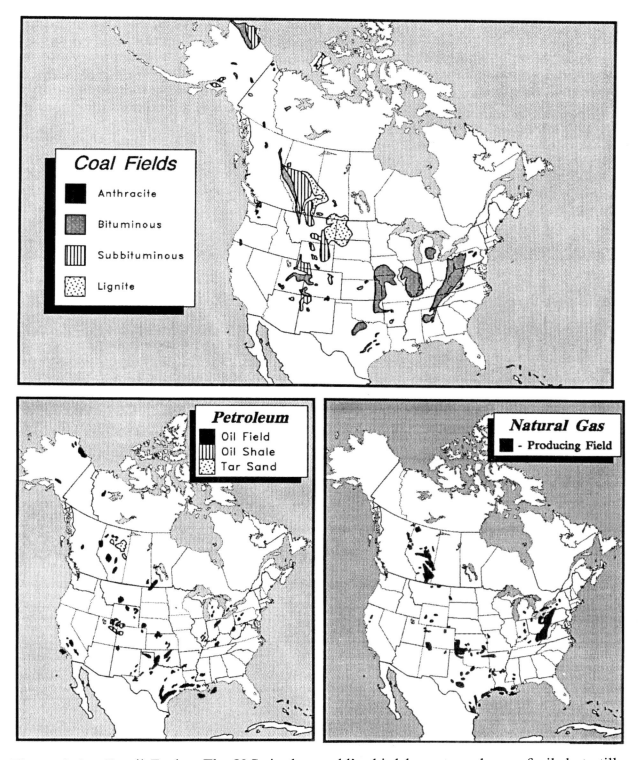

Figure 2.6 -- Fossil Fuels. The U.S. is the world's third largest producer of oil, but still must import 70 percent of what is used to meet domestic demand. The U.S. imports more from Canada than any other country.

Natural Geologic Hazards

Living on a tectonically active planet can be risky business. Earthquakes, landslides, volcanic eruptions, and tsunamis are just some of the natural hazards which result from the restless motions of the earth's great plates. By definition, **natural hazards** are extreme fluctuations in atmospheric, geologic, hydrologic, or biological systems which put humans and their property in peril because of the inability of people to adjust rapidly enough to the threat to safeguard their lives and possessions. Since these catastrophic events are known to occur only rarely, people often dismiss the possibility of these events actually happening to them. Many natural hazards can be avoided, or at least their impact can be minimized. But the **perception** of lack of immediate danger on the part of most people causes them to discount the degree of probability to which they themselves might suffer from such an event. Moreover, they are often attracted to those very locations which are highly susceptible to the occurrence of these extreme fluctuations in the physical environment. In order to minimize the consequences of these natural hazards, people have developed various **adjustments** to these events. These include protective barriers, catchment basins, special building codes, early-warning systems, property insurance, and many kinds of relief and reconstruction programs.

Among the **geologic** hazards, earthquakes have been most severe in coastal and southern California and adjacent Nevada, from Puget Sound north along the Pacific coast of British Columbia and Alaska and across the Yukon to the lower Mackenzie River Valley, from Utah north to southwestern Montana, in the central Mississippi-lower Ohio River Valleys, in eastern South Carolina and along the St. Lawrence River Valley. The sections of the United States in greatest risk of an earthquake today are found in these same general areas (Figure 2.7). Volcanoes have been a threat primarily in Hawaii and the Cascade Mountains.

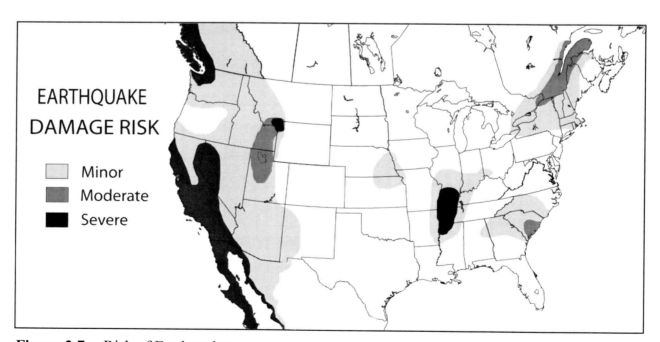

Figure 2.7 -- Risk of Earthquakes

Earthquakes

Most earthquakes are the result of the sudden release of energy from the breaking (**faulting**) and returning to the original shape of rock which has been under great pressure for many months or years as two adjacent crustal plates move toward, away from, or past each other. The **focus** is the location within the earth where the fault occurs and from where the energy is released. Energy in the form of **seismic waves**, is emitted through the interior of the earth as **primary (P) waves**, which travel fast pushing and pulling (compressing and dilating) the material they move through changing both its shape and volume, and as **secondary (S) waves**, which travel more slowly shaking the material they pass through altering its shape but not its volume. The difference in the time of arrival of these P and S waves is used in determining the distance between the recording **seismographic stations** and the **epicenter** of the earthquake located directly above the focus. If distances are computed for three stations and circles are drawn around all three using those radii, then the intersection of the three will indicate the location of the epicenter (Figure 2.8). In addition to P and S waves, there are **surface waves**, which travel over the ground like a wave at sea in an undulating motion. They can cause great damage to buildings, bridges, dams, roads, and other structures.

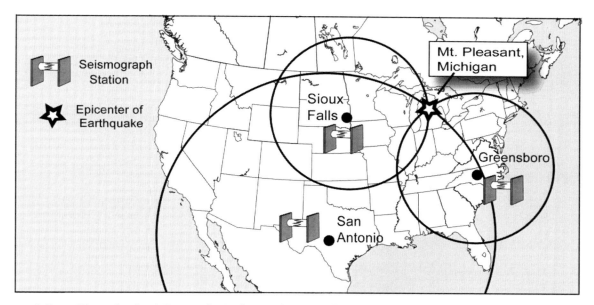

Figure 2.8 -- Hypothetical Scenario Using Triangulation to Locate Epicenter of Earthquake.

The amount of energy released, or the **magnitude** of the fault and earthquake, is measured by the United States Geological Survey (USGS) using the **Moment Magnitude scale** developed in 1979 to replace the 1930's era **Richter scale**. As this scale gives similar values to the Richter scale the popular media often erroneously reports the magnitudes calculated by the USGS as Richter Scale values. Both the Moment Magnitude and Richter scales are logarithmic so that for each increase of one magnitude, the amount of ground motion is 10 times greater and the energy released is slightly more than 30 times greater. Thus, the great Alaskan earthquake of 1964, which registered about 8.5, released more than 20,000 times more energy and created 800 times more ground motion than the moderate 1988 California quake of 5.7. Usually most moderate-to-great earthquakes are preceded by lesser **foreshocks** which indicate a larger quake might be coming and followed by numerous **aftershocks** of lower, but possibly still dangerous, magnitude.

There are several **factors related to the loss of life and property** (Figure 2.9). The most obvious is the death and destruction from cracking and crumbling buildings. Today, newer buildings in earthquake-prone areas are more likely to be constructed based on an earthquake-resistant design. But most people do not live or work in such structures. For many buildings, the composition of the earth material on which they are built can make the critical difference in the degree of damage and resulting deaths and injuries. Soft, unconsolidated material, such as recently emerged sea bottom, loess deposits (silt deposited by the wind), and man-made landfills, are subject to much more shaking than hard, solid material, such as granite. Associated landslides and ground subsidence can cause great damage to poorly constructed buildings on unconsolidated material. The severity, the focus or depth beneath the surface where the quake occurred, distance from the epicenter (the point on the surface directly above the quake), and length of time of the earthquake are also major factors.

Figure 2.9 -- Destruction of the Government Hill Elementary School by the Alaskan earthquake of 1964 (USGS)

Other causes of deaths and property damage include the **tsunamis**. These giant seismic sea waves usually result from the relative raising or lowering of the ocean floor during an earthquake. Because of their lower crests in the open ocean, they can travel nearly unnoticed across thousands of miles of ocean at 200 to 500 miles per hour (320-800 km/hr). As they approach shallow water along coasts, the distance between crests are compressed and their heights are dramatically increased. Though their speed diminishes as they near the shore, these tsunamis can reach 100 feet in height as they hit the coastline. On December 26, 2004 an earthquake off the coast of Sumatra triggered a series of tsunamis that devastated parts of Indonesia, Sri Lanka, Thailand, India, and other Indian Ocean nations. The death toll climbed to over 200,000 and the property destruction will take decades to repair. On March 11, 2011 a 9.0 magnitude earthquake near the city of Sendai, Japan, triggered a tsunami, in places over 30 feet high, that rushed inland engulfing all in its path. The combination of earthquake and tsunami killed thousands of people, left a half million people homeless, caused tens of billions of dollars in damage, and compromised the integrity of the reactors in several nuclear power plants. A short list of North American tsunamis includes: Hawaii 1946 – 151 deaths, Newfoundland 1929 – 27 deaths, Alaska 1964 – 106 deaths, and Puerto Rico 1918 – 40 deaths. In preparation the U.S. and Canada along with the other nations bordering on the Pacific Ocean have developed an extensive tsunami warning system. While warnings are not likely to greatly reduce property damage a fifteen to thirty minute walk inland would have saved most victims of a tsunami.

Major **fires** can also break out as a consequence of an earthquake and cause massive destruction themselves, as was the case in the San Francisco quake of 1906.

It was not the earthquake, but the fire – the great terrible fire – that destroyed pioneer San Francisco. For three days and three nights that awful conflagration swept the stricken city, devouring half a century's fruition of human energy, skill and ingenuity.

Fires broke out in a half dozen places shortly after the earthquake and although our excellent fire-fighters responded promptly to the call of duty, they were greatly handicapped at the very start by the lack of water, many of the mains having been broken by the temblor. Despite the firemen's heroic efforts the fire spread.

The old buildings south of Market and east of Seventh burned like so many boxes of matches, and the people fled before the ravaging elements to the nearest place of safety. Men, women and children, most of them poorly clad, clutching a family picture, carrying some relic, a bundle of bed clothes, a grip or dragging a trunk, hurried away from the scorching flames to what destinations they knew not. They were actuated by but one thought – to get away from the terrible fire.

From the *Organized Labor,* San Francisco
April 21, 28, and May 5, 1906 [Combined edition].

With so much petroleum and natural gas stored in and near cities and their pipelines running throughout the cities, a rupturing could lead to explosions and fires which could wreak great havoc. Finally avalanches, earthslides, mudflows and other mass wasting events can be triggered by geologic forces or local hydrologic conditions, such as the saturation of the subsoil. These events have occurred mainly on the steep slopes of the Cascades in the U.S. and in the Rocky Mountains in both the U.S. and Canada, but have also been noted in other sections.

Earthquakes are a virtual certainty in many parts of the U.S. and Canada but no region is more vulnerable than the Pacific coast, yet millions of people continue to live there (Figure 2.7). With major banking and trade functions of international significance, especially regarding Asia, centered in California, a major quake would not only have serious local consequences but might send financial vibrations throughout much of the world. Scientists know much more about earthquakes today. Safer building designs, earthquake alert drills and emergency disaster planning are much more widely practiced, but no one has devised an accepted reliable means of predicting when, where, and at roughly what magnitude a quake will occur. The 1989 "World Series" 7.1 quake in the San Francisco Bay area which killed over 60 people, injured more than 3,000 and caused over $7 billion in damage was not the "big one" scientists have warned about. In 1992, a 7.0 quake 250 miles north of San Francisco injured only 45 but caused $3.5 billion damage. In 1994, a 6.6 quake in Northridge about 20 miles northwest of downtown Los Angeles killed more than 30 persons and caused billions of dollars of destruction. It is important to remember that earthquakes do not kill people, buildings do. As the world's population continues to grow and to concentrate into large mega cities, such as the Los Angeles Basin and the San Francisco Bay area, the potential for unparalleled loss of life and unimaginable destruction of property only increases.

Volcanoes

Volcanoes are caused by molten magma in the earth rising from the asthenosphere toward the surface instead of cooling and crystallizing below the surface. It escapes through fractures as subdued lava flows or solidifies in the vent blocking the route to the surface. Gaseous pressure builds up behind the obstruction resulting in an explosive eruption.

The most active volcanoes in the United States and Canada are in Hawaii, the most significant being Kilauea and Mauna-Loa. In 1980, **Mt. St. Helens** in the Cascades of the U.S. exploded with such force that the top one-seventh of the mountain was blown away spewing forth an amount of material equivalent to that from the Mt. Vesuvius eruption in 79 A.D., when Pompeii was buried. Though geologists had warned of an impending eruption several weeks earlier and the federal government had established a mandated evacuation area some 57 people died. All, but four of those killed were outside of the federal evacuation zone, as the range of the destruction was considerably greater than predicted.

To the west of Oregon, Washington and British Columbia a small piece of oceanic crust, known as the **Juan de Fuca Plate,** slowly moves eastward before being subducted beneath the westward moving North American Plate. Light gaseous lava forming at a depth of some 40 miles, where the Juan de Juca Plate was melting beneath North America, rose upward through a series of cracks and vents. As it rose it cooled and began to clog the vents it was passing through. By May of 1980, the vent forming Mt. St. Helens was plugged with solidifying lava and the pressure within the mountain unimaginably intense. Just before the eruption, the pressure was so great that the north slope of the mountain bulged out nearly 300 feet (100 m) over a period of ten days. Finally, the rock could not withstand the strain and the north side of the mountain blew out. A hot cloud of gas, dust and rock fragments, known as a pyroclastic flow roared out at a speed of over 200 miles per hour (320 km/hr) and at a temperature hot enough to melt the surface rock. Trees in a 150 square mile (400 sq km) section were knocked over like matchsticks; earth, ash and forest material flowed 50 miles (80 km) downstream; Yakima, Washington, 75 miles (120 km) to the northeast, was covered with ash more than six feet (2 m) deep; and measurable amounts were carried by the winds to the upper

Mississippi Valley and the Ozarks. The eruption of Mt. St. Helens was not an isolated random geologic event, seven of the 20 large volcanoes in the Cascade Mountains of western Canada and the U.S. have erupted during the last 200 years, with Lassen Peak (1914-21) being the most recent until Mt. St. Helens (Figure 2.10).

Predictions by scientists as to whether a volcano will erupt are much more accurate than just a few years ago. An important clue to an impending eruption is increased seismic activity. Rising magma and gasses pulse unevenly toward the surface, this jerky movement through volcanic vents creates a succession of mini-earthquakes. As magma slowly rises these small quakes occur closer and closer to the surface. There is some evidence of a particular rhythmic seismic pattern prior to a major eruption. Another sign of a coming eruption is the creation and expansion of a bulge on the volcano's slope as gasses separating from the rising magma build pressure within the mountain.

Figure 2.10 -- The force of the escaping gas during the 1980 eruption of Mt. St. Helens flattened thousands of acres of forest. (USGS)

With better forecasting of eruptions now available, evacuations of those living nearby is much more likely. Unfortunately, not all volcanic events are comparable. Two volcanoes can give similar indications of a forthcoming eruption, yet only one might produce a devastating explosion. Most volcanic eruptions begin rather slowly allowing plenty of time for nearby persons to evacuate.

It is estimated that fewer than one in 20 volcanic eruptions are of the truly explosive nature as was the 1980 Mt. St. Helens event. Evacuating cities and areas the other 19 times might be viewed as excessively bothersome and costly, but one has to remember that the range of near total destruction in a major volcanic eruption can be 100 miles (160 km) or more.

Physiography

The area encompassed within the U.S. and Canada is slightly over 7.5 million square miles (19.4 mil sq km). The region extends east-west almost half way around the earth and north-south nearly 4,000 miles (6,440 km) and contains approximately 14 percent of the earth's territory, but less than six percent of the world's population. The variety of landforms and features found here are virtually endless: however, they can be divided into several general regions, or **physiographic provinces** (Figures 2.11 and 2.12).

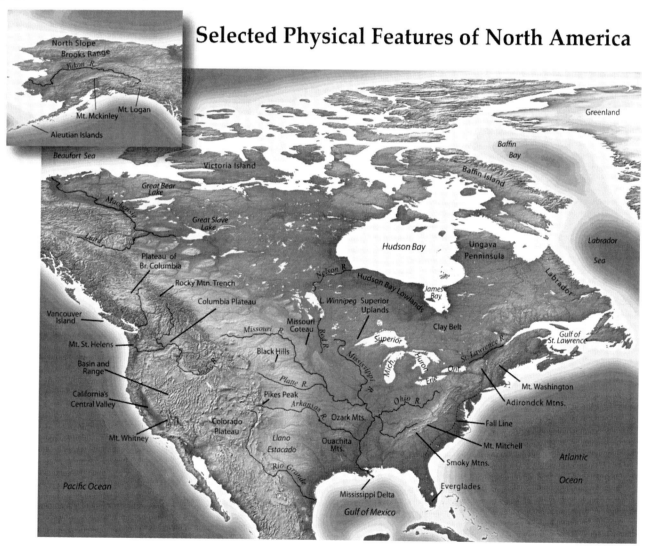

Figure 2.11—Selected Physiographic Features of North America

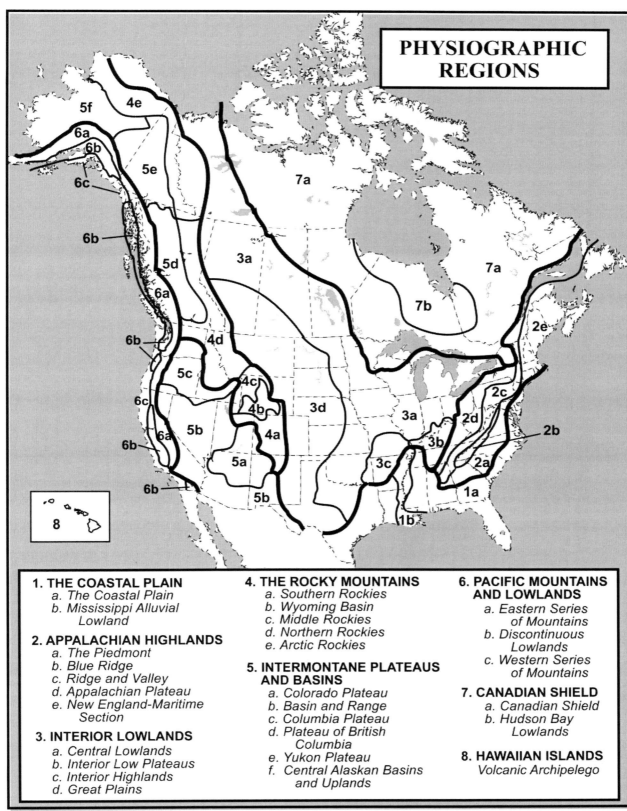

Figure 2.12 -- Physiographic Provinces and Sections

The Continental Shelf

In the south and east, the waters of the Atlantic Ocean and the Gulf of Mexico lap gently onto the nearly imperceptibly slanting coast. The submerged edge of our continent, or the continental shelf, extends to a considerable width over most of the area from Labrador to the Rio Grande before abruptly dropping down to the tremendous depths of the ocean floor. The continental shelf and adjacent Coastal Plain were formed from sediment carried to the sea by thousands of coastal rivers and streams for over 200 million years. The source of the sediment was the towering mountains that formed when ancient North America collided with Europe and Africa along the east coast and with South America along the Gulf Coast. Mountains that may have once reached 20,000 feet high have been eroded to only a few thousand feet, their granite ridges and peaks now the sparkling sand of a summer's beach.

During the Pleistocene (Ice Ages) great sheets of ice, miles in thickness, covered about one-third of the earth's surface. Today, only 10 percent of the world is covered with ice, almost all in Antarctica and Greenland. As the source of water for these continental ice caps was the oceans global sea level dropped by about 100 meters (330 feet) exposing much more of the world's coastal margins. Beginning about 10,000 years ago, as global temperatures rose, the ice caps began retreating relatively quickly and the rising ocean moved inland over the adjacent Coastal Plain. The rise of global sea level was primarily the result of the thermal expansion of the world's oceans and the continual melting of the world's ice caps over the last 10,000 years. It is important to remember that the location of the shoreline is ephemeral, on the flat coastal plain a sea level rise or drop of a few inches can move the shore in or out many miles.

Vegetation is abundant in the shallow waters of the east and Gulf coasts because sunlight can penetrate to the bottom. The profusion of vegetation supports important oyster, shrimp, clam, and fish populations. It is estimated that 80 to 90 percent of all saltwater fish are caught at depths of less than 600 feet (100 fathoms). Ancient vegetation accumulating on the sea floor and subsequently buried by sediment has formed pockets of natural gas and oil. The shallow waters of the Gulf of Mexico have made off-shore drilling particularly easy and profitable. However, as oil companies began searching further off-shore in deeper water the technologic difficulties escalated. On April 20, 2010 an oil rig leased by the British Petroleum Company, the *Deepwater Horizon*, was drilling an exploratory well in water nearly one mile deep when the rig caught fire and sank killing 11 workers and injuring 17 others. The emergency cutoff valve on the wellhead on the ocean floor failed and crude oil began spewing into the Gulf of Mexico. From April 20th until a temporary cap was placed on the wellhead in mid-July, 50,000 to 60,000 barrels of oil per day flowed into the Gulf (Figure 2.13). An armada of skimmers and floating containment booms attempted to collect the oil at sea while hundreds of miles of sand barricades were created to protect beaches, estuaries and coastal wetlands. Despite those efforts the spill caused extensive damage to coastal and marine wildlife habitats as well as fishing and tourism industries. Long term effects on the Gulf and surrounding coast are unknown.

The continental shelf underlying the Gulf of Mexico and the east coast of the United States and Canada is one of the largest remaining North American oil reserves. Despite the risks as crude oil prices rise there will undoubtedly be increasing pressure to open these and other areas to drilling.

Figure 2.13 -- A satellite image of the BP oil spill in the Gulf of Mexico in mid May 2010. In all 4.9 million barrels of oil were discharged into the Gulf making the Deepwater Horizon spill the largest in the history of petroleum exploration. Image from the Terra satellite courtesy of NASA.

The Coastal Plain

Inland from the shoreline, the same unconsolidated rock material comprising the shelf makes up the Coastal Plain This flat, gently sloping, physiographic division extends from the Rio Grande to Long Island and on to Cape Cod and Martha's Vineyard (Figure 2.14). The combination of a world-wide (eustatic) rise in the level of the oceans and the relatively flat topography of the Coastal Plain has produced a series of flooded river valleys called **estuaries.** Most notable of the estuaries formed by the rising water are Chesapeake Bay, Delaware Bay, Mobile Bay, and Albemarle and Pamlico Sounds. The area south of Cape Lookout, North Carolina had few large river valleys to flood, as a result good natural harbors are fewer here than farther north. This is a significant factor related to economic development differentials between the northeast and the southeast coast. Today, human induced global warming has accelerated sea level rise. The prestigious

Intergovernmental Panel on Climate Change (IPCC) concluded that sea level rise would probably fit in the range between 11 and 17 inches by the end of the 21st century, although 23 inches or more was a distinct possibility. In comparison global sea level rose approximately six inches during the previous century. While this may seem relatively modest such a rise on the gentle Gulf and Atlantic coasts would result in the current shoreline moving inland several miles in some areas, extensive shoreline erosion, and the loss of large areas of wetlands. The coast also becomes increasingly vulnerable to the storm surge of hurricanes (Figure 2.15).

Figure 2.14 -- The gently sloping Atlantic shore. Atlantic City, New Jersey

Figure 2.15 -- Rodanthe, NC on the Barrier Islands (Outer Banks). This group of vacation homes shown between arrows A and C were destroyed by beach erosion during Hurricane Dennis. The home marked B is shown to the left. Rapid development and the ever shifting sands of the Outer Banks and other barrier islands makes this scenario increasingly common. Courtesy USGS

From New Jersey to Texas are a series of **barrier islands,** running parallel to the coast. These islands are thought to have been formed during the most recent Ice Age when nearly a third of the world was under a sheet of ice, miles in thickness. With so much of the world's water reserves tied up in ice, sea level dropped considerably. At that time the barrier islands were probably a series of high sand dunes found on the edge of the Coastal Plain. However, as the ice began to melt, global sea level began to rise, flooding the lower area surrounding the dunes and leaving the high sand dunes as isolated islands running parallel to the mainland.

Most barrier islands, including North Carolina's **Outer Banks**, are slowly migrating toward the mainland with which they will ultimately merge. Barrier islands are particularly fragile environments vulnerable to severe damage by storms and the attempts to be developed by man. Their natural state is to be constantly shifting, a reminder that they are ephemeral structures that will last only a blink of geologic time.

During the Pleistocene Era or Ice Ages when sea level was some 200 feet lower than at present the Mississippi River carved a deep valley from what is now southern Illinois to the Gulf of Mexico. As the glacial ice melted and sea level rose the river filled the valley with alluvial deposits of sand, silt and clay. Known as the **Mississippi Alluvial Lowland** this portion of the Coastal Plain physiographic province is the broad alluvial floodplain of the Mississippi River. Running through the center of this otherwise flat floodplain is Crowley's Ridge, a thin ridge some 200 to 500 feet higher than the surrounding plain running for over 150 miles from southern Missouri to northern Mississippi (Figure 2.16).

The Mississippi River system drains approximately 40 percent of the conterminous United States. As the Mississippi River nears the sea it separates into a series of channels known as distributaries. These slow moving channels, known locally as bayou, deposit the "Muddy Mississippi's" sediment in the Gulf of Mexico forming a classic "bird's foot"

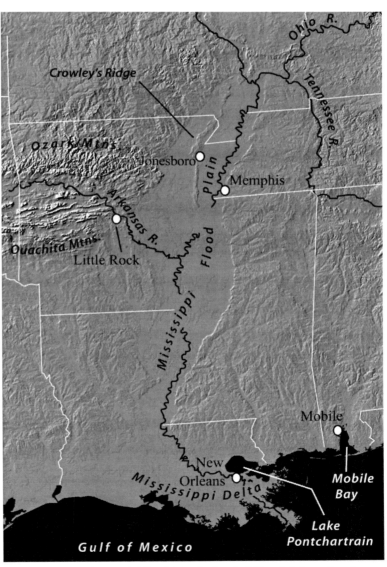

Figure 2.16 -- The Mississippi Alluvial Lowland

delta (Figure 2.17). Due to increased flood control measures, sea level rise, land subsidence, and erosion from hurricanes the Mississippi Delta has been shrinking. Starting in the mid 1950s and continuing to the mid 1970s the delta lost nearly 3,000 acres a year, since then the loss has been about 1,000 acres a year. In all, 70 percent of the land area of the delta that was there in 1932 has now been submerged, and if current rates continue, only 5 percent of the land area of the 1932 delta will be there fifty years from today. Put another way, every 35 minutes Louisiana loses one acre of land!

In an attempt to control the frequent channel shifts and **floods** associated with the Mississippi, the world's greatest system of locks, levees, and dams has been constructed. However, even this was not enough as evidenced by one of the most financially costly floods in U.S. history. The upper Mississippi and several of its major tributaries crested their banks during the late spring and summer of 1993 flooding large tracts of Illinois, Missouri, and Iowa. In order to relieve the rising pressure on the levees protecting St. Louis, the Army Corps of Engineers intentionally breeched the levee system on the Illinois side of the Mississippi River, flooding numerous small towns and thousands of acres of agricultural land.

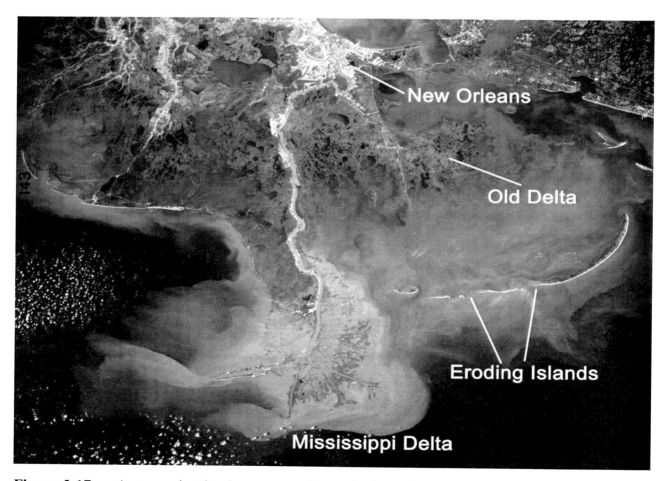

Figure 2.17 -- A space shuttle photograph of the Mississippi Delta south of New Orleans. (Image courtesy of Earth Sciences and Image Analysis Laboratory, NASA Johnson Space Center)

It is important to note that without the complex of dams and levees near Baton Rouge, Louisiana, the Mississippi would have long ago changed its course and followed a shorter route to the sea through the Atchafalaya River Valley. That result would have meant economic disaster for cities south of Baton Rouge that are currently on the river. Most important of these is New Orleans.

Throughout much of the Coastal Plain, **terraces** indicate previous shore lines. The surface material of this area has only recently been formed by the accumulation of sediment deposited by rivers as they flow to the sea. This loose sediment has been **lithified** by the compaction of overlying material and the subsequent cementing by calcium and other natural cements percolating down through the layers of deposits.

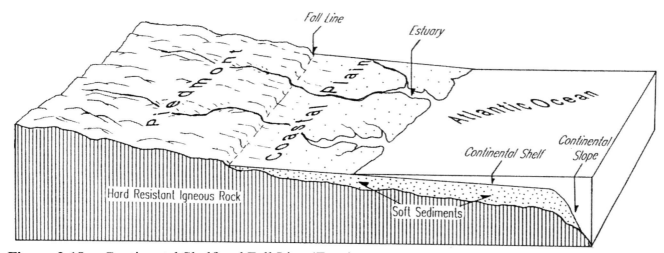

Figure 2.18 -- Continental Shelf and Fall Line (Zone)

Along the interior margins of the Coastal Plain between northern New Jersey and east-central Alabama is the **fall zone**, or **fall line** (Figure 2.18). Here, the softer, younger material of the Coastal Plain meets the harder, older rock of the Piedmont (Figure 2.19). Where rivers cross this zone, rapids and waterfalls are formed by the differential erosion caused by the varying hardness of the underlying rock material. Similar circumstances are also found in other portions of the Coastal Plain, such as near Little Rock, Arkansas.

Since early colonial days, **towns** from Trenton, New Jersey to Columbus, Georgia were established on the banks of major streams along the fall zone. Often the fall line marked the head of navigation on the river, where cargo had to change carriers, and often at the farthest point downstream for easy river crossing. The falls or rapids found here could be used for power in grist mills and later textile mills and other factories. Finally, these sites served as the main commercial outlets for the hinterland of the interior. Major fall line cities include Philadelphia, Baltimore, Washington, Richmond, and Columbia.

Figure 2.19 -- The Falls of the Potomac River is a classic fall line rapids located just upstream from Washington D.C. Here the hard resistant rock of the Piedmont (clearly visible in the upper portion of the photo) meets the soft easily eroded sediment of the Coastal Plain. The potential for water powered mills to locate here was an important consideration in the selection of the area to be the nation's capital.

The Appalachian Highlands

To the west of the Atlantic section of the Coastal Plain are the **Appalachian Highlands**, which trend generally northeast-southwest from Newfoundland to Alabama and include the Piedmont, Blue Ridge, Ridge and Valley, and Appalachian Plateau. About one billion years ago, during the formation of Pangea II, the ancestral Appalachian Highlands were born in the tectonic violence that marked the collision of North America with the African and Eurasian Plates. Five hundred million years later the scene repeated as the Appalachians were once again thrust up to towering heights when North America first collided with Europe in the north and shortly afterwards with Africa along the southeastern coast of what is today the United States. Since the demise of this last super

Figure 2.20 -- Pilot Mountain, NC -- a landmark monadnock of the North Carolina Piedmont

continent the Appalachians have been subjected to 250 million years of relentless erosional forces. The **Piedmont** is composed mainly of very old, resistant metamorphosed igneous and sedimentary rocks that changed their form under extreme heat and pressure over millions of years. These **metamorphic** rocks have been exposed by erosive forces over many centuries, so that the Piedmont has become a gently rolling **peneplain** punctuated by scattered **monadnocks,** the remnants of more resistant rock, such as Pilot Mountain, Hanging Rock, and Stone Mountain in North Carolina (Figure 2.20).

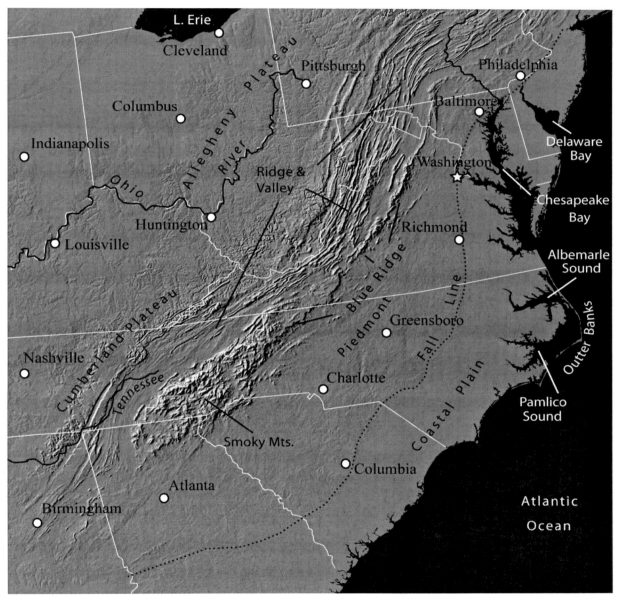

Figure 2.21 --The Coastal Plain, Southern Appalachians and Northeast Central Lowland

Farther west is the **Blue Ridge Province**, which stretches from south-central Pennsylvania to northern Georgia. The Smoky Mountains comprise the southern section of this province while the Blue Ridge Mountains form the northern portion and contain the highest peak in the eastern U.S., **Mt. Mitchell** (6,684 ft, or 2,000 m). This section of the Appalachians was one of the major obstacles delaying the westward movement of the early settlers into the interior of the continent and, thus, causing the concentration of a rather large population along the east coast. Today, the Blue Ridge still acts as a major barrier to transportation between the Southeast and Midwest, with the first connecting interstate highway not being completed until about 1980.

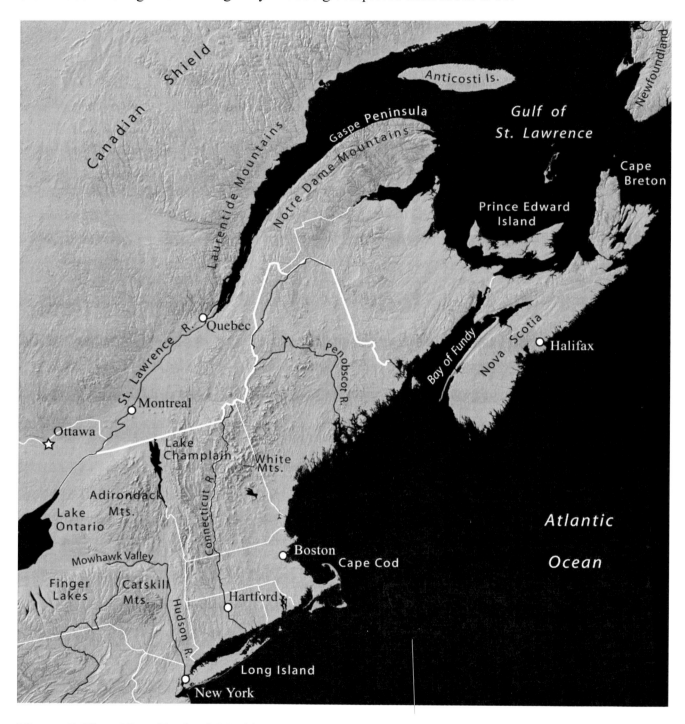

Figure 2.22 -- New England-Maritime Section of the Appalachians and the Adirondacks of the Canadian Shield.

West and north of the Blue Ridge from central Alabama to the St. Lawrence Valley is the **Ridge and Valley**, where parallel ridges of similar heights but different lengths surround beautiful valleys. From the air this region looks like a green carpet that some ancient giant has pushed against a wall, forming great parallel folds on the earth's surface. In fact, the **folded** terrain is a consequence of compression resulting from the collision of the North American, African and Eurasian crustal plates and the subsequent erosion of the last 180 million years (Figure 2.23). The more resistant rock, typically sandstone, forms the ridges and the less resistant, commonly limestone, the valley floors. Rivers are forced to flow parallel to the ridges until they encounter an unusually weak spot in the controlling ridge. Here, they can cut through forming what is known as a **water gap**. Several of the valleys and gaps, such as the Shenandoah Valley and Cumberland Gap, have served as important migration and transport routes since the early days of settlement. Agriculture is important in the fertile valleys of this region today.

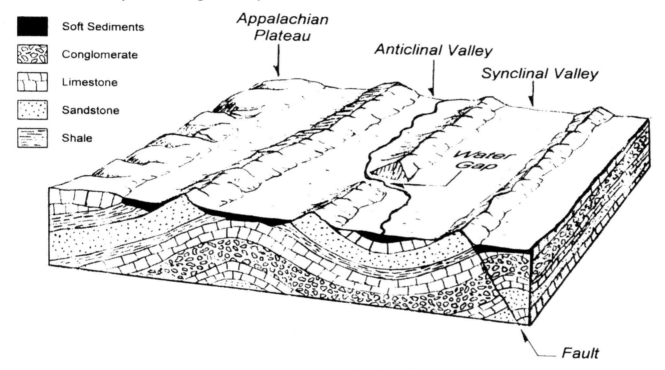

Figure 2.23 -- Geologic Structure Forming Ridge and Valley Topography

The **Appalachian Plateau** to the west was formed by the vertical uplift of horizontal layers of sedimentary rock from the collision of the North American plate with Europe and Africa. The pressure from the collision was not nearly as great as along the Blue Ridge where rock layers cracked and were then thrust over one another, nor even as great as in the Ridge and Valley where the layers were folded like the bellows of an accordion. In the Appalachian Plateau the rock layers simply bulged upward. Once raised the down-cutting of innumerable streams flowing over the soft sedimentary layers transformed the once relatively flat upland region into a rugged deeply etched landscape. The physiographic section extends from north-central Alabama northeastward into southern New York State. Northern segments of the Appalachian Plateau include the **Catskill Mountains** of southeastern New York, the **Poconos** in Pennsylvania, and the **Allegheny Plateau** of southwestern New York, western Pennsylvania, eastern Ohio and northern West Virginia. The southern reach of Appalachian Plateau province is found the **Cumberland Plateau** which stretches from southern West Virginia and eastern Kentucky, through eastern Tennessee to northern Alabama.

Both the Plateau and the Ridge and Valley contain large deposits of coal, which were formed by the burial of vast quantities of organic matter which grew in marshy downwarped troughs, or **geosynclines** millions of years ago. Later, the tectonic forces which created the Appalachian Mountains exerted tremendous pressure on this material for thousands of years forming coal. See Figure 2.6. The coal resources of this region are particularly valuable due to their relatively easy access. Coal near the surface can be removed using strip mining techniques, while the many streams in the area have cut down to the deeper layers of coal making horizontal shaft mines possible.

Three themes, all interdependent, become evident when one crosses this region: **isolation**, **coal**, and **poverty**, and the mountains are the source of all three. Their heavily dissected nature has made road construction more difficult here than in virtually any other region, with the exception of Alaska. The thin, rocky soil and steep slopes have made commercially viable agriculture nearly impossible, leaving **coal** as economic king. Coal deposits spawned a series of gritty company towns, which lasted only as long as the coal. Near the surface, the coal is strip-mined or removed by horizontal augers when the steep slopes expose the horizontal rock strata. These operations have been particularly damaging to the environment. Runoff from the mines has left many streams and rivers so highly acidic as to be virtually dead. When the coal is found at great depth, the cost has been in lives. Deep mining coal is said to be the single most dangerous occupation in the industrial world, as witnessed by the Tallmansville, W.Va mine disaster that killed twelve of thirteen miners trapped underground on January 2, 2006**.** The tragedy was made all the more cruel to the families and friends of the victims when the national media erroneously reported for several hours that twelve of the miners had survived. In the U.S., few workers were as cruelly exploited as were the coal miners of eastern Kentucky, West Virginia, and southwestern Pennsylvania, so it was no wonder that some of the earliest and bloodiest labor union battles occurred here.

In recent years the natural beauty of the region and federal and state investments in transportation infrastructure has increased the potential of tourism to play a significant economic role. White water rafting and eco-tourism have become important economic contributors in North Carolina, Tennessee and West Virginia. The beauty and milder climate of the southern Appalachian Plateau is also beginning to attract significant numbers of retirees, some escaping the cold of the northern states while others seek refuge from the heat of Florida. Despite these advances the region is still one of the poorest in the United States.

Many of the large caverns hollowed out by the effect of ground water dissolving the limestone deposits underlying the surface in much of the Appalachian Plateau and the Ridge and Valley Province have become major tourist attractions. Most notable is Mammoth Cave in Kentucky. Early guide Stephen Bishop called the cave a "grand, gloomy and peculiar place." Today, it is the world's longest known cave system, with more than 390 miles explored and mapped. The Mammoth Cave system is so extensive that it is thought that if one knew all of the connections that it would be possible to travel from the Ohio River to Georgia entirely underground. Landscapes dominated by the formation of caverns and collapsed caverns (sinkholes) are known as **karst topography.** (See BOX 2.2 for a discussion of the work of groundwater in an area of weak limestone rock.)

BOX 2.2--Karst Formations

The action of groundwater is most important in areas of soluable bedrock typically carbonate layers such as limestone or dolomite. Water percolating down from the surface may enter a layer of limestone rock through a crack in an overlying layer and begin to dissolve the easily soluable material. If the level of the water table drops or the limestone layer rises, the water will drain out carrying away some of the dissolved material and leaving **caverns** beneath the surface. As subsequent water seeps down from the surface and enters the caverns various minerals may precipitate out of solution forming beautiful hanging **stalactites** and pointed **stalagmites** on the floor. Sometimes these two features join forming **columns** (Figure 2.24). If the roof of the cavern is so close to the surface that it cannot support the weight above, the overburden can crash to the floor forming a surface depression called a **sink hole**.

Figure 2.24 -- Stalactites and Stalagmites in a Cavern

North of Long Island and east of the Hudson River Valley is the **New England-Maritime Section** of the Appalachians. Most of the area is hilly or mountainous. The Lower Connecticut River Valley and the Annapolis-Cornwallis Valley in Nova Scotia are much younger geologically and form the only extensive lowlands in this section. Like their southern counterparts these mountains were formed by continental collision of North America with the African and Eurasian plates. Unlike the southern Appalachians these mountains were subjected to the great erosional force of continental ice sheets. As the ice sheets advanced they scoured the surface beneath them, carving out numerous valleys which were later flooded by rising sea level as the ice caps melted. Most notable of these flooded valleys are Rhode Island's Narragansett Bay and the Bay of Fundy in Nova Scotia and New Brunswick. As the ice retreated it left enormous deposits of rock, sand and silt forming such noted landmarks as Long Island, Nantucket and Cape Cod. The glaciers also exposed much of the metamorphosed rock that underlies the area allowing the region to command a leading position in the quarrying of marble, slate, and granite. Agriculture is practiced in many parts of the region with dairying being most important throughout. Some specialty crops, such as tobacco, berries, and potatoes are grown.

The Interior Lowlands

To the west of the Appalachians in the United States and southern Canada are the **Interior Lowlands**. The largest section is the **Central Lowlands**, which extends from the Appalachian Plateau in the east to the first major series of **escarpments** (cliffs) in the west--including the **Missouri Coteau** of the Dakotas. Through Oklahoma, Kansas and Nebraska, the Central Lowlands and Great Plains boundary is poorly delineated. The latitudinal extent of the Central Lowlands extends from Texas in the southwest to the Arctic coast in the northwest. The northern half of the Central Lowlands bears the heavy imprint of the continental glaciers (Box 2.3) most notably the formation of the Great Lakes and tens of thousands of smaller lakes. The five Great Lakes contain nearly 20 percent of the world's surface fresh water (excluding the glacial ice caps). This abundance of fresh water is one of North America's most valuable natural resources. In addition the glaciers deposited a mantle of thick soil over much of Ohio, Indiana, Illinois, Iowa, Nebraska, the Dakotas, and Saskatchewan helping to make this region one of the premier agricultural areas in the world. In southern Manitoba is Lake Winnipeg a remnant of the vast Lake Agassiz which once stretched from South Dakota to northern Manitoba. Larger than all of the present Great Lakes put together, Lake Agassiz's waters slowly drained out leaving behind the rich "muck" that had accumulated on its lake bed. Known as the Red River Valley this former lake bed is one of the flattest and most fertile areas of North America. Most streams in this section eventually flow into the Mississippi, St. Lawrence, or Mackenzie Rivers. The downwarped geosynclines of Illinois and Ohio contain petroleum and significant quantities of coal and the north shore of the Arctic Plains of Alaska has large oil deposits (Figure 2.6).

Much of the Interior Lowlands (as well as the Great Plains region to the west) shows the imprint of the times when sea-level rose and flooded the low lying interior of the North American craton with a shallow sea. A thin sandstone layer in Kansas was once a tropical beach, while shale deposits in Saskatchewan mark a former swamp and a limestone layer in Missouri formed from seashells accumulating beneath the deep calm waters of some primeval ocean. Seas expanded and then retreated repeatedly over this region leaving behind layer upon layer of sedimentary rock. Along the shallow margins of these seas great swamps flourished. Today the vegetation of those swamps lies trapped beneath layers of sand, gravel and silt deposited by ancient rivers and has formed a variety of minerals including, petroleum, natural gas, and coal (Figure 2.6).

In the United States, most of the Interior Lowlands is drained by the Mississippi River and its tributaries. In the 1700s, it was the route used by explorers into the continent's interior. In the early

1800s, keel boats floated down the Ohio and then the Mississippi to New Orleans carrying furs and whiskey. At New Orleans, the boats would be broken up and the lumber used to build houses, while their crews would make the long trek back to Kentucky, Indiana, or Ohio on foot along the famed Natchez Trace so they could build another keel boat and float the river again. From the mouth of the Ohio River to New Orleans was a six-week float trip, while the return walk would take nearly five months. With the advent of steam came the legendary paddle wheelers. These shallow-draft vessels were ideal for the ever-changing, sand bar-filled Mississippi River. The successor to the glamorous river boats of the late 1800s might be the drabbest of all boats, the barge. One small tug can often be seen controlling a half dozen or more barges carrying the wheat of Minnesota or the coal of Kentucky. **New Orleans** was ideally situated---the products of the American Midwest flowed down the Mississippi River and out of her ports, while the fruit, bauxite, and other raw materials of Latin America moved easily across the Gulf of Mexico to be unloaded on her docks. Today, New Orleans is one of the three most important ports in the United States.

BOX 2.3--Continental Glaciation

Continental glaciers formed and moved just as mountain glaciers but continental glaciers became so great in size, depth and power that they coalesced completely covering the mountains and valleys. These ice sheets, often miles in thickness **scraped** and **plucked** the rock beneath them as they moved forward shearing off the tops of mountains and scouring out small and great lakes and disrupting the drainage pattern of thousands of streams. The material picked up by the glacier flowed with the ice and was deposited as **drift** along its margins when it melted. When the edge of the ice became stationary for periods of time as the rate of forward movement equaled the melting, deposits would become so great as to form hills, called **moraines**. The moraine found at what was the margin of the ice sheet at its greatest extent is called the **terminal moraine,** and all other moraines formed when the ice sheet paused for a period of time as it melted are called **recessional moraines** (Figure 2.25). During periods of rapid melting away of the edge, or **retreat**, the drift was dumped as **ground moraine**, forming low rolling hills.

Individual chunks of rock, or **erratics**, were also deposited, as were stratified deposits by streams. These included level outwash plains of sand and gravel, as well as **lacustrine** deposits on the bottom of pluvial/glacial lakes, plus winding **esker** ridges formed in stream tunnels within the glacier.

The most visible results of the great continental glaciers are the tens of thousands of lakes found in Manitoba, Ontario, Quebec, Minnesota, Wisconsin, Michigan and other Canadian provinces and northern U.S. states. The largest of these glacial lakes are the five Great Lakes---*Superior, Huron, Michigan, Erie,* and *Ontario*. Scoured out as the continental ice sheet advanced southward, they were subsequently filled by the torrential outwash as the ice quickly melted at the end of the Pleistocene. Today, the Great Lakes hold nearly 20% of the world's fresh surface water (other than that found in glacial ice caps).

In Canada, much of the Interior Lowlands is drained by the Mackenzie River which flows north into the Arctic Ocean or by the Red River which empties into Lake Winnipeg and then via the Nelson River to Hudson Bay.

In north-central Kentucky and central Tennessee are the **Interior Low Plateaus**. The **Cincinnati Arch**, a prominent regional uplift extends from central Tennessee through central Kentucky to northwestern Ohio. Two structural domes, the **Bluegrass and Nashville**, lie along the Cincinnati Arch. While structurally the rock layers dome upward the surface landscapes are actually basins. This is because the upwarped layers fractured and exposed softer easily eroded limestone. The eroding out of the center of the domes has produced two great basins surrounded by a high ridge. Fertile limestone soil in the **Bluegrass and Nashville Basins** is the basis of highly profitable pasture (race horses) and crop land (tobacco).

South of the Central Lowlands--in southern Missouri, northwestern Arkansas and eastern Oklahoma--are the **Interior Highlands**, which include the Ozark Plateau and the Ouachita Mountains. These two upland areas are separated by the Arkansas River Valley. The sequences of folded Paleozoic rocks found in the eastern Ouachita Mountains of Arkansas match those found in the southern Appalachians of Alabama and Tennessee. Because they date to the same period when South and North America collided, the two ranges are thought to have once been continuous. Today they are separated by a structural trough formed when North and South America later rifted apart opening the Gulf of Mexico. The great structural trough became a trap for sediment carried by the Platte, Arkansas, Missouri, Ohio, and then the Mississippi River as it made its way to the Gulf of Mexico. In Southeastern Missouri are the Saint Francois Mountains (also known as the St. Francis Mts.). Formed through volcanic and intrusive activity nearly 1.5 billion years ago, they are geologically nearly three times as old as the Ozarks or Appalachians. Although there is significant lead and zinc mining and lumbering in the hills and farming in the Arkansas Valley, as well as several successful tourism and retirement centers, much of the region suffers economically.

The Great Plains

In 1820, Major Stephen H. Long led an exploratory party across the Great Plains and despite seeing thriving corn fields of the Pawnee Indians and great herds of **bison**, he wrote in his report to the government that the area between the Missouri River and the Rocky Mountains was unsuitable for farming and on his maps labeled the region "The Great American Desert." In school atlases and textbooks, it remained so labeled for 50 years.

Today, the Great Plains stretching from Texas into southern Saskatchewan and Alberta is one of the most productive farming regions in the world. Most of the continent's **wheat** and **cattle** are produced here. This is not the small family farm; this is highly sophisticated agribusiness. Lasers guide tractors to insure the correct drainage on fields, aerial photography is taken for early detection of crop disease, and computer modems link the homestead to international commodity markets.

Natural prairie fires kept trees from covering much of the Great Plains. Fire killed the young saplings but native grasses and herbs would return with the next rain. With human occupation prairie fires were extinguished and trees invaded many areas driving out native species.

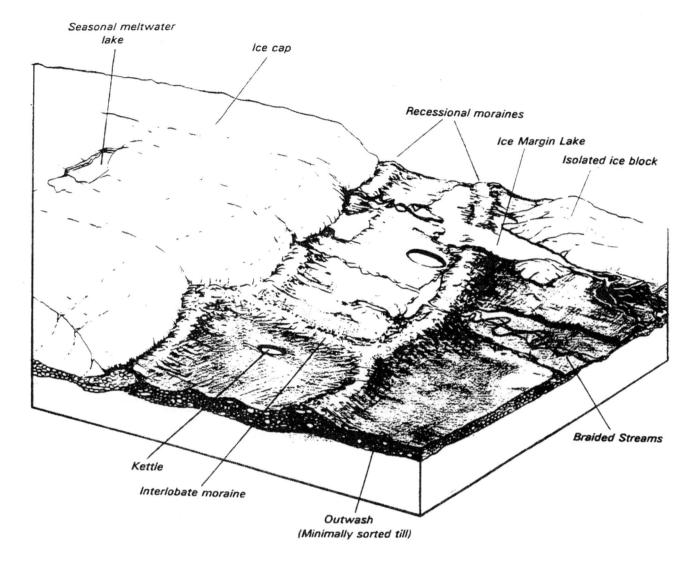

Figure 2.25 -- Continental Glacial Features (*Mark A. Patton*)

In the center of the continent the eastern boundary of the Great Plains is marked by the **Missouri Coteau,** an area stretching from southern Saskatchewan across South Dakota. The Missouri Coteau is a narrow band of upland prairie comprised of deep glacial deposits containing numerous melt water lakes, which rises about 500 feet above the Central Lowlands. In the south, the Great Plains meets the Coastal Plain along the **Balcones Escarpment** in central Texas. Formed when the rise of the Rockies pushed the flat sedimentary layers of the western portion of the ancient craton upward, the Great Plains gently tilt west to east, causing streams to flow eastward (Figure 2.26). These streams and the persistent wind have covered the Great Plains with a mantle of sediment eroding off of the Rocky Mountains to the west. In Iowa and Illinois, the original prairie grasses had been so tall that wagon trains could hide in them, while the grasses on the western margins of the plains are only a few inches high. The difference is a result of rainfall. From the Mississippi River westward the landscape becomes progressively drier. Average annual precipitation in St. Louis is 40 inches per year; in Kansas City, 30 inches; in Wichita, 25 inches; and in Amarillo, Texas, only 20 inches.

While Chicago boasts the nickname "Windy City," it is the towns of the Great Plains that truly deserve the title. Locals will tell you that on the Great Plains "the only thing blocking the wind between Texas and the Arctic Ocean is a barbed wire fence." **Weather is important here and often severe**. Tornados, blizzards, searing heat, drought, and numbing cold are all part of life on the Great Plains. A series of wet years has made millionaires of Texan, Kansan, and Saskatchewan wheat farmers, while a few dry years and the sound of the auctioneer's chant has rung out "going, going, gone" to a family's dreams. Advice to new arrivals from the earlier pioneers on the Great Plains was "to keep one eye on the banker and the other on the sky."

Most of the Great Plains are gently rolling; however, there are areas of extremely dissected terrain called **badlands topography** in Alberta, North and South Dakota, and New Mexico. Badlands typically form in semi-arid areas on soft poorly cemented sediments. The lack of continuous vegetative cover allows for the severe erosion of the surface into countless gullies and rills and knife like ridges. These geologically ephemeral landscapes are often quite spectacular.

Many people's perception of the Great Plains as being a homogenous, relatively flat and featureless region, is patently untrue. However, **The Llano Estacado** ("Staked Plains") of west Texas and eastern New Mexico is a large portion of the southern plains that matches the popular stereotype. Named by early Spanish explorers who felt compelled to place a series of stakes in the ground so they could retrace their route across what is one of the largest expanses of near-featureless terrain in the U.S. Geologically, the Llano is an uplifted plateau composed of very porous river sediments veneered by centuries of wind-blown sand. Wind was also responsible for the formation of the **Sand Hills of Nebraska**, the largest field of sand dunes in the Western Hemisphere. These dunes formed during the last 10,000 years from the immense quantity of sediment deposited by the retreating North American ice cap. Today, for the most part, they are stabilized, however, with minor changes in climatic conditions the dunes could shed their vegetative cover and again become active.

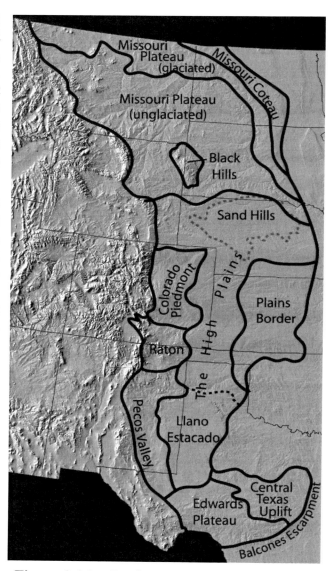

Figure 2.26 -- Regions of the Great Plains

Rising quite conspicuously on the Great Plains are the Black Hills of western South Dakota and eastern Wyoming. Geologically they are a structural dome of ancient pre-cambrian granite. The faces Washington, Jefferson, Lincoln, and Theodore Roosevelt on Mount Rushmore and some 15 miles to the southwest the form of Crazy Horse are carved in the hard resistant granite of these outliers of the Rocky Mountains.

Between 1934 and 1937, drier conditions and the conversion of millions of acres of natural grasslands into wheat fields during World War I by farmers and ranchers eager to reap the benefits of high bushel prices led to the infamous "Dust Bowl" (Figure 2.27). Wind picked up the dry soil exposed by the southern plains farmers of Texas, Oklahoma, and Kansas into monstrous clouds thousands of feet high.

> *On Sunday April 14, 1935, the sun came up in a clear sky. The day was warm and pleasant, a gentle breeze whimpered out of the southwest. Suddenly a cloud appeared on the horizon. Birds flew swiftly ahead of it, but not swift enough for the cloud traveling at sixty miles per hour. This day, which many people of the area readily remember, was named "Black Sunday".*
>
> *By May, it seemed like the wind and dirt had been blowing for an eternity. Rain was an event occurring only in dreams. It was a year of intensive dirt storms, gales, rollers and floods mixed with economic depression, sickness and disaster. It was a year of extreme hardship, but surprisingly the vast majority of the people stayed. By 1935, the unusual had become the usual, the extreme became the normal, the exception became the routine.*
>
> --- Paul Bonnifield   *The Dust Bowl, Men, Dirt and Depression*

Figure 2.27 -- Stratford, Texas April 18, 1935. Hundreds of people reported that they believed that the world was coming to an end when this black blizzard engulfed their town for days. Photo from the George E. Marsh Album, NOAA

After the 1930s Dust Bowl, millions of trees were planted as wind blocks and over 170,000 wells were drilled. Providing water for those wells are a series of **aquifers**. The largest, the Ogallala, underlies much of the Great Plains of the United States. Over one fourth of all of the irrigated land in the United States uses the water of the Ogallala. Unlike the water table which is formed by local rain percolating down through the soil and accumulating on top of the underlying bedrock, an aquifer's water may originate hundreds of miles away. This is because an aquifer is a layer of water slowly flowing through permeable rock or gravel sandwiched between impermeable rock layers above and below it (Figure 2.28). On the Great Plains, the permeable, water-filled rock slopes gently up to the west eventually reaching the surface on the eastern slope of the Rocky Mountains. Here, water infiltrates into the rock layer and slowly moves down and eastward. It is estimated that the water being pumped out of the eastern edge of the **Ogallala** may have begun as snow or rain over 60,000 years ago. Unfortunately, the rate at which the water is being pumped out of the aquifer is far faster than the rate of recharge from the mountains and so the great Ogallala aquifer is already beginning to run dry in small areas of the Great Plains and for large portions of the southern Great Plains. At the current rate of use, it is estimated that six percent of the area of the Ogallala will run dry every 25 years. The potential loss of even a small part of the Ogallala is of great national concern as agricultural products are one of the few sectors where the U.S. exports far more than imports. The loss of water from the Ogallala would require a greater emphasis on water conservation and on crops, such as grains, requiring less rainfall which might drop productivity nearly 80 percent.

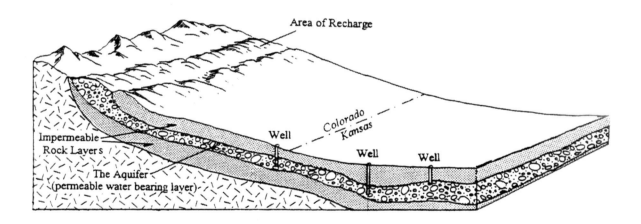

Figure 2.28 -- An Aquifer.

The Rocky Mountains

To the west of the Great Plains section of the Interior Lowlands are the Rocky Mountains, stretching from central New Mexico to Point Hope in Alaska. The meeting of the Great Plains and the Rockies is generally breathtaking with the mountains rising abruptly thousands of feet above the Plains. Through Colorado and southern Wyoming this rise is along a relatively straight line called the **Front Range** (Figure 2.28). The Rockies exhibit both high peaks and rugged relief and stand as a major barrier to east-west movement on land. This is especially critical in the United States, since so much inhabitable territory and so much of the population are to the west of the mountains. The major break in the Rockies in the United States is the **Wyoming Basin**, which has been important for transcontinental transportation since the early days of exploration and settlement. The Mormon, Oregon, and California Trails, the Pony Express, the Union Pacific (the first transcontinental railroad), and Interstate highway 80 all have used this route. Petroleum and coal production and ranching are major contributors to the economy. From Alaska to Mexico the Great Continental Divide runs along the crest of the Rocky Mountains. East of the divide in the contiguous United States rivers flow to the Gulf of Mexico while rivers west of the divide flow into the Pacific Ocean. In Canada and Alaska rivers to the east flow into the Arctic Ocean and those west of the Great Continental Divide empty into the Pacific.

The **Southern Rockies** which stretch from southern Wyoming into New Mexico, contain many of the highest peaks in the contiguous United States, such as Pikes Peak. A series of basins, called **parks**, provide pasture for summer grazing and hay for winter feed to support cattle and sheep production. The seasonal migration of livestock up the mountain for summer grazing and then back down as temperatures drop is called **transhumance**. The winter snow pack that accumulates in the Southern Rockies is the source of four of the great rivers of North America. the Rio Grande, Colorado, Platte, and Arkansas Rivers. To the west through the Grand Canyon flows the Colorado River. Many

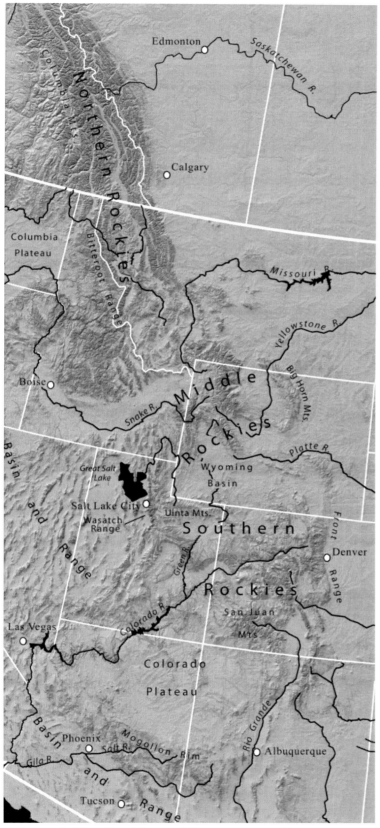

Figure 2.28 -- Rockies and Intermontane Plateaus

of the cities of the Southwest, including Los Angeles, Phoenix and Las Vegas rely heavily upon the Colorado for water. South through central New Mexico, the Rio Grande irrigates cotton fields and supplies the water needs of Albuquerque and El Paso before turning east and becoming the U.S. Mexican border. To the east flows the Arkansas through eastern Colorado, Kansas, and Arkansas before joining the Mississippi River. The Platte flows across the High Plains of Nebraska to join the Missouri River a little south of Omaha. While water is undoubtedly the most important export of the Southern Rockies, the region also contains important deposits of molybdenum, uranium, silver and other minerals (Figure 2.4).

The ranges of the **Middle Rockies** cover the northwest quarter of Wyoming and extend into northeastern Utah, eastern Idaho, and southern Montana. The volcanic origin of much of this area is dramatically demonstrated in Yellowstone National Park where **geysers**, such as Old Faithful, and hot springs number in the thousands. Geysers occur when groundwater seeping down through cracks in the rock becomes heated well above the boiling point by a subterranean magma chamber. The superheated water is held under pressure by the weight of the water above. Eventually, though, the heating process creates enough force to blow out the water in the crack above it in a dazzling display. At high elevations, small valley glaciers have added beauty to the Grand Tetons and other ranges by carving knife-like ridges and jagged peaks. Phosphate, silver, and lead deposits are economically important in this area.

The **Northern Rockies** stretch from central Idaho to northern British Columbia. They are bordered on their east by the Great Plains in the south and by the Central Lowlands in the north. To their west the **Rocky Mountain Trench** separates them from the **Columbia Mountains** and the **Cassiar Mountains**. The Rocky Mountain Trench running from Flathead Lake in Montana to the Liard River of northern British Columbia is a striking 900 mile long valley formed primarily by faulting. The Trench provided a natural north south transportation route and is the headwaters of the Kootenay, Fraser, Peace, Columbia, and Liard rivers.

The Northern Rockies were formed when small slivers of land were added one after the other to the coast of ancient North America in a process called **accreted terrane**. The compressional forces melding these pieces to the continent folded and faulted the mountains to great heights. The Northern Rockies are composed of layered sedimentary rock such as limestone and shale, whereas the Middle and Southern Rockies are comprised primarily of igneous and metamorphic rock such as gneiss and granite. Active alpine glaciers are found throughout the Northern Rockies and have sculpted these mountains into one of the most beautiful landscapes in the world. Jasper and Banff National Parks in Canada and Glacier National Park in the U.S. are just a few of the outstanding scenic attractions. Copper, lead, silver and zinc make this a notable mining area.

The major break in the Rockies in Canada occurs between the Northern and the Arctic Rockies, where the **Liard River** winds through the mountains toward the Mackenzie River to the east. This passageway is used by a section of the Al-Can Highway leading from Whitehorse in the Yukon to Fort Nelson in British Columbia.

The **Arctic Rockies** include the Mackenzie Mountains and the Brooks Range (Figure 2.29). The Brooks Range, trending east-west effectively separates the Arctic Coastal Plain from the interior of Alaska. Only a single gravel road crosses the Brooks Range, a chain stretching a distance greater than that between Washington, D. C. and Chicago, Illinois.

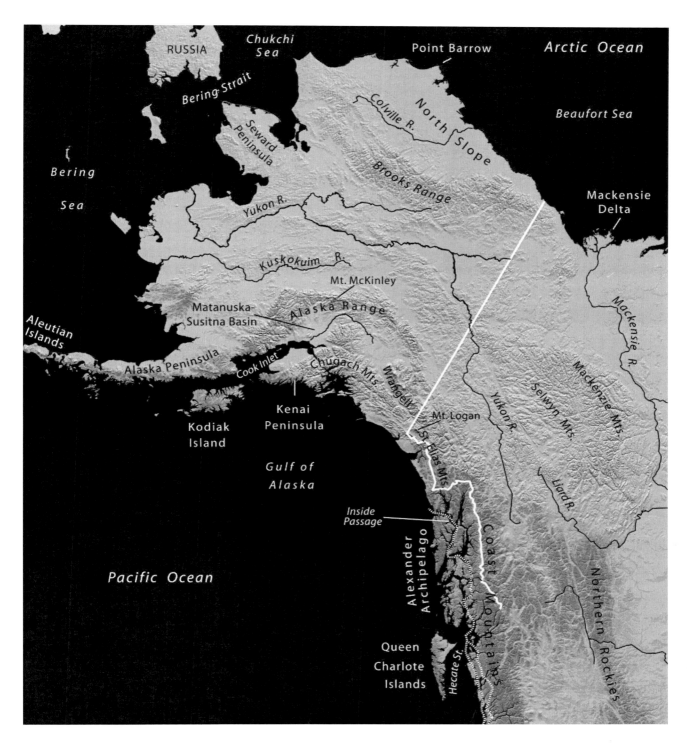

Figure 2.29 -- The Arctic Rockies and other significant physical features of Alaska, the Yukon and the western portion of the Northwest Territories.

The Intermontane Plateaus and Basins

Westward from the Rockies lie the Intermontane Basins and Plateaus, which reach from Mexico to the Bering Strait. The **Colorado Plateau** is located west of the Southern Rockies in parts of Colorado, New Mexico, Arizona, and Utah. The topography is generally flat and there is very little vegetative cover since precipitation is less than ten inches annually. Streams have cut deep canyons through the soft horizontal rock strata in this Desert Climate. At one time, this area was sea floor, as evidenced by the sea shell-rich limestone layers and strata of marine shales laid down in the shallow swampy areas of a retreating ocean. Tremendous tectonic pressure has caused the region to slowly rise. As this regional uplift occurred, streams responded by eroding downward. The result is a series of spectacular deep canyons which dissect the Colorado Plateau and draw millions of tourists annually.

The evidence for numerous stages of vertical uplift of the horizontal strata over hundreds of millions of years is found most dramatically in the **Grand Canyon**. As the land slowly rose the Colorado River cut a deep gorge over one mile deep. As streams do not develop tight meanders unless they are flowing over relatively flat topography, the presence of deeply entrenched meanders is good evidence that at one time this area was nearly at sea level.

Figure 2.30. -- The Goosenecks of the San Juan River – Located in the heart of the Colorado Plateau these entrenched meanders indicate a slowly rising landscape.

They are also evidence that the region rose very slowly as rapid upheavals would have destroyed the stream patterns long before they could become incised into the landscape (Figure 2.30). About a third of the Colorado Plateau is in Indian Reservations and nearly another fourth is public land. Some agriculture and mining is practiced.

The largest portion of the The Intermontane Plateaus and Basins province is the **Basin and Range Section**. Lying to the east of the Cascades and the Sierra Nevada Ranges, the Basin and Range includes virtually all of Nevada and the adjacent areas of eastern California and western Utah as well as Southern Arizona and New Mexico and a small part of western Texas. The Basin and Range province has fascinated geologists as it appears that it the entire region is being stretched. The western edge of the Basin and Range is marked by the Sierra Nevada Mountains, which mark the western edge of the North American Plate. As the Pacific Plate and North American Plates slide by one another, it is thought that they periodically "catch" or "snag" eventually they will break free, but not before slightly stretching and thus thinning the slower moving North American plate. It is estimated that the Basin and Range region has been stretched to nearly twice its original size and consequently is only half its original thickness. As this thinner crust is pulled apart, blocks of material slip downward in what is known as normal faulting. This type of faulting produces a **horst and graben** landscape. The horsts are the linear ridges of the region and the grabens form the, valley floors. Over time, material washing off of the mountains filled the valleys creating a region of long linear mountain ranges separated from one another by flat plains. Much of this area has **interior drainage**, meaning that the rivers do not flow out of the region but rather empty into local low-lying pockets where the water evaporates or forms shallow salty lakes, especially in the part of the Great Basin centered on Nevada. The extent of vertical faulting that has occurred is seen in the proximity of Mt. Whitney to Badwater Basin in Death Valley. At 14,494 feet, Whitney, the highest peak in the 48 contiguous states, is a mere 85 miles from Badwater Basin, at 280 feet below sea level, the lowest point in North America.

Irrigated agriculture, ranching, and mining are important in various parts of the Basin and Range section. With the exception of the Las Vegas and Reno areas this is one of the least inhabited regions of the U.S. The federal government retains ownership of the vast majority of the Basin and Range. Its vast size and sparse population has been utilized for atomic weapons testing in the 1950s and 1960s, testing of secret aircraft as in the case of the famous Area 51 in Nevada, and most recently for the disposal of spent fuel from nuclear reactors and other sources.

North of the Basin and Range Section in southern Idaho and eastern Oregon and Washington is the **Columbia Plateau**. The Columbia and Snake Rivers have cut magnificent gorges through this plateau which was formed by layer upon layer of lava that flowed out of huge fissures in the earth during the last 50 million years. The most recent flow occurred a mere 1,000 years ago. The source of the massive lava flows appears to be a relatively stationary hot plume that is located in the mantle directly beneath the North American Plate. As the North American Plate moved westward it over rode the hot plume in western Oregon. As the North American Plate continued its westward journey the effects of the hot spot were felt progressively further east. A line tracing younger and younger volcanic activity can be drawn from the Coast of Oregon across eastern Oregon's famed lava beds through the lava cliffs of Hell's Canyon in Idaho to Crater's of the Moon National Park's stark volcanic landscape in central Idaho. Today, the hot spot is located beneath Yellowstone National Park in northwest Wyoming and is responsible for the geysers, thermal pools and mud pots that have made the park famous. The main type of economic activity on the Columbia Plateau is farming with an emphasis on grains and fruits. Irrigation is very important in this semiarid area and grazing, lumbering, fishing, and mining are also pursued.

North of the Columbia Plateau is the **Plateau of British Columbia**. This region, cut by the Fraser River and its tributaries, is more dissected and rugged than the plateaus to the south. Little of the region is flat; rather, it consists of rolling hills and low lying mountains, all less than 6,500 feet (2000 meters). Lumbering is the main economic activity throughout the Interior Plateau, but farming is important in the south in the Okanagan and Fraser River Valleys.

To the north is the **Yukon Plateau**, which stretches the length of Canada's Yukon Territory into eastern Alaska. Like the Interior Plateau of British Columbia the Yukon Plateau is heavily dissected leaving little flat topography. The main livelihood of most of the people is mining. West of the Yukon Plateau are the **Central Alaskan Basins and Uplands**, which are drained by the Yukon River. In this section, mining, trapping, and fishing are the main activities.

The Pacific Mountains and Lowlands

West of the Intermontane Basins and Plateaus are the **Pacific Mountains and Lowlands**. Three generally north-south trending divisions constitute this physiographic province: an eastern and a western series of mountains separated by a series of discontinuous lowlands. Like much of the Rocky Mountain region this area is composed of accreted, or exotic, terrane.

The Eastern Series of Mountains

These ranges extend from the Sierra Nevada to the Aleutian Islands (Figure 2.31). Stretching north-south over 350 miles, California's Sierra Nevada, Spanish for "Snowy Mountain," is a massive block of granite, called a **batholith**. Some 200 to 80 million years ago as the eastern portion of the Pacific Plate was being subducted beneath the crust of the North American Plate some of the lightest of the melting subducted material attempted to rise through the overlying crust. Most of these **plutonic** intrusions cooled slowly at great depth forming granite. Much later the granite of these multiple **plutons** was pushed upward to form the Sierra Nevada.

The **Sierra Nevada** contain **Mt. Whitney**, the highest peak in the lower 48 contiguous states (Figure 2.31). Glaciers have carved magnificent scenery out of the western slopes of the Sierras, as in Yosemite National Park (Figure 2.32). The mining of gold in these mountains started the famed 1849 California Gold Rush. Today, lumbering and tourism dominate the economic landscape of the Sierra Nevada range and at times the two industries clash. The mountains are home to some of the largest trees in the world including the massive Sequoia and decisions on which areas will or will not be open to lumbering are always controversial. One of the greatest resources of the Sierra Nevada is the heavy snow pack that falls each winter. Water from the melting snow supplies much of the irrigation needs of agriculture in the Central Valley of California as well as drinking water for San Francisco, San Jose, Los Angeles, San Diego and hundreds of other coastal towns.

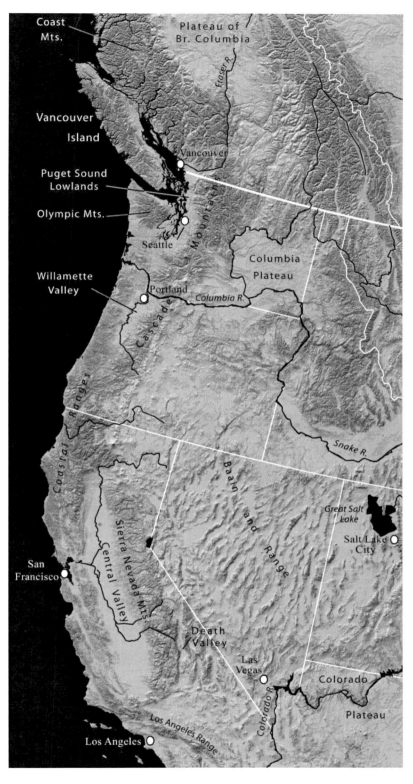

Figure 2.31 -- U.S. Pacific Coastlands and Intermontane Plateaus and Basins

To the north are the **Cascade Ranges**. They include a series of volcanic cones, such as Mt. Hood, Adams, and Rainier. The volcanoes of the Cascades are all potentially active as was vividly demonstrated by the violent eruption of Mt. St. Helens in 1980. In 2004, Mt. St. Helens again spewed forth dust and ash but so far no cataclysmic eruption has followed. Famed Crater Lake in southern Oregon occupies a six mile wide **caldera** formed during the eruption of ancient Mt. Mazama nearly 7,000 years ago. The roughly circular depressions known as caldera form when a crater collapses into the underlying void created when great masses of material are violently blown out of a volcano. Protruding out of the lake is Wizard Island, a new volcanic vent and vivid evidence that Mt. Mazama may be sleeping but is not dead (Figure 2.33). The Columbia River cuts through the Cascade Mountains on its journey to the Pacific. Lumbering is the leading economic activity throughout these mountains, although environmental concerns coupled with the rise of tourism during recent years have limited the extent of the cutting which undoubtedly would have taken place otherwise.

Farther north are the **Coast Mountains of British Columbia**, which are separated from the Cascades by the deep gorge cut by the Fraser River. These mountains often plunge directly down into the sea. Ancient glaciers, flowing down through the pre-existing river valleys on their way to the sea, broadened

Figure 2.32 -- Famed Half Dome towers over Yosemite Valley. The distinctive "U" shaped trough was carved by a glacier that flowed through the valley some 10,000 years ago. Each year nearly 4 million visitors come to Yosemite National Park.

Figure 2.33 -- Wizard Island in Crater Lake. The lake fills the ancient volcanic caldera and has been measured to a depth of nearly 2000 feet (608 meters) making it North America's deepest lake.

and deepened the valleys. (See BOX 2.4 for a discussion of mountain, or valley, glaciation.) The rising ocean has filled these valleys to create a beautifully **fiorded** coastline. The rivers rushing down to the sea have been utilized effectively in providing water power locally for industry, such as the production of aluminum at Kitimat. Lumbering is of utmost importance throughout much of the area and mining is practiced in a few places. Fishing along the coast and in the Fraser River, plus agriculture in that valley, are additions to the local economy.

In southern Alaska, the **Alaskan Range** contains the highest point in North America, Mt. McKinley (20,320 ft, or 6,096 m). The few people inhabiting the Alaskan Peninsula and the Aleutian Islands depend primarily on the sea and on military bases for earning a living.

BOX 2.4--Mountain Glaciation

More than 10,000 years ago during the Pleistocene era, commonly called the Ice Ages, more snow fell in the high mountains than melted during the short summer season. In small high depressions called **cirques** layer upon layer of snow would accumulate year after year. The snow at the bottom of the cirque would eventually be changed in form by the pressure of the overlying snow layers. Gradually the deep snow became harder, more resistant, and began to flow. Now glacial ice it would often moved down slope pushed by the weight of the snow over it. During the Pleistocene a multitude of glaciers flowed down through pre-existing stream carved valleys of the high mountains or northerly ranges of North America. Flowing like a thick plastic they scraped and plucked rock from the sides and floor of the valleys. The eroded material or **till** would accumulate along the sides of the glacier in linear mounds called **lateral moraine or** along the snout of the glacier where the deposited till formed **terminal moraines.** Typically glacial carved valleys have a **U-shape** profile with sharp knife-like ridges (**arêtes**) separating parallel glacial valleys (Figure 2.34). Often previous smaller river tributary valleys were not deepened as much as the main one and, thus, were left as **hanging valleys**, often with waterfalls, above the main valley floor (Figure 2.34). The main result of mountain glaciation is a jagged sculpted landscape often choked with unconsolidated mounds of till.

Figure 2.34 -- The Athabasca Glacier in the Columbia Ice-field of Jasper National Park.

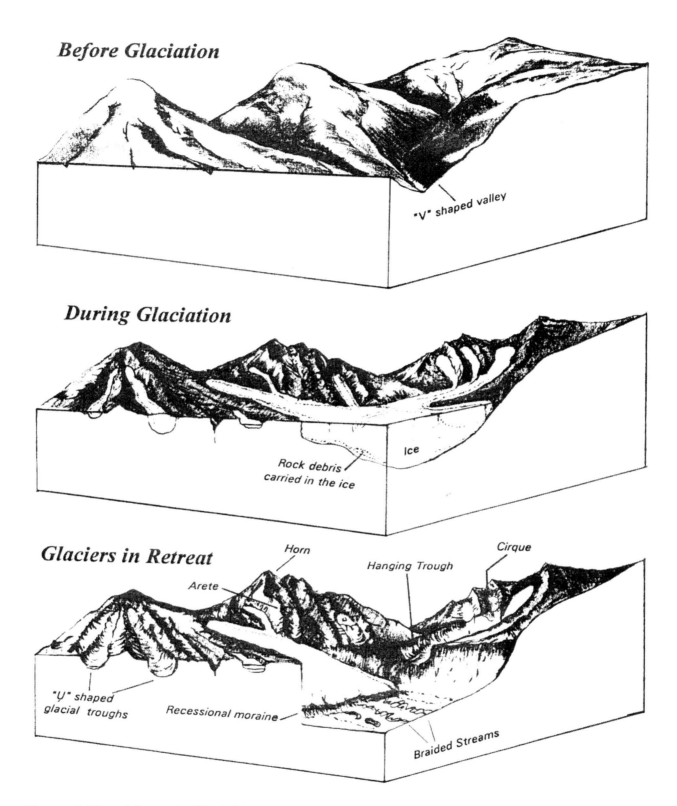

Figure 2.35 -- Mountain Glacial Features (*Mark A. Patton*)

The Western Series of Mountains

Running along the entire western edge of North America from the Mexican border to Alaska are a series of coastal mountains periodically broken by valleys formed by rivers as they enter the Pacific Ocean. The southernmost of these highlands are the **Los Angeles Ranges**, which surround the Los Angeles Basin and the adjoining coastal plain on three sides. Streams, many of them flowing only during the wet winter months or during the spring from snow melt, have filled the basin with fertile alluvium washed from the surrounding hillsides. Agriculture, timber industries, mining (drilling), manufacturing, and service industries combine to support a major economy in these lowlands. Since the end of World War II agriculture has steadily diminished as fruit trees have given way to urban expansion. Today, over 13 million people live in the Los Angeles Basin

To the north are the **Coast Ranges of California**. The most noted feature of this range is the San Andreas Fault. The geological instability of these areas can be seen in the recent earth tremors in various parts, such as the 1994 Los Angeles quake which registered 6.6-6.8 on the Momement Magnitude scale and which caused over $30 billion in damage. (See BOX 2.5 for a discussion of earthquakes and transform faults.)

Interrupting these hill lands are several valleys and basins. San Francisco Bay severs the mountains into the Northern and Southern Coast Ranges. Into San Francisco Bay flow the two great rivers of the Central Valley, the San Joaquin and the Sacramento. The bay area is the main economic center of the Coast Ranges of California. Wine production and fruit and vegetable growing are important in many of the coastal valleys. In general, the Southern Coast Ranges are steep but not very high, most peaks are less than 6000 feet. The northern Coast ranges are higher and significantly wetter. Here are found the famed Redwoods, the tallest tree species on earth.

The **Coast Ranges of Oregon and Washington** are cut by the Columbia River Valley. This section of the Columbia Valley is a classic submerged coastline. As the great ice caps melted at the end of the Pleistocene global sea level rose and drowned the portion of the Columbia River Valley as it entered the ocean. More hydroelectric power is generated by the 14 dams on the Columbia River than any other river in North America. In addition, there are numerous other hydroelectric plants on the Columbia's tributaries. Lumbering and some agriculture are practiced within this section. In the northwestern corner of the United States are the Olympic Mountains. Lumbering is of great importance here also. Across the Strait of Juan de Fuca, the Western Series of mountains form islands, such as **Vancouver** and **Queen Charlotte**. Agriculture and lumbering are important in the southern part of Vancouver Island and fishing is excellent in the adjacent waters.

The **Wrangell-St. Elias Range** in southeastern Alaska and the southwestern corner of the Yukon Territory contain some of the highest peaks in North America, including Mt. Logan (19,850 ft, or 5,955 m), the highest peak in Canada and the second highest in North America. The **Chugach Mountains** and **Kodiak Island** complete this western mountain system.

BOX 2.5--Earthquakes and Transform Faults

Along the western coast of North America is a series of fractures (**faults**) in the earth, where two plates are moving laterally against each other (Figure 2.36). As the rock is distorted by the pressure exerted, **strain** increases in the rock. Eventually, the rock cannot withstand the pressure and will lurch forward suddenly, which is an **earthquake**. Energy waves are sent out in all directions from the point where the break occurred, or **focus**. The point on the surface directly above the focus is known as the **epicenter** of the earthquake. These **seismic waves** cause the destruction on the land and can also create giant sea waves, or **tsunamis**, which can travel hundreds of miles and wreck great havoc. The epicenter's location is determined by drawing circles from three seismic stations, with the radius of each circle being the distance from the station to the quake. The epicenter will be the point of intersection of the three circles. The amount of ground motion that occurs during an earthquake (the **magnitude**) is expressed as a **logarithmic** value on the **Moment Magnitude scale**. Thus, an earthquake with a value of 7 has ten times the ground motion as one with a value of 6 and 100 times that of a quake registering 5 on the scale. Earthquakes with a value of 7 can cause major damage and those with a value of 8 are considered catastrophic. Moreover, each increase of one on the scale means 30 times more energy released. Thus, 30 times more energy is released by a 7 quake than a 6 and 900 times more energy by a 7 than by a 5. **NOTE:** The use of the Moment Magnitude scale or its more famous predecessor, the Richter scale as commonly interpreted by the media today, is being questioned by a growing number of scientists, since ground motion is not directly correlated with the destructive power of earthquakes.

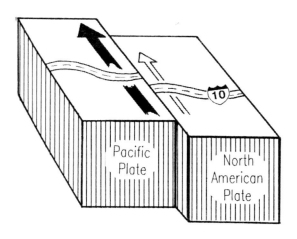

Figure 2.36 -- Transform Fault Boundary in California. Both the North American and Pacific Plates are drifting northwest; but, the Pacific Plate is moving faster.

Discontinuous Lowlands between the Mountains

The southernmost lowland section is the **Central Valley of California**, which is drained by the Sacramento River in the north and the San Joaquin in the south. This flat alluvium filled valley is roughly 450 miles long and 40 to 60 miles wide to the east are the Sierra Nevada. Farming in the Central Valley has helped California to become the leading agricultural state in the United States. It is estimated that a fourth of the food eaten by Americans is grown in the Central Valley of California. The northern half of the Central Valley receives about 20 inches of rainfall a year, while Bakersfield in the southern half averages less than seven inches a year. As a result, the Central Valley relies heavily on irrigation for its agricultural production. In recent years, large tracts of rich farmland in the Central Valley have been converted into housing subdivisions as hundreds of thousands of Californians moved inland willing to trade three-hour work commutes for affordable homes.

The **Willamette Valley-Puget Sound Lowland-Georgia Trough** of Oregon, Washington and British Columbia is a broad valley flanked on the west by the low lying Coastal Ranges and on the east by the rugged Cascade Mountains. The cities of Portland, Seattle and Vancouver are found in this lowland trough--in all three-fourths of the population of Oregon, Washington and British Columbia live in these valleys. Physical factors, including rich soil, mild temperatures and plentiful rain make for excellent agriculture, especially hops, vegetables, and fruit. The topographic depression continues north through the Strait of Georgia. Through the hundreds of islands between Seattle and Skagway, Alaska winds the **Inside Passage** (sometimes called the Inland Passage) a coastal waterway for vessels seeking protection from the storms of the open ocean. In recent years, it has become an important route for the cruise ship trade bringing tens of thousands of tourists each summer to view the beautiful fiorded coast, active glaciers and whales. The Inside Passage connects the many isolated towns of the Alaskan panhandle and the coast of British Columbia. These towns including Alaska's capital, Juneau, rely heavily on shipping as there are no roads connecting them to the outside world.

The St. Elias Range separates the lowlands of British Columbia from the **Southern Alaskan Basins,** including **the Matanuska-Susitna Basin, Cook Inlet** and the **Shelikof Strait.** The **Matanuska-Susitna Basin,** or **Mat-Sur** as it is known locally, is the main agricultural area in Alaska and contains Anchorage, the state's most populous and most industrialized city. For these reasons and Juneau's isolation, there has been discussion of moving state government operations to this area.

The Canadian Shield

The Canadian Shield is located north and east of the Interior Lowlands (Figure 2.37). Most of this province is found in Canada, with two small extensions into the United States, the **Adirondacks** of northeastern New York and the **Superior Upland** in northern Minnesota, Wisconsin, and Michigan. The region is composed of the oldest rock on the continent. The continental glaciers had their origins here and moved outward in all directions scraping off nearly all pre-existing hills and soil. Today's rather level topography and numerous lakes attest to the erosive power of the glaciers. (See BOX 2.3 for a discussion of the work of continental glaciation.)

Mineral deposits of significant quality and quantity have been exposed at the surface by the erosive glacial action. The basis of the economy throughout most of this region is the great coniferous forests of the south and the widespread mineral deposits. The thin soil cover, plus the harsh climate, severely limit agriculture. The **Clay Belt** is geologically different from the Shield, but is surrounded by it. The region is an area of highly fertile gray clay soils deposited on the bottom of a large glacial meltwater lake that once existed in northeast Ontario and western Quebec. During and immediately following World War I, the Canadian government encouraged immigrants and returning soldiers to settle in the Clay Belt based on the agricultural potential of the soils. Unfortunately, the fertility of the soils could not overcome the shortness of the growing season and, by the mid 1930s, virtually all of the pioneer agricultural settlements had been abandoned. With predictions of global warming, there is renewed interest in the Clay Belt for commercial agricultural.

Figure 2.37 -- The Canadian Shield in Southern Ontario

Bordering the southern shore of Hudson Bay and James Bay are the **Hudson Bay Lowlands**, North America's largest wetlands region. A relatively flat poorly drained region crossed by numerous broad slow moving streams, it is sparsely populated. Much of the region is covered with **muskeg** or bogs. Like a wet soggy blanket, the muskeg are composed of only slightly decayed vegetative matter and sphagnum moss. The moss can absorb 15 to30 times its weight in water and with the cool temperatures minimizing evaporation rates the region is continually spongy in the summer and early fall before freezing solid in the winter. The region produces peat moss and has significant oil and gas deposits. The western portion of the lowlands include important maternity grounds for Polar Bears. Late forming ice on Hudson Bay has placed the Polar Bear in desperate straits and has made the Polar Bear an international symbol of the consequences of global climate change. Churchill, Manitoba on the west coast of Hudson Bay lies at the northern end of the Hudson Bay Lowlands. Projections for the shrinking of the extent of permanent sea ice on the Arctic Ocean has led to a great deal of interest in establishing a shipping route between the Arctic Russian seaport of Murmansk and the deep ocean port in Churchill. Dubbed the **Arctic Bridge** minor amounts of shipping has already made this Arctic crossing.

Hawaiian Islands

Located 2,300 miles west of the California coast are the Hawaiian Islands. The eight large volcanic islands that comprise the 50th U.S. state are the southern most links in the Hawaiian–Emperor Seamount chain that stretches nearly 3800 miles (6000 km) to the Aleutian Islands of Alaska (Figure 2.38). All of these islands were formed as the Pacific Plate slowly moved over a hot, relatively stationary mantle plume found beneath the oceanic crust. The hot plume burns a hole

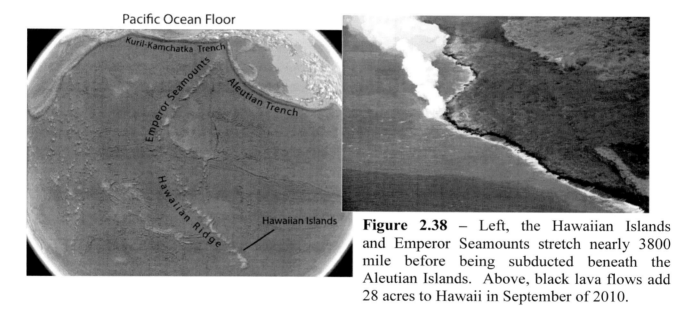

Figure 2.38 – Left, the Hawaiian Islands and Emperor Seamounts stretch nearly 3800 mile before being subducted beneath the Aleutian Islands. Above, black lava flows add 28 acres to Hawaii in September of 2010.

through the thin crust passing overhead creating a passage for magma to flow upward creating a submarine volcano. Some of these volcanoes have grown large enough to rise to the oceans surface forming what are known as "**hot spot islands.**" Evidence for this idea came from the radioactive isotope dating of the volcanic rock making up each of the Hawaiian Islands and the Emperor Seamounts. The research revealed that as one moves from the southern most island toward the northwest the islands become progressively older. In addition, only the southern most islands are still volcanically active. The age of the volcanic rock on each island also allowed geologists to determine the rate that the Pacific Plate is moving over the hot mantle plume at the rate of approximately 3.3 inches a year.

Currently, the hot plume lies beneath the Big Island of Hawaii, but as the plate slowly moves away a new island is being born. Named Lo'ihi, it is still a submarine volcano some 3000 feet beneath the surface, but some day it may build up enough height to poke through the waters of the Pacific to become the newest link in the Hawaiian chain.

PHYSIOGRAPHY REVIEW

1. According to the theory of Plate Tectonics, why and upon what do the earth's crustal plates float?

2. How and when was the great central core, or craton, of North America formed?

3. Describe the Appalachian Mountains of 250 million years ago. How were they formed and what did they look like?

4. Describe the process by which the Rocky Mountains were formed?

5. What are the seven major physiographic provinces of North America?

6. What is the *Fall Line*, how was it formed, and what has been its economic role?

7. Why are there so many lakes in Canada and the Northern tier of American states and approximately what percent of the world's fresh water (not counting ice caps) is held in the five Great Lakes?

8. What are the major depositional features associated with glaciation and what are the major erosional features? How was each formed?

9. What type of fault is the San Andreas and why are earthquakes associated with it? In what direction is each plate moving?

10. How do scientists determine the epicenter of an earthquake? What factors are related to the loss of life and property by earthquakes?

11. Other than coastal California, what other regions of the U.S. and Canada are at moderate or severe risk from earthquakes?

12. Why did the north slope of Mt. St. Helens bulge out over 300 feet prior to the eruption of May 1980?

13. Locate each of the physiographic provinces. Then locate each of the following and note how they were formed.

Cascades(Mt. St Helens)	Columbia Plateau	Balcones Escarpment
Mississippi Alluvial Lowland	Outer Banks	Ridge and Valley
Monadnocks (Pilot Mt.)	Appalachian Plateau	Sand Hills of Nebraska
Colorado Plateau	Columbian Plateau	Basin and Range
Bluegrass & Nashville Basins	Missouri Coteau	The Clay Belt
Badlands Topography	Saint Francois Mts.	Inside Passage Fiords
Mt. Whitney and Death Valley	Crater Lake Caldera	Adirondacks
Superior Uplands		

PHYSIOGRAPHY EXERCISE I

1. ON THE ATTACHED MAP, LABEL AND DRAW (in blue) THE FOLLOWING RIVERS:
   - A. Mississippi
   - B. Ohio
   - C. Missouri
   - D. Hudson
   - E. Tennessee
   - F. St. Lawrence

2. LOCATE AND LABEL THE FOLLOWING CITIES IN RED:
   - A. Greensboro, NC
   - B. Atlanta
   - C. New Orleans
   - D. St. Louis
   - E. Detroit
   - F. Cleveland
   - G. Chicago
   - H. New York City
   - I. Boston
   - J. Memphis
   - K. Pittsburgh
   - L. Miami
   - M. Minneapolis
   - N. Washington, DC
   - O. Houston
   - P. Quebec
   - Q. Montreal
   - R. Toronto

3. FOR EACH OF THE PHYSIOGRAPHIC REGIONS LISTED BELOW ANSWER THE QUESTIONS AND <u>CAREFULLY</u> SHADE THEM IN ON THE PHYSIOGRAPHIC MAP USING THE SUGGESTED COLOR.

A. COASTAL PLAIN (*Shade regions on map of the Eastern United States – Figure 2.39*)

(1) Continental Shelf (do not color)--the submerged edge of the continent. During the Pleistocene, was more or less of the continental margins exposed? __1__.

(2) Coastal Plain (yellow)--The islands that parallel the coasts of New Jersey, North Carolina and Texas are known as __2__. These islands are migrating in which direction? __3__.

(3) The Mississippi Alluvial Lowland (orange-yellow)--The Mississippi Flood Plain south of the confluence of the Mississippi and Ohio Rivers is an exceptionally fertile region. Farmers and river men have watched the River constantly move like a wiggling snake in its flood plain. Man has attempted to restrict its wanderings and flooding. Currently, the river flows from Baton Rouge to New Orleans and through its delta to the Gulf of Mexico. But, without man's help, the course of the Mississippi River below Baton Rouge would flow through the valley of the __4__ river (label and draw this river on the map in blue). What are two reasons that the Mississippi Delta is rapidly shrinking? __5__ and __6__.

B. APPALACHIAN HIGHLANDS (*Shade regions on map– Figure 2.39*)

(1) The Piedmont (light green)--This region is composed of old, metamorphosed rock. At places, small knobs (such as Stone Mt., GA; Pilot Mt., NC; or Looking Glass Rock, NC) of highly resistant rock stand above the general landscape. They represent the last remains, or cores, of an ancient mountain chain that once covered the region and are called __7__. The line that divides the Piedmont from the Coastal Plain is called the __8__. List two reasons why so many cities are located along this line: __9__ and __10__. Name three major cities located on this line: __11__, __12__, and __13__.

(2) The Blue Ridge (blue)--The Blue Ridge rises abruptly above the Piedmont. The highest peaks in the eastern U.S. are here, including __14__ the highest point in the East. The southern portion of the Appalachian Highland and all of the Blue Ridge were formed when North America first collided and later separated from __15__.

(3) The Ridge and Valley (blue-green)--The tremendous compression caused by the great continental collision forming the Blue Ridge resulted in a more gentle folding of the rock layers farther west. The folding rock layers look as if someone had pushed a loose carpet against a wall. The tops of the folds cracked and were subject to greater erosion. While almost all of the rock overlying the region is sedimentary in nature, there are significant differences between sedimentary rock types in their erosional rates. Rock such as __16__ eroded down quickly to form the valley floors, while resistant rock like __17__ remained to form the ridges. Rivers trapped between the ridges will flow parallel to the ridges until they encounter a weak spot where they can cut through. The places where rivers eroded through the ridges are known as __18__ and were major routes in the westward migration. Name two of these famous breaks __19__ and __20__.

(4) The Appalachian Plateau (green)--This region looks very little like the stereotypical flat-topped plateau. Originally, when tectonic pressure slowly uplifted the thick, flat sedimentary layers which form the Appalachian Plateau, it might have been quite flat. However, after the uplift, the numerous streams of the region began to cut down through the soft rock until they had formed one of the most dissected of all physiographic regions in North America. One of the most common sedimentary rocks found in this region is __21__. Where subterranean water encounters this rock, it can easily dissolve it to form caverns. Sometimes the caverns collapse forming "sinkholes" on the surface. A landscape of caverns, sinkholes and other solution landforms is known as a __22__ landscape.

(5) New England-Maritime Section (green-blue)--This is the oldest section of the Appalachian Highlands, having formed nearly 440 million years ago in a collision with __23__.

C. INTERIOR LOWLANDS (Shade regions on map of Central United States – Figure 2.40)

(1) Central Lowlands (light red)--This is the largest region of the Interior lowlands stretching from the Arctic Ocean to Texas. Flat to gently rolling it is one of the richest agricultural regions in the world. The covering of sedimentary rock is testament to periods in the past when much of the region was covered by shallow seas. The shale and coal deposits formed in __24__ areas, sandstones indicate ancient __25__, and limestone areas of __26__. The northern half of the region was heavily glaciated; moraines, eskers and drumlins are found throughout the northern half of the Central Lowlands. The most notable feature are the hundreds of thousands of lakes left by the retreating glacier. They range in size from small ponds to the Great Lakes. Of all the world's fresh surface water (other than the glacial ice caps), what percentage is found in the 5 Great Lakes? __27__.

(2) Bluegrass and Nashville Basins (dark red)--This region is a gently rising dome whose core was composed primarily of limestone. As the limestone core cracked, it was easily eroded creating a depression or basin in the middle of the dome surrounded by a low ridge of

hills/mountains. The eroded limestone has left fertile soils. What unique agricultural industry has become associated with the lush grass growing on these limestone-based soils? _____28.

(3) Interior Highlands (light orange-red)--This region encompasses the Ozark Plateau and Ouachita Mountains separated by the Arkansas River Valley. Like the Bluegrass and Nashville Basins, they were formed initially by a doming of the earth's surface. However, instead of a basin, there are the St. Francis Mountains. What accounts for such a dramatic difference? 29__.

(4) Great Plains (pink)--The Great Plains are composed of sedimentary rock layers, mainly Cenozoic in age. These layers rise gently from about 2000 feet on their eastern edge to nearly a mile where their sedimentary layers lay on the flanks of the Rocky Mountains. Perhaps, the greatest difference between the Central Lowlands and Great Plains is in the amount of precipitation received. The Great Plains in general receives less than __30__ inches per year, resulting in a short grass prairie (as opposed to the tall grass prairie farther east) with trees being relegated to areas along streams and rivers. The eastern boundary of the Great Plains in the north is marked by the __31__, which rises about 500 feet above the Central Lowlands. In the south, the Great Plains meets the Coastal Plain along the __32__ in central Texas. Through Oklahoma, Kansas and Nebraska, the Central Lowlands and Great Plains boundary is poorly delineated. The western boundary of the Great Plains is abrupt and dramatic, as the Rocky Mountains rise some thousands of feet above the rolling prairie. In areas where the thick protective grasses have been broken, the soft, recently deposited sediment, has been deeply and dramatically eroded into what is known as __33__.

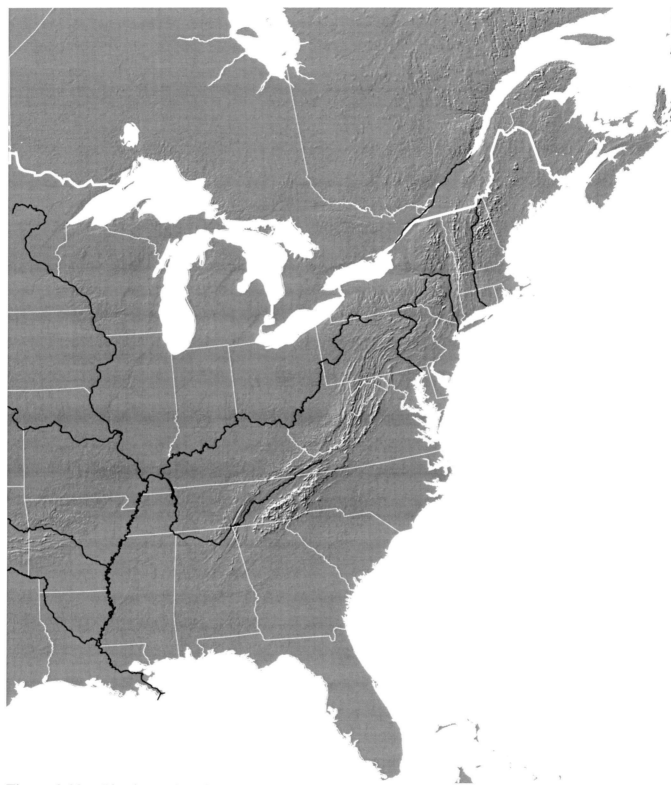

Figure 2.39 -- Physiography of the eastern United States and southeastern Canada

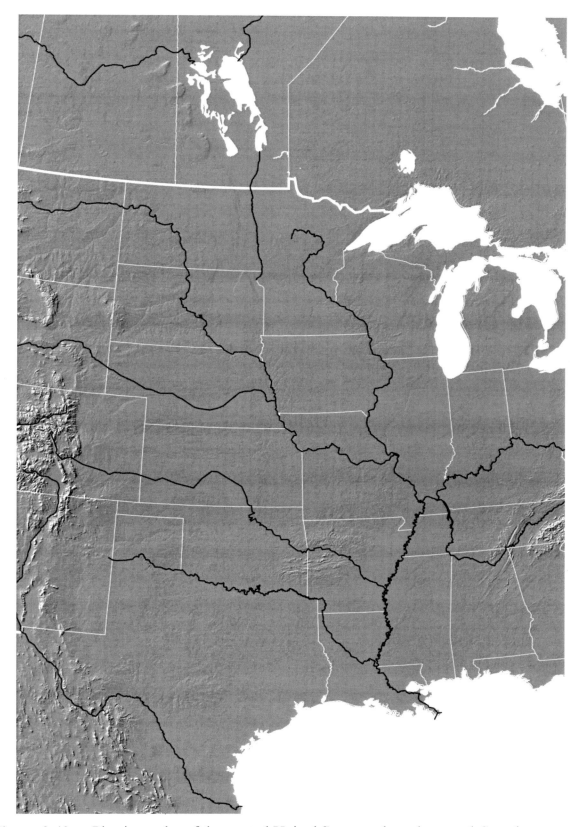

Figure 2.40 -- Physiography of the central United States and south-central Canada

Name _____

ANSWER SHEET -- PHYSIOGRAPHY EXERCISE I

1. _____

2. _____

3. _____

4. _____

5. _____
   _____

6. _____
   _____

7. _____

8. _____

9. _____
   _____

10. _____
    _____

11. _____

12. _____

13. _____

14. _____

15. _____

16. _____

17. _____

18. _____

19. _____

20. _____

21. _____

22. _____

23. _____

24. _____

25. _____

26. _____

27. _____

28. _____

29. _____
    _____
    _____

30. _____

31. _____

32. _____

33. _____

PHYSIOGRAPHY EXERCISE II

1. ON THE ATTACHED MAP (Figure 2.41), LABEL & DRAW (in blue) THESE RIVERS:

    A. Missouri
    B. Colorado
    C. Columbia
    D. Green
    E. Rio Grande
    F. Snake
    G. Red (north)
    H. San Joaquin
    I. Saskatchewan

2. LOCATE AND LABEL THE FOLLOWING CITIES IN RED:

    A. Kansas City
    B. Denver
    C. Seattle
    D. Portland
    E. Salt Lake City
    F. Dallas
    G. Phoenix
    H. Vancouver
    I. Los Angeles
    J. San Francisco
    K. San Diego
    L. Oklahoma City
    M. Vancouver
    N. Calgary

3. ANSWER THE FOLLOWING QUESTIONS AND COLOR IN EACH OF THE PHYSIOGRAPHIC REGIONS WITH THE SUGGESTED COLOR.

   ### A. THE ROCKY MOUNTAINS

   (1) The Rocky Mts., stretching from New Mexico to Alaska, were formed as the North American Plate moved westward and collided with oceanic crust moving eastward from the __1__ beneath the Pacific Ocean. The colliding oceanic crust was subducted beneath the edge of the continent with most of it melting and returning to the earth's mantle. However, as in the case of the Sierra Nevada Mts., some of the lightest of the magma rose upward from the descending plate. These huge masses of magma, called __2__, forced their way up through the continental crust with most cooling before reaching the surface. The result are immense pockets of buried __3__, an igneous rock that took millions of years to cool and solidify. Today, erosion has exposed these massive rock intrusions, from Southern California to Alaska. Folding and faulting of the continent from the collision of the plates combined with the rise of the less dense magma formed the earliest Rocky Mountains in the same fashion as the present day __4__ mountains of South America are being formed. About 180 million years ago, the north Pacific probably resembled the southwestern Pacific Ocean of today, full of island arcs moving away from an oceanic spreading center. As the Pacific Plate of that time moved eastward into the oncoming North American Plate, these island arcs were carried, one after the other, to the subduction zone. Because they were composed of lightweight materials, they were not pulled down beneath the continent but were crushed and fused onto the western edge of North America. Over a period of 100 million years, about 40 island arcs, or microcontinents, were added to North America in this way. They are called __5__, referring to the fact that they were formed elsewhere in the world and were added to the North American continent.

   (2) The Southern Rockies (green-blue)--From New Mexico to Southern Wyoming, this portion of the Rockies contains many of the highest peaks in the conterminous U.S. Here,

among the lofty San Juan, Sangre de Cristo and Front Range Mountains, four great rivers are born. The __6__ moves through great dams and the Grand Canyon to the Pacific Ocean, the __7__ flows south to irrigate the cotton and fruit of New Mexico and Texas. To the east, through Kansas wheat fields rolls the __8__. Finally, the __9__ wanders across Nebraska to join the Missouri.

(3) The Wyoming Basin (yellow-green)--This basin separates the Southern Rockies from the Middle Rockies. This major break in the mountains has been utilized for transcontinental transportation since the early days of exploration. Wagon train routes, the Pony Express, railroads, and interstate highways all have used this route to connect the east coast with the west.

(4) The Middle Rockies and Northern Rockies (blue)--North of the Wyoming Basin begin the Middle and Northern Rockies. These mountains extend north to the border of British Columbia and the Yukon Territory, where the Liard River separates them from the Arctic Rockies. The Liard River flows east and joins the __10__ River, the second largest river (by drainage area or length) in North America after the Mississippi River.

B. THE INTERMONTANE PLATEAUS AND BASINS

(1) Colorado Plateau (red)--This roughly circular region centered on the "Four Corners" (the point where the states of Arizona, Utah, New Mexico, and Colorado come together) began to rise gently about 5-10 million years ago. The slow rise of the region is evidenced by the numerous __11__ found on rivers like the San Juan, Green or Colorado in the Grand Canyon. This flat plateau with its spectacular canyons (Grand Canyon, Zion, Bryce and many others) has numerous volcanic cones scattered over its area. These volcanic remnants, including the towering Shiprock of northwest New Mexico, Vulcan's Throne in Grand Canyon National Park, Sunset Crater National Monument and Valley of Fire State Park in central New Mexico are all evidence of the tremendous force that is pushing this region upward.

(2) Basin and Range (orange)--South and west of the Colorado Plateau is a unique area called the Basin and Range. This sparsely populated arid region is characterized by __12__, referring to the fact that the streams do not flow out of the region but rather empty into low-lying pockets where the water evaporates or forms shallow salty lakes. As the Pacific Plate slides northwest along the San Andreas fault, it has been dragging North America along with it for the past thirty million years. As a result, North America has been "stretched" in the Basin and Range Province leaving the crust unusually thin and cracked. The cracking has allowed for pieces of the crust to drop forming a horst and __13__ topography, which is the result of normal faulting. Many geologists believe that the stretching and thinning of the region have roughly doubled its size.

(3) Columbia Plateau (purple)--Found in eastern Washington and Oregon and southern Idaho is the Columbian Plateau. This plateau was formed from repeated flows of lava from great fissures in the crust. The most recent of these lava flows occurred only 1,000 years ago, and there is no geologic reason why additional flows could not occur today. The Snake and Columbia Rivers have cut deep gorges through the lava flows.

C. PACIFIC MOUNTAINS AND LOWLANDS

(1) Eastern Series of Mountains (light blue)--This series of north-south trending mountains includes the Sierra Nevada, Cascades, Coast Mountains of Br. Columbia and the Aleutian Islands of Alaska. All of these ranges are accreted terrane. The Sierra Nevada Mountains tower above the Central Valley of California. The highest peak in the 48 conterminous U.S. states, __14__, is located here, as are Yosemite, Sequoia and Kings Canyon National Parks. To the north of the Sierra Nevada Mountain are the Cascades. This range includes a series of spectacular composite volcanoes, including Mt. Rainier, Mt. Hood, Crater Lake and Mt. Adams. The fact that all of these peaks are potentially active was vividly illustrated in May of 1980 with the violent eruption of Mt. St. Helens. These composite cones exist because far below them the small __15__ plate is slowly being subducted.

(2) Western Series of Mountains (brown)--This series of mountains lies along the western margin of North America. The southernmost are the Los Angeles Range which rings the Los Angeles Basin, an area about the size of the Greensboro Triad, containing over 15 million people. Material washing off of the Los Angeles Range has collected in the basin, at one time making it a prime agricultural region. Today, due to the population pressure, little is left of the massive orchards that covered the area 30 years ago. To the north are the Coast Ranges of California. These low lying hills mark the path of the San Andreas Fault, a __16__ fault. The Pacific Plate on the western side of the San Andreas Fault is slowly drifting to the __17__, while the North American Plate on the eastern side of the San Andreas is moving to the __18__ at a much __19__ rate. North of San Francisco, the San Andreas runs out to sea. The Western Series of mountains continues as the Coast Ranges of Oregon, Washington and British Columbia. These low-lying mountains are cut by the Columbia and Fraser Rivers. In British Columbia, the mountains are actually a series of islands, including the two largest, __20__ and Queen Charlotte, lying just off the mainland.

(3) Discontinuous Lowlands (green)--Lying between the Eastern and Western Series of mountains are a series of interrupted lowlands running from southern California through southern Alaska. The southernmost and largest is the __21__ the most important agricultural region in the most important agricultural state in the U.S. The Willamette Valley-Puget Sound Lowland of Washington and Oregon is also an important agricultural region, as well as the major commercial/industrial center of the U.S. Northwest. The lowlands continue across the border into Canada. Here is located __22__, one of the world's most beautiful cities, lying at the mouth of the __23__ River in the lowlands with the mountains to the east and the Juan de Fuca Strait to the west. Northward into Alaska's "panhandle," the discontinuous lowlands are known as the __24__ because ships can sail for hundreds of miles along the coast, protected by the countless islands found there. Finally, the last major segment of the discontinuous lowlands is the __25__ Valley, Alaska's primary agricultural region and its population center.

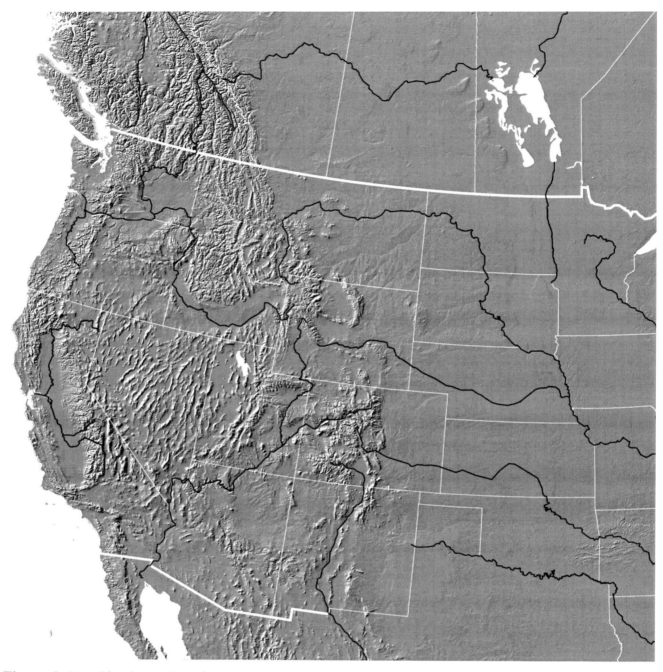

Figure 2.41 -- Physiography of the western United States and southwest Canada

Name _____

ANSWER SHEET -- PHYSIOGRAPHY EXERCISE II

1. _____

2. _____

3. _____

4. _____

5. _____

6. _____

7. _____

8. _____

9. _____

10. _____

11. _____

12. _____

13. _____

14. _____

15. _____

16. _____

17. _____

18. _____

19. _____

20. _____

21. _____

22. _____

23. _____

24. _____

25. _____

Figure 3.1 -- Hurricane Dennis (seen here) sat off the North Carolina coast for 9 days, saturating the eastern third of the state, before finally making landfall as a tropical storm on Sept. 5, 1999. Ten days later Hurricane Floyd made landfall near Wilmington, NC with winds clocked at nearly 130 mph. Floyd's most dangerous punch however, was its rain. In some areas 15 to 20 inches of rain fell in a 12 hour period. Quickly the Tar, Neuse, Roanoke, and Pamlico Rivers overflowed their banks in what was considered to be a 500 year flood event. This one-two hurricane punch killed 51 people and was the most costly disaster in North Carolina history (image courtesy NOAA).

CHAPTER THREE

WEATHER, CLIMATE, VEGETATION AND SOILS

Weather and Climate

Sitting on the northern tip of Canada's Ellesmere Island the tiny village of Alert is the northern most settlement in the world. Just over 4,100 miles south lies Key West, Florida the southernmost settlement in the continental United States. This immense latitudinal extent of the landmass encompassing the U.S. and Canada is the major reason why they contain such a variety of climatic regions. For the eastern two-thirds of the U.S. and Canada, the primary change to climate is that of temperature. Simply put as you travel pole ward the climates become cooler. Places in the low latitudes normally have minimal temperature ranges. As water is a moderating influence on temperature change, areas near the oceans typically experience less seasonal temperature variation than those farther inland. Most of the continent lies in the **Prevailing Westerlies** so that weather systems move from west to east. Much of the moisture originating from the Pacific Ocean falls on the windward slopes of the western mountains. In a process known as **orographic** rainfall, the wind rushes up the mountains causing barometric pressure to drop, the air cools and the water vapor carried off the Pacific condenses and falls as rain or at higher elevations snow. The air, now considerably drier, warms as it descends the **leeward slopes** (the side protected from the prevailing winds) resulting in a drier and warmer area known as a **rain shadow**. Thus, west coast cities such as Portland and Seattle located on the windward slopes of the coastal mountains are famous for their rainfall totals, while eastern Washington and eastern Oregon are semi-deserts. With the western mountains effectively blocking precipitation from reaching the interior from the Pacific and the prevailing Westerlies preventing moisture from the Atlantic penetrating very far inland, the major source of moisture for the eastern United States and adjacent Canada is the Gulf of Mexico. As air moves northward from the Gulf, the Westerlies and Jet Stream direct it toward the east. As a result, the southeast and east coasts record a great deal of precipitation; however, the prevailing winds carry most moisture away from the Great Plains, which remains rather dry.

Air Masses

Air resting upon the open ocean of the Arctic will become cold and moist, while air over the deserts of northern Mexico will become warm and dry. The longer air lingers over an area, the more closely its temperature and humidity characteristics resemble the region it covers. A large body of air that develops relatively homogeneous temperature and humidity characteristics from the surface, or **source region**, beneath it is called an **air mass**. Air masses are classified as *Tropical* if their source region is in the low latitudes and *Polar* if their source region is in the high latitudes. Air masses whose source regions are the oceans are categorized as *maritime*, and those that form over large land masses are classified *continental*. Four general types of air masses are possible, maritime-tropical (mT), maritime-polar (mP), continental-tropical (cT) and continental-polar (cP). Because warm air can hold more moisture than cold air, marine tropical air masses contain far more water vapor than marine polar ones, though either would contain more moisture than continental air masses. Water vapor is a moderating influence on an air mass' temperature; thus, continental polar air is normally far colder than marine polar air and continental tropical air is far warmer than marine tropical air. Seven major **air masses** influence weather patterns in North America. The **continental polar** air mass originating over northern Canada and the **maritime tropical of the Gulf of Mexico** are the two most important for the most populous eastern two-thirds of the United States and southeastern Canada (Figure 3.2).

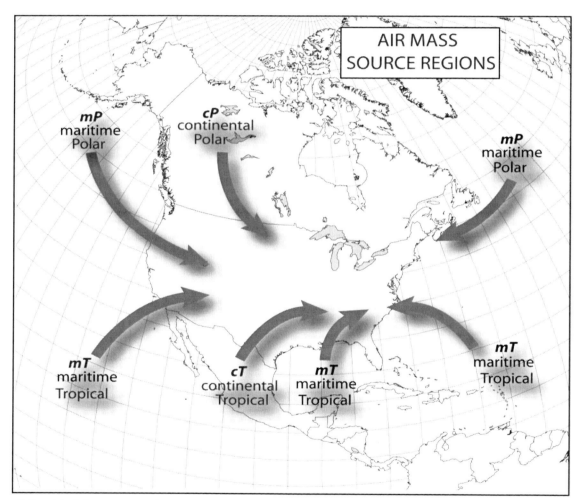

Figure 3.2. Air Masses

In winter, the continental polar air mass moves south out of Canada bringing frigid, dry air which occasionally results in freezing temperatures as far south as Miami. In summer, this air mass usually remains far to the north as the maritime tropical of the Gulf invades the northern United States and southern Canada. Along the **zone of contact** where these two air masses meet, the warm, moist air from the south rises over the cold, dry air from the north. This results in the formation of a low pressure center. The rising air cools and the moisture it is carrying condenses causing increasing clouds and possible **cyclonic** precipitation (Figure 3.3). The low pressure storm system is blown generally eastward by the Prevailing Westerlies so that eventually much of the eastern U.S. and Canada are affected. As high pressure builds in behind the low and follows its eastward journey, clear skies and drier air replace the cloudy, more moist conditions. Approximately 20,000 feet above the surface lies a ribbon of fast flowing air circling the globe, known as the **Jet Stream** (Figure 3.3). The Jet Stream steers air masses across the continent. In the winter time, the Jet Stream slides further southward and brings cold arctic air to the continental U.S. in the summer, it retreats to northern Canada and is not a significant factor for most North Americans. If one visualizes an air mass as a large dome of air being pushed by the Prevailing Westerlies and/or the Jet Stream, the leading edge of that dome is called a front. If the dome is colder than the surrounding air, then it is a **cold front**, and if warmer air is in the dome then it is a

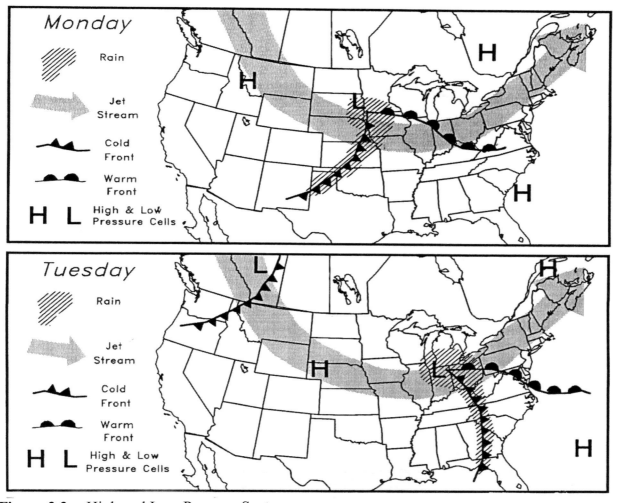

Figure 3.3 -- High and Low Pressure Systems

warm front. If the dome of air is not moving then the edge of the dome is referred to as a **stationary front.** Cold fronts tend to bring rainfall because as the cold dome moves into a region it forces the air that is in front of it to rise up and over the cold, creating a trough of low barometric pressure along the advancing front. As the warmer air rises over the front, it cools and condensation of water vapor is likely to occur. After the front moves through, surface conditions are typically cool and relatively cloud free.

In western North America, the **maritime polar air mass of the north Pacific** and the **maritime tropical air mass of the south Pacific** shift pole ward in the warmer months, along with the Prevailing Westerlies and their attendant high pressure cell, resulting in dry weather in California and limited precipitation from northern California to southern Alaska. During the cooler period of the year, however, the air masses and wind and pressure systems shift south, bringing moisture to southern California and increased precipitation to coastal sections farther north.

Atmospheric Hazards

Hurricanes

The violent circular, tropical storms called **cyclones** in the Indian Ocean and **typhoons** in the western Pacific are known to North Americans as **hurricanes**. Forming over large bodies of warm water (at least 80 degrees Fahrenheit), these turbulent giants derive their energy from the latent heat of condensation. Air, in contact with warm tropical water, heats and begins to rise in a slow vortex. Moist air from all points flows in to replace the ascending air. Water vapor carried aloft with the rising air condenses, releasing more heat--allowing the air to rise even faster. The faster the air rises, the faster it must be replaced. When the air rushing in to fill the void left by the rising air reaches 74 miles per hour (119 km/hr), the storm is classified as a true hurricane (Table 1).

Table 1.

The Saffir-Simpson Hurricane Scale
(from the National Oceanic and Atmospheric Administration)

Category One Hurricane:
    Winds 74-95 mph (64-82 kt or 119-153 km/hr). Storm surge generally 4-5 ft above normal. No real damage to building structures. Damage primarily to unanchored mobile homes, shrubbery, and trees. Some damage to poorly constructed signs. Also, some coastal road flooding and minor pier damage.

Category Two Hurricane:
    Winds 96-110 mph (83-95 kt or 154-177 km/hr). Storm surge generally 6-8 feet above normal. Some roofing material, door, and window damage of buildings. Considerable damage to shrubbery and trees with some trees

blown down. Considerable damage to mobile homes, poorly constructed signs, and piers. Coastal and low-lying escape routes flood 2-4 hours before arrival of the hurricane center. Small craft in unprotected anchorages break moorings.

Category Three Hurricane:
Winds 111-130 mph (96-113 kt or 178-209 km/hr). Storm surge generally 9-12 ft above normal. Some structural damage to small residences and utility buildings with a minor amount of curtain wall failures. Damage to shrubbery and trees with foliage blown off trees and large trees blown down. Mobile homes and poorly constructed signs are destroyed. Low-lying escape routes are cut by rising water 3-5 hours before arrival of the center of the hurricane. Flooding near the coast destroys smaller structures with larger structures damaged by battering from floating debris. Terrain continuously lower than 5 ft above mean sea level may be flooded inland 8 miles (13 km) or more. Evacuation of low-lying residences with several blocks of the shoreline may be required.

Category Four Hurricane:
Winds 131-155 mph (114-135 kt or 210-249 km/hr). Storm surge generally 13-18 ft above normal. More extensive curtain wall failures with some complete roof structure failures on small residences. Shrubs, trees, and all signs are blown down. Complete destruction of mobile homes. Extensive damage to doors and windows. Low-lying escape routes may be cut by rising water 3-5 hours before arrival of the center of the hurricane. Major damage to lower floors of structures near the shore. Terrain lower than 10 ft above sea level may be flooded requiring massive evacuation of residential areas as far inland as 6 miles (10 km).

Category Five Hurricane:
Winds greater than 155 mph (135 kt or 249 km/hr). Storm surge generally greater than 18 ft above normal. Complete roof failure on many residences and industrial buildings. Some complete building failures with small utility buildings blown over or away. All shrubs, trees, and signs blown down. Complete destruction of mobile homes. Severe and extensive window and door damage. Low-lying escape routes are cut by rising water 3-5 hours before arrival of the center of the hurricane. Major damage to lower floors of all structures located less than 15 ft above sea level and within 500 yards of the shoreline. Massive evacuation of residential areas on low ground within 5-10 miles (8-16 km) of the shoreline may be required

Storms affecting the Gulf and Atlantic coasts of the U.S. and Canada usually develop between $5°$ and $20°$ North latitude off the coast of Africa and move west by the Trade Winds into the Caribbean (Figure 3.4). After forming, these storms initially drift slowly in a westerly direction; as long as they stay over warm water, they gather strength. As they gain in intensity, their track begins to curve gradually pole ward toward cooler water or land, where, cut off from their energy source, these giants weaken and dissipate.

All hurricanes serve the useful purpose of transferring the hot air of the overheated tropics to cooler, more pole ward locations. However, for those in the path of the most violent of these storms, there is often a price to pay for this overall beneficial act of nature. Of the approximately 100 such storms which originate in the summer and fall each year, on average fewer than ten evolve into hurricanes with a minimum speed of 74 miles per hour (120 km/hr), although winds can reach speeds of nearly 200 miles per hour (320 km/hr). These storms have an average radius of 200 miles (320 km) from the center (**eye**), so that an extremely large area can be impacted. Although the wind around the eye might be strong, the center, some 10 to 15 miles (16-24 km) wide, is an area of calm rising warm, moist air being drawn in from the surrounding ocean. Many people are injured when they venture outside after the winds temporarily subside as the eye passes over them. They are trapped in the open, as the winds suddenly pick up again and whirl deadly debris through the air.

People along the coasts are most vulnerable to these storms. Since the hurricane is spiraling counterclockwise in the northern hemisphere, the most dangerous location in which to be is to the east of the storm's eye. Not only would such a location receive the highest winds, but these winds would also push the sea in front of them producing a wall of water, or **storm surge**. If the storm surge hits the coast about the time of high tide, then water 20 to 30 feet (6-9 m) high moving at a high speed could hit coastal property full-force causing intense destruction. In fact, the storm surge results in much of the property damage and nearly all of the deaths caused by hurricanes.

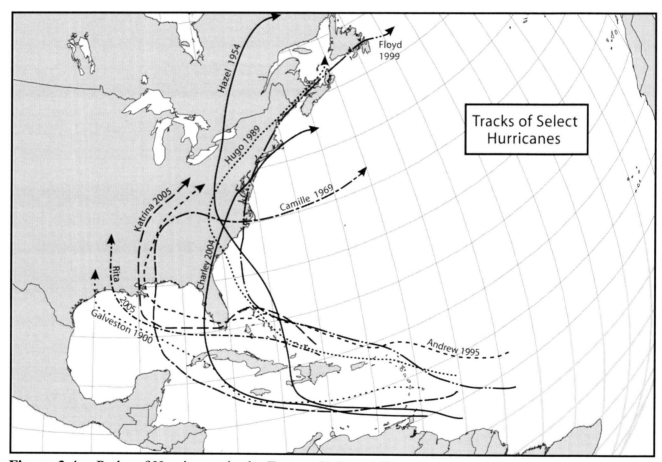

Figure 3.4 -- Paths of Hurricanes in the Eastern U.S. and Canada

Just over 100 years ago on September 8, 1900 a category 4 hurricane roared over the island city of Galveston, Texas. With winds in excess of 130 mph and a storm surge of 15 feet the unsuspecting inhabitants of the island had little chance. When it was over, more than 8,000 were dead and what had been the largest city in Texas was virtually gone. This single event cost more American lives than all subsequent hurricanes combined. With the advent of satellite images, Doppler radar, and a global network of weather stations reporting the minute by minute location of these giant storms, the death toll of Galveston is not likely to be repeated in the U.S. However, these monster storms, are still deadly and the potential dollar loss from hurricanes grows each year as the value and number of beachfront housing units increases at unprecedented rates.

In 1969, **Camille,** a category 5 storm, came onshore near New Orleans, moved up the Mississippi Valley to Cairo, then east through Kentucky and Virginia killing over 250 people. Hurricane Hugo, which came inland at Charleston, S.C. then moved through Charlotte, N.C. and southwestern Virginia in October 1989, was the strongest to hit the Atlantic Coast in 35 years, killing fewer than a dozen people but causing over $5 billion in property damage. Just since the landing of Hurricane Hugo the number of persons living along the Atlantic-Gulf coast has approximately doubled. Authorities are concerned that an early major storm coming ashore during the peak summer vacation period could result in a human and a financial disaster.

During the 2004 hurricane season, four major hurricanes (**Charley, Frances, Ivan and Jeanne**) swept through Florida in August and September. It was estimated that one in five Florida homes was damaged and 117 Floridians lost their lives. The price tag of 42 billion dollars for the 2004 hurricane season eclipsed the previous record of 35 billion dollars set by hurricane **Andrew** in 1992. When Andrew, a category 5 storm, hit the U.S. it leveled Homestead, Florida south of Miami before continuing across the Gulf of Mexico and striking south-central Louisiana. As devastating as the 1992 and 2004 seasons were, it is the 2005 Atlantic hurricane season that will be longest remembered. There were a record 26 named storms that year with three becoming category-five hurricanes **Rita, Wilma** and **Katrina**.

Wilma became the strongest hurricane on record in the Atlantic Basin with a pressure of 882 mb breaking the old record set by **Gilbert** (888 mb) in 1988, but it was **Katrina** with the most deadly punch. When Katrina came ashore its **storm surge** filled Lake Pontchartrain which rose quickly breaching the levee system protecting New Orleans and flooding most of the city (figure3.5). Much of New Orleans lies in a depression between Lake Pontchartrain to the north and the Mississipppi River to the south. Once the flood waters entered the city they had to be artificially pumped out, a process that took months to complete. Katrina killed over 1800 people and displaced over one million people. Financially the costliest natural disaster in U.S. history, the final price tag is difficult to calculate with estimates varying between 85 billion and 200 billion dollars.

While coastal communities are typically most vulnerable to hurricanes, the effects of these storms can reach far inland. As the hurricane comes onshore, the winds slow down because of land friction and the storm losing its source of strength, the warm ocean water. However, wind speeds can still remain between 50 and 100 miles per hour (80-160 km/hr). Heavy rains causing widespread flooding can also occur. In 1954, hurricane Hazel came onshore in the Carolinas and then moved north into Canada, where flooding caused over 80 deaths in Toronto alone. In 1999 hurricanes Dennis and Floyd teamed up to create the most costly disaster in North Carolina history. Making landfall only ten days apart the torrential rainfalls of this one-two punch caused unprecedented flooding in North Carolina leaving 51 dead and tens of thousands homeless. The state of North Carolina has yet to fully recover from this six billion dollar disaster (Figure3.1).

Figure 3.5 -- Flooding in New Orleans from Hurricane Katrina. Federal, state and local agencies were widely criticized for their lack of preparations, for the slow and inadequate response to the disaster, and for the lack of coordination among the various relief agencies. Charges of cronyism, incompetence and racism (New Orleans was nearly 70% African American) filled the national media (photo courtesy of NOAA/National Weather Service).

    There have been numerous attempts to limit storm damage along the coast, but constructing buildings at a safe distance from the beach has **not** usually been one of them. Instead, hotels and condominiums have increasingly been erected within only 50 feet (15m) of the beach. In order to protect costly investments, people have built **seawalls** between their buildings and the beach. Unfortunately, these result in further beach erosion in front and, thus, ultimately greater vulnerability for buildings. **Groins** are often extended out from the beach to catch drifting sand in order to build up one's beach. This, of course, robs the property down-current of its supply of sand, thus depleting that beach. In order to compensate, the person next door must then erect a groin to capture some sand to build his beach. This does not necessarily result in a beautiful beach. The combination of developers wanting to maximize profits by building as many units as close to the ocean as possible, plus beach residents and visitors wanting to live on--and not just near--the beach, have produced a perilous condition for the next major hurricane.

Tornadoes

Tornadoes are typically short-lived, small, but extremely powerful storms. They are mainly associated with advancing cold fronts on warm, moist air masses in the central U.S. during spring (April-June) (Figure 3.6). However, they also develop in convectional storms of mid-summer and are often by-products of hurricanes. Actual wind speed measurements within a tornado funnel have never been made. Instead tornado wind speeds have only been estimated indirectly through the use of Doppler radar or have been estimated by the level of damage done by a tornado. The widely used Fujita classification scale is based on the observed damage caused by a tornado (Table 2).

Table 2.

Fujita Tornado Damage Scale

Category F0: Light Damage (<73 mph); Some damage to chimneys; branches broken off trees; shallow-rooted trees pushed over; sign boards damaged.

Category F1: Moderate Damage (73-112 mph); Peels surface off roofs; mobile homes pushed off foundations or overturned; moving autos blown off road.

Category F2: Considerable Damage (113-157 mph); Roofs torn off frame houses; mobile homes demolished; boxcars overturned; large trees snapped or uprooted; light-object missiles generated; cars lifted off ground.

Category F3: Severe Damage (158- 206 mph); Roofs and some walls torn off well-constructed houses, trains overturned; most trees in forest uprooted; heavy cars lifted off ground and thrown.

Category F4: Devastating Damage (207- 260 mph); Well-constructed houses leveled; structure with weak foundations blown off some distance; cars thrown and large missiles generated.

Category F5: Incredible Damage (261- 318 mph); Strong frame houses lifted off foundations and swept away; automobile sized missiles fly through the air in excess of 100 meters (109 yards); trees debarked; incredible phenomena will occur

Tornadoes which do touch down can create a path of nearly total destruction from a few hundred yards to nearly a third of a mile wide. Some tornadoes pop up and down like a giant pogo stick, while others have been known to stay on the ground for over 20 miles (32 km). Tornadoes generally move forward at speeds of 25 to 35 miles per hour (40-56 km/hr). However, winds within the funnel can exceed 400 miles per hour (640 km/hr). The area covered might not be wide, but those small areas affected can be completely devastated (Figure 3.7). On one April day in 1974, over 300 people died as a result of a series of tornadoes from Georgia to southern Canada.

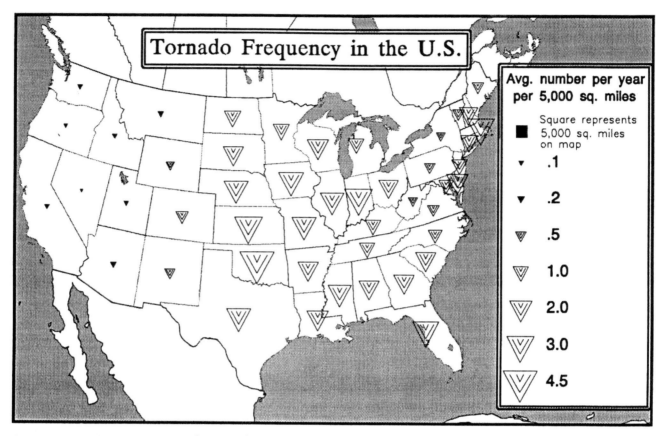

Figure 3.6 -- Average Annual Tornado Frequency

In early 1994, NASA launched the first GOES (Geostationary Operational Environmental Satellite), the most advanced weather satellite ever constructed. Today, four GOES satellites provide continuous coverage of the U.S. and considerable surrounding environs. One of the primary functions of these satellites is to track hurricanes and to monitor storms with the potential of spawning tornadoes. These NOAA satellites have improved the current lead time for warning of important storms. When conditions are favorable for the development of a tornado, a **tornado watch** is given for the affected area. Only when one has actually been detected is a **tornado warning** announced. One flaw in the warning system is that not everyone would be listening to the radio or television. Another danger is that by the time the message is relayed from the observer to the radio and television audience, the warning could be too late. It should be remembered that just because one tornado has passed by the danger is not over as there could be others nearby, since they often appear in clusters Even with the new satellite and **Doppler radar** technology providing greater accuracy of tornado forecasts, there is still relatively little time for evasive action. Storm cellars and other protective measures can only be useful if one has enough warning to reach them. The most sophisticated technology can still give only a few minutes warning of an impending tornado.

Figure 3.7 -- Tornado near Anadarko, Oklahoma in 1999 (NOAA)

Thunderstorms and Hail

While not as spectacular as tornadoes or hurricanes, thunderstorms are responsible for more deaths than their more notorious cousins. These quick developing storms can produce flash flooding, hail, and spectacular lightning strikes. Nearly 150 flash flood deaths each year are due to thunderstorms and lightning strikes are responsible for an additional 80 fatalities. Hail damage typically totals over one billion dollar annually. Compared to hurricanes, thunderstorms are quite small averaging only 15 miles across and much shorter lived, averaging only 30 minutes. Thus, while a summer thunderstorm was bringing intense winds and hail to one part of town the other side of town could be sunny and relatively calm. At any moment in time it is estimated that 1,800 thunderstorms are occurring on our planet. In the U.S. over 1,000 thunderstorms a year are classified as severe and capable of developing winds in excess of 100 mph. All of North America experiences thunderstorms but, they are far more common in the southeastern states, particularly Florida.

Hail is normally a very small, isolated event of short duration. It occurs most often in spring and summer and is associated with violent thunderstorms. Usually from two or three acres to one or two square miles are affected in an area. Occasionally, they are more widespread. In a 1994 storm, marble-size hail accumulated to a depth of over five inches in parts of Omaha, Nebraska and there have been confirmed reports of individual hail stones larger than a softball (Figure 3.8). Hail storms usually last only a few minutes, but can do great damage to crops and automobiles. Each year on average, Canada suffers at least $100 million in crop and livestock damage, while the U.S. figure is more nearly one billion dollars.

Hail is **formed** by strong updrafts carrying rain aloft through air which is below the freezing mark, so that it freezes before falling again and collecting more super-cooled water on the hailstone, which can be thrust upward again where another layer of ice is formed. This process can occur several times, with larger and larger hailstones being created. Eventually the hailstone will fall to earth when it becomes so large that the rising air is incapable of keeping the stone aloft.

Automobiles and some livestock can be moved to shelter when a hailstorm threatens, but crops cannot be protected. In hail prone areas farmers with many acres under cultivation often spread their most vulnerable crops to several nonadjacent fields. Tobacco, fruits, and vegetables are particularly vulnerable, but most crops can be damaged.

Figure 3.8. On the left golf ball size hail. Note the concentric rings of ice. Each ring indicates a time the stone fell through the atmosphere only to be pushed back up by the rising air in the thunderstorm cell. Eventually so much ice is added that the uprising air cannot hold the hail stone aloft. Imagine the force necessary to keep the grapefruit size hailstone, shown in the photo on the right, from falling (courtesy NOAA/National Weather Service).

Droughts

The drought of 2007–2008 was one of the most severe droughts of the past 100 years, particularly in the Southeast. At one point, over 40 percent of the U.S. was classified as being in either "exceptional" or "extreme drought," the two most severe classes. Record high temperatures in Georgia and the Carolinas, coupled with decades of rapid population growth, made the effects of the lack of rain particularly damaging. The great **drought of 1988** was the most recent and the most severe of a series of three much drier years during the 1980s (Figure 3.9). Different parts of the United States and Canada had the driest conditions in different year. The 1988 drought was the worst since the 1950s. There had also been a severe drought in the mid-1930s, dramatized so well by John Steinbeck in *The Grapes of Wrath* (Figure 3.10). The parts of the U.S. most affected by the 1988 drought stretched from northern Georgia across the Appalachians to Lake Ontario, from western Indiana into Minnesota and Kansas, in the eastern two-thirds of Texas and adjoining southeastern Oklahoma, from central Utah northeast into the Canadian Prairie Provinces, and throughout much of the Pacific coast states The extensive use of the Ogallala aquifer for irrigation of the Great Plains, together with U.S. government relief programs and insurance, have lessened the

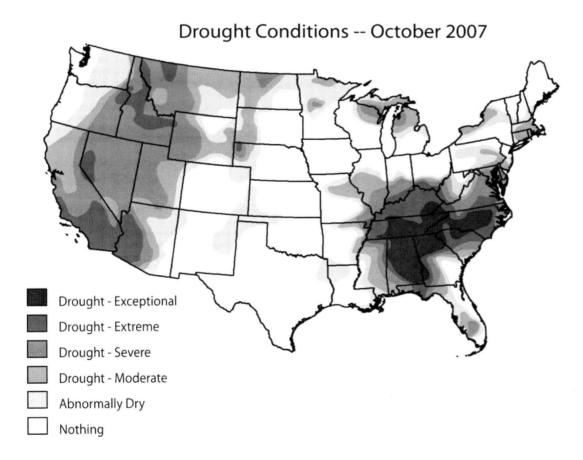

Figure 3.9-- The Drought of 2007-2008 was most acute during October of 2007. Data U.S. Drought Monitor online archives.

economic impact of the more recent droughts. During the summer of 1988, about half of the states asked for emergency drought relief and Congress initiated legislation to provide aid to farmers hurt by the extremely dry conditions. One method of helping was to use an unneeded $4 billion in crop subsidies set aside for low farm prices to alleviate some of the losses brought by the drought.

The primary **impact of drought** is usually on agriculture, though industrial and residential sectors are also affected. Since the United States and Canada are the world's two largest food exporters, a sizable decline in food crop production in these two countries means there will be much less available to be given as aid to poor lands as well as less to be sold abroad. In addition, the prices of affected food crops and livestock increase. As prices rise, poor people here and abroad suffer. Long-term effects of the 1988 drought were also apparent as many dairy and cattle farmers sold their livestock because of lack of feed, with many farmers leaving agriculture permanently.

In addition to agricultural production problems from the 1988 drought, many cities had to ration water to residences and businesses. Manufacturing plants had to reduce their hours of operation, resulting in less production and reduced income for workers. The Mississippi River was also adversely affected, reaching its lowest level in a century, thereby sharply curtailing shipping on the river. Governors of states along the Mississippi River asked the governors of the Great Lakes states and the premiers of the adjacent provinces of Canada to allow Congress to transfer sufficient water from the Great Lakes to raise the river about a foot so that most shipping could resume. The chief executives from the states in the Great Lakes area stated that this would be unwise because it might have an adverse impact on shipping in their region. Fortunately, the recently completed Tombigbee canal system was able to carry most of the vessels around the shallow portions of the Mississippi so that shipping could continue.

Most meteorologists believe that the foundations of the 1988 drought can be traced to the warm water current, **El Nino**, off the coast of Ecuador and Peru two years earlier. Instead of the jet stream taking its normal course across the United States bringing needed rain from the Gulf of Mexico, this river of air divided into two parts with one swinging far to the north into Canada and the other remaining to the south in the Gulf coast area. Another factor was the spread of a large vortex of high pressure which spread from the Midwest to the East stabilizing over the eastern two-thirds of the United States from June until late August. This both added to the high temperatures and to the drought conditions. While the threat of drought was possibly of a temporary nature, many scientists predict that the abnormally high temperatures would continue into the next century as the greenhouse effect warms both the United States and Canada, along with many other parts of the world. As it turns out, the 1990s were the warmest years of the 20th century and global sea level showed a marked increase. The first decade of the 21st century have seen global temperatures continue to be above normal.

One reason that the droughts of the mid-to-late 1980s and the 2007-2008 could be considered worse than that of not only the mid-1950s but also the mid-1930s is that the population of the United States and Canada has grown considerably. There were nearly 100 million more people in the U.S. and Canada by late 1980s than in the mid-1950s and 140 million more than were there for

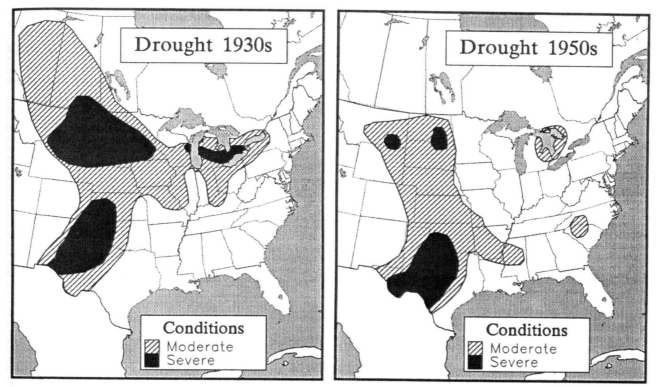

Figure 3.10. Areas Affected by the Droughts of the 1930s and 1950s (After J. Borchert, Annals, Association of American Geographers, 1971)

the drought of the mid-1930s. Another 65 million people were in the U.S. and Canada during the 2007-2008 drought than were here for the droughts of the mid-1980s. Moreover, per capita water usage had also increased by several times. Consequently, severe droughts in the twenty-first century mean much greater competition for the available water.

There will, undoubtedly, be future droughts of varying degree. The realization of this should alert public officials and citizens to begin now to develop a long-term strategy for regular water conservation, plus emergency plans for severe droughts.

Floods

All natural streams flood. When flooding occurs along a single small stream, it is normally the result of a short-lived intense period of rain, a cloudburst causing water to rush into a stream faster than it can be carried away. This kind of event is called a flash flood and can be locally devastating, since there is typically little warning. Urban areas are particularly vulnerable to flash flooding because in cities forest and grasslands have been replaced with impermeable parking lots, roads, and roof tops. Water which once would have soaked into the ground, where plants would use much of it and the remainder take days or weeks to reach the stream, now washes quickly over the surface to enter all at once into the stream channel.

Flooding of large rivers or basins is a result of prolonged periods of precipitation over a large portion of the watershed or massive rapid snow melt. The conditions for either of these events occur primarily in the early spring in Canada's most populated sections, in winter along the U.S. Pacific coast and in the spring and summer in the eastern states. The most financially costly flood in North American history occurred in the summer of 1993 in the Missouri and Mississippi River Valleys of the Midwest. An abnormally wet spring in the basins of both the upper Missouri River and the upper Mississippi spelled disaster for the people living downstream, particularly the area near St. Louis, where the Missouri and Mississippi Rivers flow together. Damage from the destruction of crops, homes, and even entire cities were in the billions. While forecasters accurately predicted the danger weeks in advance, the magnitude of the flood was so great that there was nothing anyone could do to stop it. While prevention was not possible, the early warning undoubtedly kept the death toll amazingly low and allowed many people to salvage some of their belongings.

Global Climatic Change

The abnormally high temperatures beginning in the 1980s led to speculation that increased carbon dioxide in the atmosphere caused by the ever greater burning of fossil fuels had finally brought about the often discussed **greenhouse effect**, where long energy waves radiated from earth, after having been converted from shorter incoming rays from the sun, are trapped by the higher carbon dioxide levels and raise the average planetary temperature. Since 1880, the year that modern scientific instrumentation became available to monitor temperatures precisely, a clear warming trend is evident, though there was a leveling off between the 1940s and 1970s (Figure 3.11). Each of the last 13 years (1997-2009) has been among the 14 warmest years on record. With the increase in temperatures there has been unprecedented increases in the melt rate of the world's glaciers which coupled with the thermal expansion of the world's oceans has led to a rise in global sea level, in some regions low lying coastal regions have been inundated. Temperature increases have been greatest in the polar and sub polar regions, where the permanent sea ice has been shrinking at alarming rates. If the current trend continues there could be times of the year when it would be possible to sail to the North Pole without encountering ice by mid-century. While the shrinking sea ice in the Canadian and Alaskan Arctic is devastating to much of the arctic wildlife and indicative of greater global problems on the near horizon it may also allow for the age old dream of a Northwest Passage from Europe to the far east to become a reality. As Icelandic President Olafur Ragnar Grímsson noted the route was becoming a "trans-Arctic Panama Canal".

By the late 1970s, another threat from man-made pollutants had been detected. Escaping chlorofluorocarbons (CFCs) from refrigerants and aerosols were carried aloft eventually reaching the stratosphere. Once in the stratosphere the CFCs were quite effective in depleting the protective layer of ozone found there.. When ultraviolet radiation strikes a CFC molecule one chlorine atom shears off. The free chlorine atom may then hit an ozone molecule, which consists of three oxygen atoms, and capture one of the oxygen atoms. This destroys the ozone molecule by turning it into oxygen. The resulting depletion of the **ozone layer** in the stratosphere permits more of the sun's short ultraviolet rays to reach the earth. These UV rays are a potential health risk, particularly for

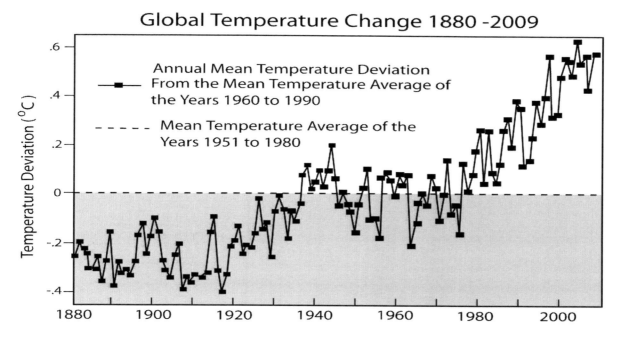

Figure 3.11 Global temperature change relative to the average annual temperature for the years 1950 to 1980. Data courtesy of NASA's Goddard Institute for Space Studies.

melanoma (skin cancer). In 1987, in response to a dramatic seasonal depletion of the ozone layer over Antarctica and northern North America, diplomats in Montreal forged a treaty, the Montreal Protocol, which called for drastic reductions in the production of CFCs. With European nations, Canada, and the U.S. taking the lead, CFCs were phase out of production. By 1995, no new CFCs were being manufactured however, large quantities are still leaking from older appliances, cars, and landfills. In addition, as CFCs have a lifetime of about 20 to 100 years those placed in the atmosphere decades earlier will continue to damage the ozone layer for a number of years to come.

Climatic Regions

The United States and Canada contain most of the main world **climates** (Figure 3.12). Only the topical, rainy climates are not found within either of these two countries.

Eastern and Northern North America

In the eastern two-thirds of the continent south-to-north variations in climate are primarily differences in temperature, especially those of winter. The **Subtropical Savanna Climate** is found only in southernmost Florida, where the average temperature for the coldest month is above 64.4°F (18°C) and the cooler months have a distinct dry season.

To the north is the **Humid Subtropical Climate**, with its hot summers, mild winters and year-round precipitation. Its northern border is marked by the 32°F (0°C) average **isotherm** for the coldest month. An isotherm is a line connecting points having the same temperature. In the Humid Subtropical climate, a great variety of fruits and vegetables, along with cotton, tobacco, rice, corn, soybeans, and other crops are grown. In the southern portions of this climatic zone, warm-weather tourism is a nearly year-round business.

To the north of the Humid Subtropical Climate are humid but more continental climates. Extending west to about the 100th meridian is the **Humid Continental, Warm (Long) Summer Climate**. As in the Humid Subtropical region to the south, the hottest month averages over 71.6°F (22°C) and there is precipitation throughout the year, but summers are shorter and winters are longer and colder, with the average temperature of the coldest month falling below 32°F (0°C) and more of the precipitation falling as snow. This climate roughly corresponds to what is called the **Corn/Soybean/Hog Belt**. However, in recent years new hybrid seeds have made it possible to produce a mature corn crop farther north.

Still farther to the north is the **Humid Continental, Cool (Short) Summer Climate**. The average temperature for the warmest month falls below 71.6°F (22°C) and winters are even longer and colder. This region corresponds generally to the **Hay and Dairying Belt**, the dominant agricultural activities. Specialty crops, especially fruits and vegetables, are also important in certain locales, particularly near lakes which moderate the spring and fall temperatures.

Farther north and in all but the northernmost sections of Canada and Alaska is the **Subarctic Climate** where the average temperature is over 50°F (10°C) for only one to four months and winters are very long and severe, though summers are mild. In this region is the greatest annual range in temperature in North America. This is the result of a combination of its pole ward and interior location. The lack of maritime influence stems from both the distance to the sea and the sheltering effect of the western mountains. There is very little agriculture and most income is derived from mining operations.

The northernmost climate in North America is the **Tundra**, where the average temperature for the warmest month is below 50°F (10°C). This 50°F **isotherm** is generally associated with the so-called **tree line**, pole ward of this line trees do not grow. In general this is a region of bitterly cold, long winters and brief, cool summers. The sun is below the horizon for most of the day in the winter and when it does appears it hugs the horizon giving off only a feeble warmth and diffused light. In the summer the sun is almost always above the horizon, but again never very high so its ability to warm the landscape is severely restricted. Precipitation is limited in the tundra because the air is simply too cold to hold much moisture; however, evaporation is also severely limited by the cold temperatures so the region actually has a moisture surplus.

Western North America

In western North America, variations in climate result more from differences in elevation and the locational relationship to mountain ranges than to latitudinal change. The north-south trending

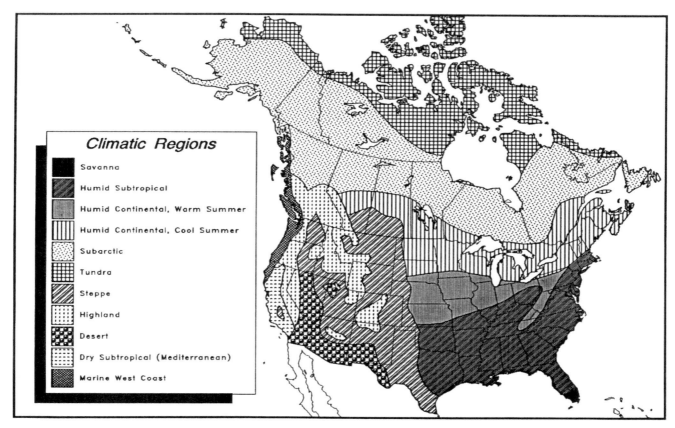

Figure 3.12 -- Climates

Coastal Ranges, the Sierra Nevada-Cascades, and the Rockies catch most of their moisture on the western slopes **orographically**, but as the air descends and warms along the eastern slopes, little precipitation occurs. In the southwest, where a high pressure cell also blocks moisture for part of the year, it is very arid, with less than ten inches (25.4 cm) of precipitation falling and evaporation exceeding precipitation. The slightly higher, less protected sections which remain in the Prevailing Westerlies year round are semi-arid with 10 to 20 inches of rainfall (25.4-50.8 cm) annually. These **Desert and Steppe Climates** dominate the western third of North America south of the 52nd parallel, except for the high mountains and coastal sections. Livestock grazing is important, especially in the Steppe Climate, and irrigated crops are produced in river valleys and in other locations where water can be brought by pipeline. In the wetter margins of the Steppe region, wheat growing is the dominant type of agriculture.

The **Highland Climate**, which borders the Desert and Steppe regions, are so noted because there is no common temperature or precipitation pattern throughout. As altitude increases, temperature declines. On the windward slopes, precipitation increases with altitude until temperatures become so cold that further cooling does not yield greater amounts. On the leeward slopes, little precipitation occurs. Generally, only in the highland basins where grasslands are found are livestock brought from drier lowlands for grazing during the warmer months, an activity referred to as **transhumance**.

The **Mediterranean**, or **Dry Subtropical**, **Climate** is found in most of California west of the Sierra Nevada where the pole ward shifting of the high pressure cell over the area in summer causes clear, dry conditions and the shifting south of the Prevailing Westerlies in the cooler months brings precipitation. These shifts, especially where the dry season is more severe in the south, have complicated the lives of those who have settled the brush-covered hill and canyon lands. Here, forest and brush fires frequently claim numerous residences and, later, downpours on the denuded, burned-over slopes wash the topsoil along with the homes to lower levels. California has used irrigation in both its Mediterranean and drier climates in the Central and Imperial Valleys to produce more agricultural goods than any other state. Its market extends beyond the borders of this most populous state in the nation to the Midwest and Atlantic Coast states.

The **Marine West Coast Climate** stretches along the Pacific coast from northern California to southern Alaska. As in the Humid Subtropical and Dry Subtropical Climates, the average temperature for the coldest month is above 32°F (0°C). However, in contrast to the other two climatic regions, the Marine West Coast Climate has an average temperature for the warmest month below 71.6°F (22°C), which has generally prohibited the production of a mature corn crop, though this is becoming increasingly possible with new hybrid seeds. Dairying and fruit and vegetable growing have long been the agricultural mainstays of the region. Mild temperatures and the highest precipitation in North America make this a major lumbering region.

Natural Vegetation and Soil Patterns

The soil and natural vegetation patterns are generally similar to the climatic regions. Little natural vegetation exists in the most populous and agriculturally developed areas today, so that these patterns represent earlier conditions.

The formation of soil types is primarily a result of two factors, climate and time. The relationship of soils to climate can be seen in the general distribution of **pedocals,** soils high in calcium and **pedalfers,** soils rich in iron and aluminum. In the east and north, pedalfers form where there is plenty of available precipitation to leach out soluble salts, including calcium, potassium, nitrates, and phosphates, leaving the soils acidic and nutrient-poor. To make these acidic soils more productive eastern farmers typically add lime to their fields to raise the pH level of the soils. On the other hand, in the southwest and interior, where it is significantly drier, pedocals have formed due to the lack of removal of the soluble salts. Without rainfall to leach out soluble salts the soils typically are quite alkaline. To lower the pH of these soils farmers will often spray ammonium sulfate. The material may have begun as beach sand, dissolved limestone or an alluvial gravel deposit; it does not matter; in the end it will be a pedalfer or pedocal because of the climate under which it formed. Vegetation is also controlled to a great extent by climate; thus, there is a high correlation between vegetation type and soil type (Figures 3.14 and 3.15).

The geographic distribution of a plant or animal species is called its **range** and is dependent on the specie's **tolerance** of environmental conditions and **competition** from other plants and animals. Climate, soil type and other environmental components can be thought of as permissive factors. Not being able to tolerate any of an area's environmental conditions will preclude a species from existing there. However, being able to tolerate all environmental conditions does not necessarily mean that a plant or animal will in fact exist in a particular place. It is a plant or animal's ability to compete for resources with other species that are also tolerant of local conditions that determines which species will and will not flourish. There are numerous examples of plants and animals introduced to a region from elsewhere that "compete" better than native species for resources and, thus, flourish at the expense of those native species. A long list of **"exotics"** have invaded the North American continent, including cheatgrass, Russian thistle, salt cedar, the English starling, prickly pear and kudzu (Figure 3.13). The unchecked growth of exotics often means that they develop into serious pests, for which federal, state, and local governments spend billions of dollars annually attempting to control their spread.

Figure 3.13 -- Tractor spraying herbicides on Kudzu infestation (Image courtesy of the USDA).

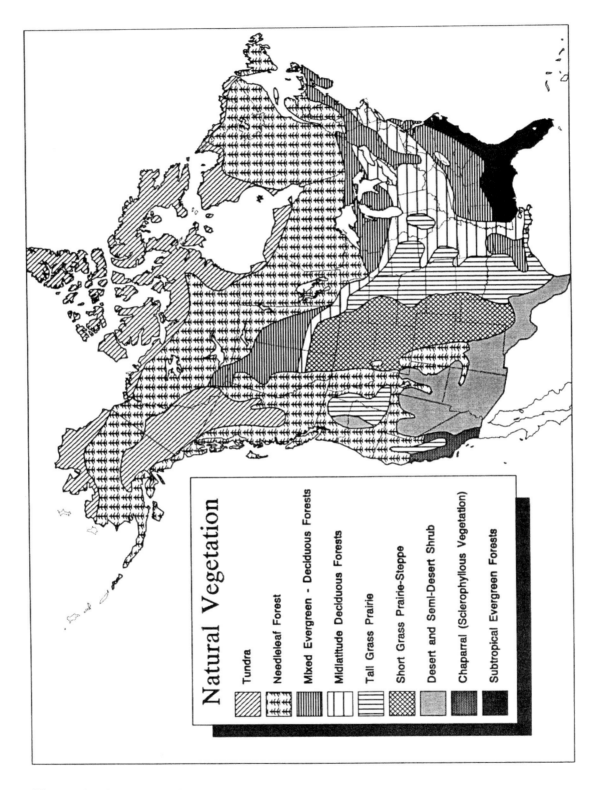

Figure 3.14 -- Natural Vegetation

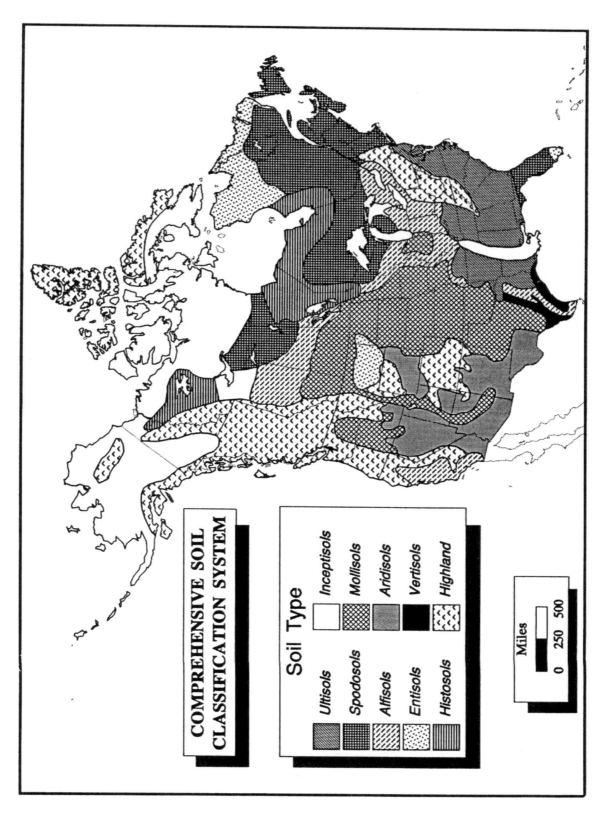

Figure 3.15 -- Major Soil Groups

Major Biomes

The following sections describe the major **biomes,** or plant and animal communities, that cover North America. While finer divisions can be made, biomes are generally classified as forest, grasslands, tundra and deserts. It is important to note that biomes are impermanent. While the composition of a plant community may remain stable for hundreds or thousands of years, change is inevitable. Natural change invariably leads from simpler to more complex communities. Man has had tremendous influence on the natural vegetation. For example, Southern forests have seen oak, hickory and other hardwoods replaced with fast-growing loblolly pine. No area of North America has seen greater biome alteration by the hand of man than the Great Plains. The Great Plains have seen almost all of their native grasses replaced by domestic grasses, such as corn and wheat, while native grazing animals like antelope and bison have been superceded by the cow.

The availability of water is a major factor in determining the distribution of plants. Plants that actually live in the oceans or lakes such as algae or sea weed are classified as **hydrophytes**. **Hygrophytes** are well adapted to environments that are normally quite wet, such as rainforests, swamps, or marshes. Hygrophytes, such as cattails, rushes, and mangroves can tolerate short periods of being dry, but not extended periods. Various cactus, mesquite, salt brush and other plants well adapted to dry conditions are known as **xerophytes.** Most other plants are **mesophytes,** they develop in areas having neither extreme arid nor extreme wet conditions.

Forests

The eastern United States and most of Canada are humid, forested and covered with **pedalfer** soils. Most of the Coastal Plain section of the Humid Subtropical Climate east of the Mississippi River Valley is characterized by **needleleaf evergreen coniferous** (cone-bearing) forest as well as broadleaf evergreens such as magnolia and mountain laurel.. In the Piedmont and the less humid inner margins of the western Coastal Plain, deciduous trees, which drop their leaves in cooler months, and evergreen trees become intermingled in a **mixed forest**. The warm summers, mild winters and year-round precipitation have led to the formation of **Ultisols** in the both the Piedmont and Coastal Plain. Ultisols are normally quite red in color, indicative of their high iron and aluminum content, they are also nutrient poor and have a distinctive layer of clay. To remain agriculturally productive, they are heavily fertilized to make up for the loss of nutrients from extensive leaching. The Mississippi Valley is covered with **alluvium,** sediment deposited during the frequent floods of the Mississippi River and its tributaries. These alluvial soils, a form of **Inceptisols,** have been laid down only recently, so leaching has not had much time to remove nutrients or develop soil horizons. They are highly productive agricultural soils.

In the Mississippi Alluvial Lowland, the Appalachians and the Interior Low Plateaus of the Humid Subtropical Climate, as well as the wetter parts of the Humid Continental, Warm (Long) Summer Climate, **deciduous** forests dominate. Viewing of the turning of the leaves of deciduous trees, such as maple, birch, and oaks has become a major tourist attraction in New England and the Appalachian Highlands. North and west of the Appalachian Mountains, **Alfisols** are found. These soils have developed under cooler conditions than those to the south, are less leached and, thus, are more fertile. A distinctive clay layer forms at depth.

In the wetter sections of the Humid Continental, Cool (Short) Summer Climate is a **mixed forest**. The area is a transition from the needleleaf evergreens dominating to the north and the broadleaf deciduous trees found to the south. This area is largely underlain with **Spodosols**, which are acidic and leached like the Alfisols. However, because of cooler temperatures, they have a slower rate of plant decay, resulting in a thick "litter" layer on the surface.

Most of the area of Subarctic Climate is **needleleaf evergreen** forest, called **taiga** in Russia and **boreal** forest in Canada. This is the simplest assemblage of plants in any major biome. Almost all trees are needleleaf coniferous (cone-bearing), and the number of species is quite limited. Often, a single variety of fir, spruce or pine will extend for hundreds of miles. In regions of extreme cold winter temperatures there are stands of **larch**, a variety of **needleleaf deciduous** tree. Larch are far more common in Russia's Siberia. In the plains section between the Canadian Rockies and the Canadian Shield is an area of mixed forest. West of this area in the colder Yukon Plateau and the Alaskan Range are more elementary herb-like plants. **Spodosols** extend from the Great Lakes to east of James Bay, as well as being west of central Hudson Bay. These are separated by **Histosols** in the area from the Hudson Bay Lowland to Lake Winnipeg, where this "bog soil" forms under locally poor drainage conditions. The boggy Histosols also occur in the lowland from the Mackenzie River Valley in the west to Great Slave Lake in the south and Great Bear Lake in the north. **Alfisols** are found in the mixed forest section between Lake Winnipeg, the Rockies and Lake Athabasca.

The Marine West Coast Climate, with its persistent orographic precipitation and mild coastal temperatures, has allowed for the growth of some of the world's most spectacular trees, including the famous redwoods of northern California and the Douglas Fir of coastal Oregon and Washington. These needleaf evergreens rise over 300 feet through the dense Pacific fog and can live for thousand of years.

The Mediterranean Climate of southern California supports a mix of dwarf oaks and broadleaf shrubs called **chaparral.** Severe water shortages during the dry summer months limit these areas to drought-resistant, drawf trees, that are widely spaced. In the valleys, chaparral vegetation is underlain primarily with **Alfisols**, but in the highlands **mountain soils** predominate.

Tundra

The western Subarctic Climate region and the Tundra Climate north and west of Hudson Bay has **Inceptisols** with their poorly defined horizons, while the Tundra east of Hudson Bay is underlain by **Entisols**, which are among the youngest soils on earth. The Tundra Climate is characterized by **tundra vegetation** of mosses, lichens, and heaths. The soils of the Tundra and northern Subarctic Climates have a **permafrost** condition, where the active top layer thaws during the warmer months. The passive bottom layer remains frozen, thus preventing the filtering downward of water. Since much of the Tundra is relatively flat, the presence of the permafrost layer results in large areas of **bogs** and standing water during the short summer season. Exasperating these conditions is the fact that most of the rivers of the Tundra flow northward. When the summer melt comes it is the southern stretches that thaw first. Blocks of ice flowing in the rivers often collect in jumbled masses forming temporary ice dams that cause the water to spill over great areas.

Grasslands

West of the humid, acidic soils are those which developed under drier conditions. As mentioned earlier, these alkaline soils are often called **pedocals** because they have accumulations of calcium near or at the surface. In the drier margins of the Humid Continental, Warm (Long) and Cool (Short) Summer Climates and the wetter sections of the Steppe Climate are tall **prairie grasses** in the east and shorter grasses in the west. These are underlain by **Mollisols**, which have calcium deposits and a dark, thick top horizon of **humus**--organic matter decomposed by plants and animals: the taller the grasses, the deeper and denser the roots and the darker the humus. Mollisols are also found in the Steppe region of eastern Oregon and Washington. In general, Mollisols are highly productive agricultural soils.

Early European settlers on the tallgrass prairie found the tangled root masses so thick that conventional plows could not penetrate them. The introduction of steel tipped plows opened the prairie for cultivation. Strips of sod, jokingly known as "Nebraska Marble" were used to build homes on the prairie. Sod homes provided excellent insulation, were virtually tornado proof, easy to construct and inexpensive. Their major drawbacks were that in general they required constant repair and that rainwater would often percolate through the sod roofs to drip from the ceilings for days after heavy rainfalls.

Of the 400,000 square miles of tallgrass prairie that once covered the North American continent, less than four percent remains, primarily in the new Tallgrass National Preserve in the Flint Hills of Kansas. The transformation of the prairies has been more thorough than that of any other region. Virtually all of the native grasses and flowers have been replaced by their domesticated cousins corn, wheat, sorghum, soybeans, canola, and sunflowers. The once vast herds of grazing animals including bison and antelope have been replaced with cattle.

Deserts

The Desert Climate and the drier margins of the Steppe Climate are underlain with **Aridisols**, where calcium and other salt accumulations are significant. As noted drought-resistant plants called **xerophytes** have adapted to the protracted dry conditions of the desert in a variety of ways. Some have developed tap roots extending to incredible depths to reach subterranean water supplies. Succulents, such as prickly pear and saguaro cactus, have spongy, fleshy stems where water is stored. Others have waxy leaves to prevent moisture loss by transpiration and still others have developed very light green or silver leaves that reflect sunlight allowing the plant to stay cool. One very unique adaptation involves the reproductive cycle of some drought-tolerant plants. When rain eventually does come to the desert these plants germinate, flower, bear fruit and disperse their seeds in only a few days. The seeds may remain dormant for months or years waiting for the next rain.

WEATHER, CLIMATE, VEGETATION AND SOILS REVIEW

1. In what major wind belt does the continent lie? How does that effect our weather patterns, especially rainfall amounts across the continent?

2. What are the three main types of rainfall (precipitation) and what processes cause each one?

3. What is an air mass and what are the major source regions for North America?

4. What is the primary climatic factor that explains the variation of climatic regions in the eastern part of the continent? And in the west?

5. What agricultural belts are associated with the *Humid Subtropical, Humid Continental-Warm Summer,* and *Humid Continental-Cool Summer* climates?

6. Explain the formation of the western deserts and steppes.

7. Why does southern California have distinct wet and dry seasons and what is the effect of these seasons on the population.

8. Where are the largest trees in the world found? What are the climatic conditions that allow for such incredible growth?

9. What two factors determine the distribution or range of plant and animal species?

10. Give examples of the following: a hydrophyte, mesophyte, xerophyte, broadleaf deciduous tree, evergreen needleleaf tree, evergreen broadleaf tree, and needleleaf deciduous tree.

11. Which natural vegetation region has very little species diversification?

12. Which natural vegetation region has been almost entirely replaced with man introduced species? What are the animal and plant species that were introduced by man in this region?

13. What is an *exotic species*? Why do they have the potential to become such great pests? Give several examples of exotics gone berserk.

14. What are the two factors that determine what type of soil will be formed in any area?

15. What is the primary difference between soils of the eastern half of the continent and those of the western half (not including the coastal areas north of San Francisco or the Tundra)?

16. What soil type covers much of the eastern Great Plains? Why is it so fertile and why is it so deep?

17. Explain the following:

    hail formation   storm surge   seawall and groin   Jet stream

    zone of contact   El Nino   greenhouse effect

18. Explain the differences in areal extent, direction of movement and warning time for hurricanes and tornadoes.

NAME _____

WEATHER, CLIMATE, VEGETATION AND SOILS EXERCISE

Use the following map and your text to answer the questions in this exercise. You will also need an atlas.

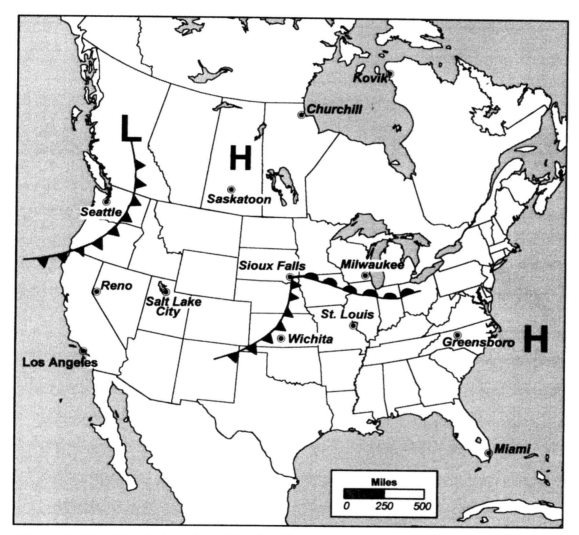

Figure 3.16. -- North American Weather Patterns

1. From Wichita to Sioux Falls the atmospheric pressure would be low, why? _____
   _____
   _____
   _____

2. What city is likely to experience cooler temperatures tomorrow? _____

3. What city is likely to be warmer tomorrow? _____

4. What two factors are probably responsible for the cold front near St. Louis to be moving toward the east?
   _____
   _____

5. What type of air mass is most likely covering Seattle? _____

6. Of all the cities labeled on the map which do you suspect has the coldest winter temperatures? _____.

7. Of all the cities on the map which do you expect has the smallest seasonal temperature range? _____.
   Why? _____
   _____
   _____

8. Why *might* the cold front shown in British Columbia, Washington and Oregon *not* bring rainfall when it arrives in Reno, Nevada?
   _____
   _____
   _____

9. What is the climatic classification for the Los Angeles area? _____

In this climatic type, the summer season is normally quite arid. Why?

_____

_____

10. What are the two controlling factors in the formation of soils? _____

    and _____.

11. Describe the climate, soil type and natural vegetation for Greensboro, N.C.

    climate _____,

    soil _____,

    natural vegetation _____.

12. A farmer near Cleveland would likely to fertilize his/her fields with

    _____ in order to _____ the soil's pH level. While a

    farmer in the prairies of Colorado would be more likely to put _____

    on his/her fields in order to _____ the soil's pH level.

13. Give an example of each of the following:

    Needleleaf evergreen _____   Broadleaf evergreen _____

    Needleleaf deciduous _____   Broadleaf deciduous _____

    Hygrophyte _____   Hydrophyte _____

    Mesophyte _____   Xerophyte _____

14. What are the two factors that limit the *"range"* of any plant species?

    _____ and _____.

15. Which area of natural vegetation in North America has the *least* species diversity?

    _____

16. What soil type is most closely correlated with the Humid Subtropical Climate Region?

    _____.

17. The Steppe Climatic Region is primarily covered with what type of soil and would naturally support what type of vegetation? soil_____; vegetation _____

18. Which region has the smallest percentage of its land covered in natural vegetation?

    _____

19. Explain why there are so many bogs and swampy areas in the far northern regions of the continent, especially on relatively flat areas. _____

    _____

    _____

    _____

    _____

20. What are two reasons why droughts could be more devastating in the near future?

    _____

    _____

    _____

    _____

    _____

21. From the following list of North American cities select the one having the following climate, vegetation and soil types, You may need an atlas!

City Choices

Greensboro, NC
Chicago, IL
St. John's, NF
Vancouver, BC
Toronto, Ont.
Denver, CO
Kansas City, MO
Amadjuak (Baffn Island)
Los Angeles, CA
New Orleans, LA

a. Humid Continental Warm Summer, midlatitude deciduous forests, mollisols _____

b. Mediterranean climate, chaparral vegetation and alfisol soils _____

c. Steppe climate, short grass prairie and highland soils _____

d. Subarctic Climate, needleleaf forests and spodosols _____

e. Humid Subtropical climate, mixed evergreen/deciduous forests and ultisols _____

f. Humid Continental Cool Summer, midlatitude deciduous forests and alfisols _____

g. Tundra climate and vegetation type with inceptisols _____

h. Marine West Coast climate, needleleaf forest, highland soils _____

i. Humid Subtropical climate, midlatitude forest with inceptisols
_____

j. Humid Continental Warm Summer, tall grass prairie with Mollisols _____

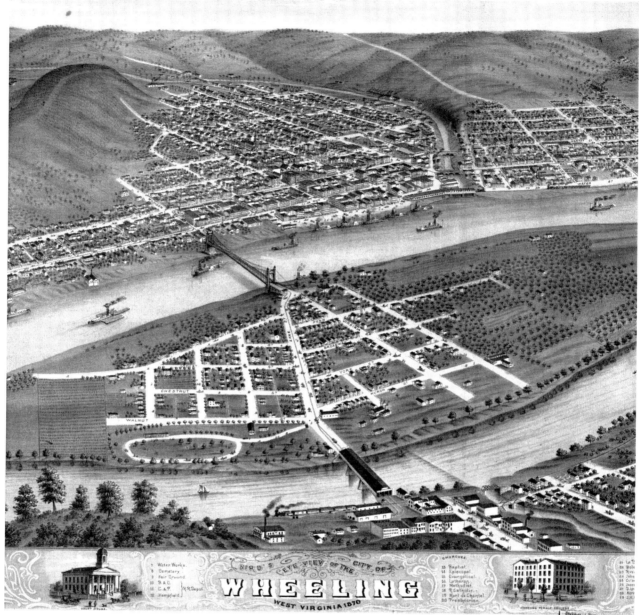

Figure 4.1 -- A section of Wheeling, WV drawn in 1870. Panoramic maps like this (also known as bird's-eye views, perspective maps, and aero views) were highly popular. The trade mark of these maps was the high level of detail obtained by the artist/cartographer walking the streets to individually sketch every building in town. Approximately 5,000 U.S. and Canadian towns and cities were drawn in this style between 1850 and 1920. Amazingly about half of these maps can be attributed to just five itinerant artist/cartographers! The views were used to promote the city and reflected great civic pride. They were often underwritten by individual subscriptions, real estate firms, and railroad companies, who were also major landholders (courtesy the Library of Congress)

CHAPTER FOUR

HISTORICAL DEVELOPMENT: SETTLEMENT and EXPANSION

In discussing the historical development of the United States in his book *America and Americans*, John Steinbeck wrote that "America did not exist. Four centuries of work, of bloodshed, of loneliness and fear created this land." The human occupance of America is a drama of many migrations by different peoples into and throughout an unfamiliar and uncharted land. So varied were the climates, soils, physiography and other physical elements that many types were unknown to the newcomers and, thus, demanded an early willingness and ability to adjust to the environment. Those who could not adapt quickly and adequately enough either died, moved on, or returned to their place of origin. The main challenge to most new Americans was the natural environment, but often other people were the deciding factor. The fights between people of different origins sometimes proved more decisive than the struggle of the individual against nature.

The Original Inhabitants: The Native Americans

The land mass encompassing the United States and Canada is believed by most authorities to have been inhabited by humans for at least 30,000 years; and in late 2004, evidence of the use of charcoal along the Savannah River dating back 50,000 years was presented by an archaeologist. Probably the first migrants to this area came from eastern Asia during the great Ice Age, which terminated about 10,000 years ago. At that time, the water level of the oceans was lower because of the great accumulation of moisture in the large continental ice sheets (glaciers). The relatively lower sea level exposed land connecting Asia to North America at the Bering Strait, thus allowing people to walk into this area. Later, when the ice melted and the sea rose, this land-connector was submerged beneath the water. Waves of migrants pushed south, eventually spreading across all of present-day Canada and the United States. Others continued south into Central and South America.

When the Europeans began probing North America in the 16th century, it has been estimated that over 3.5 million Native Americans inhabited this region. For more than 30,000 years their ancestors had explored the continent and had developed various ways of living. They represented many different ancestral backgrounds and languages. They also settled in widely scattered sections of the continent with its great variety of climates, soils, vegetation, and topography. Thus, diverse cultural and economic systems developed throughout the region. The linguistic pattern was highly complex, with 56 language families containing hundreds of languages and dialects.

The pattern of economic activities can be simplified into meaningful spatial groupings. Clark Wissler has identified six major food areas: the caribou, salmon, wild seeds, intensive agriculture, bison, and eastern maize (Figure 4.2). Most of Canada was occupied by the **caribou** (American reindeer) **hunters** scattered through the coniferous forest. In the northern part near the Arctic waters, the Eskimos hunted the caribou in the warmer months, but when cold weather forced the animals farther to the south, the natives turned toward the sea for their food. Other groups who lived farther inland depended to a greater extent on the caribou, as well as moose, deer, and other land animals. Some of them also caught a variety of fresh-water fish. The dog was the only domesticated animal in North America and was found mainly in Canada.

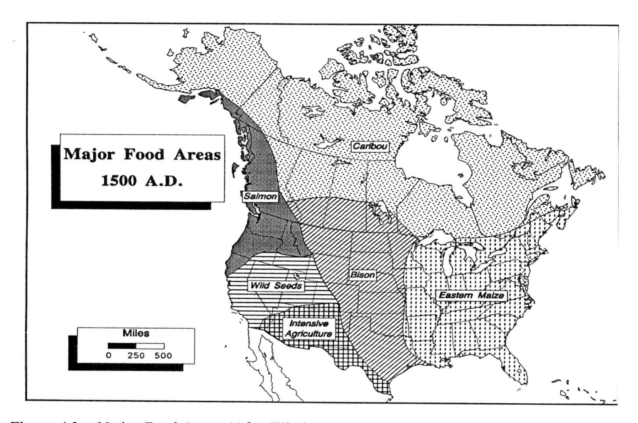

Figure 4.2 -- Native Food Areas (After Wissler)

To the southwest of the caribou area, along the Pacific coast and inland for some 400 miles (644 km), from northern California to the Yukon, the **salmon fishers** lived. Both the coastal and inland peoples participated in the annual salmon-run fishing. The fish were dried and pounded into a fine powder for storing. During the rest of the year, the coastal tribes generally continued to fish for other varieties, while those in the interior hunted deer, bear, rabbit, and other animals and gathered numerous kinds of roots and berries.

South of the salmon region was the **wild seeds** area. In the hill lands of California west of the Sierra Nevada, the acorn was the most important food. It was beaten into a flour and washed with hot water in order to remove the tannic acid and then made into bread or cake. In addition to the acorn, various seeds and roots were gathered and fish were caught. To the east of the mountains in the Great Basin, neither the acorn nor many berries grew. Thus, these tribes had to depend on wild seeds and roots, some rabbit and fish, and even insects in some parts.

South of the wild seeds area was the **intensive agriculture** region. It extended through Central America into the Andes of South America. In the Salt River Valley and some other valleys of the southwest, maize, beans, squashes, melons, and sunflower seeds were raised by natives who lived in villages of flat-roofed adobe or stone houses (often multi-storied) called **pueblos** (Figure 4.3). Spade-like tools with footrests, fertilization with human and animal manure, and irrigation methods were used in this area. Crafts of pottery-making and weaving were also developed.

Figure 4.3 -- The Anazasi People occupied the famous cliff dwellings at Mesa Verde, Colorado from 600 to 1300. Abandonment of the site was probably due to extended drought.

In the eastern foothills of the Rockies and in the Great Plains were the **bison**, or buffalo, lands. The bison were first hunted by nomadic pastoral peoples who had to capture the animals without the aid of horses. Only after the horse was obtained from the Spaniards in the early 17th century did the natives of the Great Plains--and other Native Americans who consequently migrated there--become capable of killing large numbers of bison without setting up large cages. The dog, found in the northern half of this area, was the only domesticated animal. Although most of the tribes were nomadic, in the eastern humid margins of the region a transitional zone of sedentary farmers supplemented their food by periodic hunting trips for buffalo.

Finally, additional rainfall in the territory to the east of approximately the 20-inch (50.8-cm) rainfall line (isohyet) in the United States and in southeastern Canada allowed more dense settlements. The **eastern maize** Native Americans, who inhabited grasslands in large forest openings established by annual burnings of the trees, lived in tepees and more permanent housing. Because the region was largely forested, cut and burn agriculture was practiced. Trees and brush were cut annually and burned to make grasslands suitable for the growing of field crops. Many lived in sedentary settlements and practiced communal farming. In addition to maize, other agricultural products consumed included squashes, beans, wild rice, and maple sugar in the north and millet, melons, sweet potatoes, gourds, squashes, and tobacco in the south. Various roots and berries, plus deer, wild turkey, and fish were also eaten. The most highly advanced culture in this region was centered on the estimated 40,000 mound builders of Cahokia (near East St. Louis) in the central Mississippi Valley along the Illinois-Missouri border.

European Exploration and Settlement

To reach North America, there were two logical **routes** for European sailing vessels. The first was across the North Atlantic. Beginning in Scandinavia or the British Isles, explorers used the Shetland Islands, the Faroe Islands, Iceland, Greenland, and finally Newfoundland as a series of giant stepping stones. Leif Erickson used the island stair steps to land in Labrador nearly 500 years before Columbus' famous voyage. In 1960, the site of an ancient Viking colony called L'Anse aux Meadows was discovered on the northern most tip of Newfoundland. The site represents the only widely accepted pre-Columbian European contact in North America.

The second route to the western continent was to sail south along the coast of Europe and northwest Africa until the Trade Winds would catch the sails and drive the ships across the Atlantic to the Caribbean Sea. In 1492, Columbus propelled by the Trade Winds made landfall on the island of San Salvador in the Bahamas. A European cartographer, **Waldseemuller**, named the new lands America in honor of **Americo Vespucci.** Vespucci has often been criticized for embellishing his role in the early voyages to the new world, but recent research indicates that it was others who exaggerated his contributions. In fact, Vespucci made two voyages to the New World between 1497 and 1503 and may well have made two others (Figure 4.4). For the next 100 years, explorers from Spain, England, and France, following one of these two routes, probed and charted the new lands.

Spanish Claims

Although the 15th and 16th century superpowers made claims and overlapping counterclaims to the American continent, the Spanish dominated the Caribbean Basin and the lands surrounding the Gulf of Mexico, later expanding into the Southwest of today's United States. Among the early Spanish adventurers (Figure 4.4) were Ponce de Leon, who explored the Atlantic coast of Florida, Pineda, who sailed along the entire Gulf coast, de Vaca, who moved inland from Galveston Bay across south Texas to the southern border of New Mexico, and Gordillo, who investigated the coast along the Carolinas to about Cape Lookout (North Carolina). In the 1540s, de Soto encountered settlements of mound builders while marching from Tampa Bay to North Carolina, then southwest across northern Georgia, Alabama, Mississippi, and Arkansas. After his death near modern Natchez,

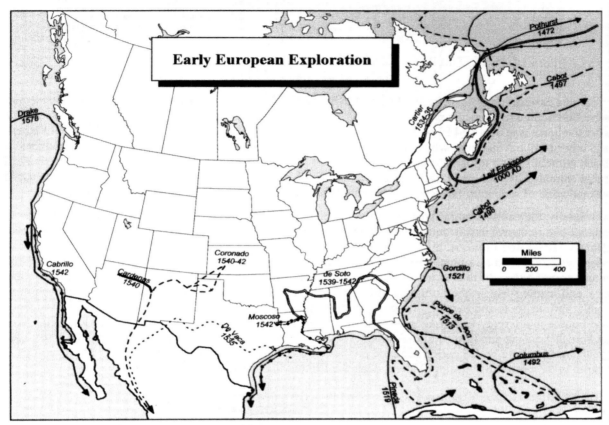

Figure 4.4 -- European Exploration

Mississippi, his lieutenant, Moscoso, continued the journey across northern Louisiana into east Texas before returning to the Mississippi River and following it to the Gulf of Mexico. About this same time, Coronado was exploring from New Mexico to Kansas, while his lieutenant, Cardenas, took a group of soldiers west across northern Arizona where he cursed the great chasm blocking his continued exploration to the west—he had discovered the Grand Canyon. Meanwhile, Cabrillo had sailed north along the California coast as far as San Francisco Bay. By the beginning of the 17th century, however, Spain's St. Augustine (founded in 1565) was that country's only permanent settlement in what would become the United States (Figure 4.5). Between 1769 and 1776, Spain established several missions from San Diego to San Francisco. Although the Spanish had established a major presence in California by the last quarter of the 18th century, Russia had crossed the Bering Strait in 1741 and soon entered Alaska and coastal Canada. They eventually claimed not only these areas but also most of the Columbia River basin and the northern California coast south to their settlement at Fort Ross, some 70 miles north of San Francisco Bay.

French Settlement

The first French settlement was founded by Champlain at Port Royal (Annapolis, Nova Scotia) in 1604-05 and was supported mainly by agriculture and fishing (Figure 4.5). Although Cartier moved

Figure 4.5 -- Early European Settlement

into the interior in the mid-1530s, sailing up the estuary of the St. Lawrence River to the site of today's Montreal, it was not until 1608 that the French established Quebec on an island in the St. Lawrence River Valley. The site for the town was considered favorable because it was located at the head of the estuary where the river channel became narrow, had a good harbor, and had, topographically, a good defensive position (later proven not good enough). This was also the site farthest downstream that could control access into the St. Lawrence River valley. Unfortunately, the river could not be used for transportation for nearly half of the year because it was frozen. The French established trading arrangements with several Native American tribes. Fur trade became the main basis for the continued French interest in this part of the world during the next century.

While those entering the English territory were confined by the forests, the natives and the rugged Appalachians, the French were able to continue their exploration of the continental interior by using the St. Lawrence–Great Lakes-Mississippi River system of waterways. The French pushed farther inland, exploring the area between Lake Ontario and the Ottawa River in the early 1600s. The French further implanted themselves in the lower St. Lawrence River valley by founding Trois Rivieres (1634) and Montreal (1642). (See Figure 4.5.) By 1660, the French had control of the St. Lawrence River valley, the Great Lakes area and maritime Canada.

Some French farmers remained in the lower St. Lawrence River valley, while explorers traveled nearly the entire length of the Mississippi River by 1682. The French were, perhaps, the greatest users of portages (the act of carrying boats and goods across low divides between water courses) for their fur trade and exploration. The most important routes leading into the heart of the Interior Lowlands used portages at the southern end of Lake Michigan from the late 1680s to the late 1710s and portages between the Maumee and Wabash rivers from that time till the end of their rule in this part of North America. The French established numerous forts, such as Fort Ponchartrain (Detroit) and Fort Duquesne (Pittsburg) at strategic sites between the Appalachians and the Mississippi River to protect their trade routes. They founded New Orleans in 1718 and St. Louis in 1764 along the Mississippi River (Figure 4.5).

The permanent French settlers in the lower St. Lawrence River and lower Mississippi River valleys established a settlement pattern known as long lots, a system which had been developed in Europe in the 11th century. This system gave access to the river to a large number of people, with most of one's property extending far inland from the river to the higher forested ridges in a narrow band 200 to 250 feet (50-75 m) wide and about ten times that long. As population increased and roads became more important, the long lot system was pushed inland in successive parallel series of long lots laid out with the houses along the roads. This land use pattern is still visible in the province of Quebec today (Figure 4.6).

English Dominance

The English located their first permanent settlement at Jamestown, Virginia (near Williamsburg) in 1607 (Figure 4.5). The position chosen on the James River demonstrated several major geographical advantages and disadvantages. One advantage was that the site was along a river which

Figure 4.6 – The imprint of the French long lot system is clearly visible in this photograph taken of the agricultural fields along the St. Lawrence River near the village of St. Vallier, Quebec by an astronaut on the International Space Station in May of 2010. Image courtesy of the Image Science & Analysis Laboratory, NASA Johnson Space Center. Photo ID -- ISS023E054697 (http://eol.jsc.nasa.gov)

provided easy transportation to England and to the interior. Secondly, it was nearly surrounded by water, so that it was easier to defend. Finally, boats could get rather close to shore because of the deep water. One disadvantage was that the low, level terrain was rather swampy. Secondly, the settlers had to drink water that was salty because of the high water table and the ocean tide extending beyond this point, thus allowing the infiltration of sea water into the ground water. Finally, the fairly dense forest offered cover and protection for approaching enemies from the interior.

Plymouth was established as the first settlement along the northern coast in 1620. The site was on a sandy hook that stretched out into the Atlantic. It had a good deep harbor, a good water supply for drinking and cooking, a favorable defensive position, and initially, a good basis for agriculture. However, the limited hinterland could not support a large population. Thus, some of the people moved on to found Salem (1626) and Boston (1630).

The Dutch, led by Henry Hudson, founded New Amsterdam at the mouth of the Hudson River on Manhattan Island and another at present-day Albany just south of the confluence of the Hudson and Mohawk Rivers. The former provided protection from European rivals entering the Hudson River valley and the latter location controlled one of the major access routes into the fur-rich interior. During this same period, the Dutch expanded their territory by establishing posts about 30 miles (48 km) up the Connecticut River at present-day Hartford and at the confluence of the Schuylkill and Delaware Rivers near present-day Philadelphia. These two sites were potentially advantageous in regard to fur trading, but were strategically vulnerable, not being located at the mouths of the rivers where access could be controlled.

The main emphasis of the French and Dutch was on fur trading, whereas the English promoted agricultural settlements, while still engaging in the fur business. During the 1630s, the English strengthened their holdings in New England by building a fort at the mouth of the Connecticut River, thus cutting off Dutch access to the Atlantic Ocean and their supplies from abroad. Settlers from the Boston area were then sent into the valley to establish farming communities based on the more fertile soils found there. The Dutch withdrew. During this time, another group from England was settling in Maryland just north of the mouth of the Potomac River. Also, Swedes came into the area surrounding Delaware Bay, but were overtaken by the Dutch in 1655. Thus, the Dutch territory included New Jersey and eastern New York south of Lake George, which had settlements of Germans and Swedes in the Delaware Valley. The English, consequently, were bordered on the north by the French and on the south by the Spanish, but were divided into two separate areas by the Dutch. The English considered the division of their colonies by the Dutch to be detrimental to their colonial objectives. As a result, in 1664, the English forced the Dutch to surrender their claims. This gave England control over all the territory east of the Appalachians between southern Georgia and southern Maine. By then, people from nearly 20 countries were living within these borders. Those entering the English territory were confined by the forests, the natives, and the rugged Appalachians to the areas of the eastern Coastal Plain, Piedmont, and sections of the Ridge and Valley. By 1670, the Hudson's Bay Company of Britain had established a foothold in the Hudson Bay area, claiming all the land drained by all the river systems flowing into it.

In 1713, Great Britain forced France to relinquish her claims to Nova Scotia and the vast watershed of Hudson Bay. After the fall of Quebec (1759) and Montreal (1760), the French and Indian War between England and France soon ended. In the 1763 Treaty of Paris, France ceded all her lands east of the Mississippi River and in Canada to Britain. In that same year, Spain surrendered Florida to Britain. Thus, England controlled all the territory in Canada east of the Rocky Mountains and all that is now the United States east of the Mississippi River.

New England. Although the English domain was unified after 1664, the colonies in the north, middle, and south were diverse in their economic and cultural patterns. In New England, most of the people lived in small towns and were engaged mainly in fishing, manufacturing (mainly handicrafts), lumbering and trade with England. Although agriculture was attempted here soon after the arrival of the first settlers, it did not prove very successful because of the combination of cool, short summers and thin, rocky soils. Most farming was subsistence, with maize (corn) the main food. Other crops were rye, barley, oats and buckwheat. Very few places of commercial production existed. One indication of the rocky soil is in evidence today by the many stone fences in that region. From the time of the earliest settlers in New England, the sea continued to increase in importance because of the environmental constraints on agriculture. Fish and whale products were exchanged for imported products, such as sugar, molasses and manufactured goods. This trade was part of a complex multi-triangular pattern, including ports in England, the Mediterranean, West Africa, the West Indies, and the colonies in America (Figure 4.7). Manufacturing began early in New England, with shoes and linen, woolen and cotton textiles having been initiated in the first half of the 17th century.

The Middle Colonies. The middle colonies were inhabited mainly by families on small individual farms. Soils and climate were more favorable to agriculture than in New England, and a livestock/general farming economy developed. Subsistence growing of maize and wheat became particularly important. The long rifle and the early covered wagon were also developed in this area. Several cities were also developing, such as New York, Philadelphia, and Baltimore. From this area,

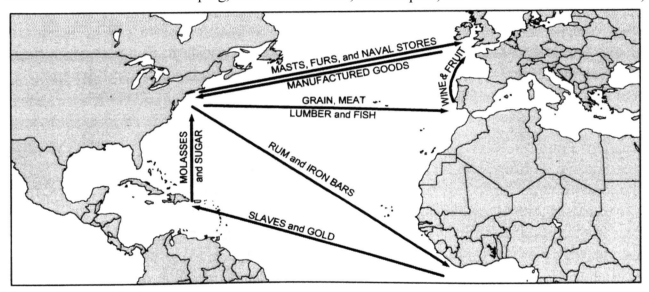

Figure 4.7-- Multi-triangular Trade Routes

major early pioneer trails extended west blazed by the Germans into eastern Pennsylvania, where they became known as "Pennsylvania Dutch" of the fertile Lancaster County area. British troops built Forbe's Road through the mountains of southern Pennsylvania to Ft. Duquesne (Pittsburg) in 1755 and Braddock's Road through the hills along the Potomac Valley of Virginia and Maryland in 1758 (Figure 4.5).

The Southern Colonies. In the southern colonies commercial plantations fronting on rivers pouring into the Atlantic Ocean became the most significant type of settlement. Soils were rather fertile initially, precipitation was plentiful, especially during the early part of the growing season, which was long and hot. In addition, large land-grant estates and a large market in Europe were key factors in the establishment of the plantation economy and the institution of slavery. Only five years after the founding of Jamestown, the colonists began growing tobacco commercially in Tidewater Virginia, and within only another seven years, the first boat containing black Africans landed. Tobacco was to be the major export of this section for many decades and, being a labor-intensive crop, demanded a large number of cheap workers. Although the first blacks were brought in as indentured servants, they were to become so necessary to the plantation economy that their status was later changed to slave. This was to develop into one of the most significant influences on southern--and national--economic, social, and political life, having now lasted for more than three and a half centuries. Cotton, rice, and indigo soon became important crops in the South, and all used slave labor. In 1790, the first U.S. Census recorded the number of blacks to be 750,000, or almost one-fifth of the population. This was likely a conservative count because slaves were property on which taxes had to be paid, so owners did not admit to having any more than they felt they must. About 95 percent of the blacks were found in the South, mainly as laborers on plantations. Even though slave trading was outlawed in the U.S. in 1805, the practice of slavery continued for nearly 60 years.

Climates in Canada were unfavorable for plantations. Thus, slavery was much less important than in the southern colonies. There were, perhaps, 5,000 slaves in Canada in 1790, but by the early 1800s, slavery had been all but abolished. Several thousand blacks from the United States fled north to Canada to obtain freedom before the Emancipation Proclamation of 1863. (See Box 4.1 for a discussion of the development of slavery and life for the early African Americans.)

Many small farmers in the Coastal Plain could not compete with the large-scale plantation agriculture dominated by a single crop and using slave labor and, therefore, moved inland into the Carolina and Virginia Piedmont, which was largely settled by the middle of the 18th century. In addition, several groups of poor newcomers to the middle colonies had moved down the Shenandoah Valley and then through the water gaps and the wind gaps to the east and the southeast into the Piedmont, where they not only found cheap land but also abundant game and fish. Many of these people represented a great variety of religious groups, such as the Quakers and the Moravians. Fur trading was also established in the last quarter of the 17th century with Savannah as the major port. Naval stores using pitch from pine trees also became an important export from Carolina--and stuck to the heels of those in the area. Thus, the nickname "Tar Heel" was applied to those settlers from North Carolina.

The Birth and Territorial Expansion of the United States

Several decisions by the British Parliament began to lead to unrest in the colonies. First, the British Proclamation Line of 1763 impinged upon the rights of the colonists by preventing them from moving west of the Appalachian Mountains. Next, the Sugar Act of 1764 set off a chain reaction of economic decline in numerous aspects of life in New England. This was followed by several other tax laws which led to further dissatisfaction and eventually to revolution. Although the turning point in the war was fought at Guilford Courthouse near Greensboro, N.C. in early 1781, and the last battle was fought at Yorktown, Virginia later that year, the Treaty of Paris did not officially end the conflict until 1783. By this time, the Americans were beginning to follow the

BOX 4.1 – African American Life in the Colonial South

In 1619, the first African Americans stepped ashore at Jamestown, Virginia. But unlike most of the whites who preceded them, the African Americans began their life in America as indentured servants rather than free men. An indentured servant was one who signed a contract to work for a few years in return for passage to the New World. Thus, they could gain their freedom after the contract period. These Africans were brought to the English colonies in order to provide a large supply of cheap workers for the labor-intensive plantation production of tobacco and later to grow rice, indigo, sugar, and cotton.

With the introduction of sugar cultivation to islands in the Caribbean in the early 17th century, Africans were imported as slaves by the French and Spanish. Slavery had not been used by the English, but had its origin during the Middle Ages when large numbers of Slavs (from which the word slave is derived) were abducted from the Balkan Peninsula and forced to work on sugar plantations on islands in the Mediterranean Sea. For several decades, Africans on the Southern plantations were treated the same as indentured white servants, thus gaining their freedom after the contract period. Because of the economic success of the plantation economy, the freeing of these indentured servants was considered highly unsatisfactory and slavery was instituted. It was soon deemed to be an economic good, and shortly thereafter was supported by most religious groups as a social good. In 1661, Virginia passed the first law dealing with slavery. In 1705, slaves were proclaimed by the southern colonies to be a form of property and, thus, not subject to any rights.

For nearly 200 years, the Caribbean and Brazil provided the southern colonies with an ever-increasing number of enslaved Africans. Since they were brought to the U.S. from many parts of Africa, they were often unable to communicate with one another in any native tongue. Slaves were denied the right to go to school, own property, or marry. Any children born to a woman slave were deemed legally the slaves of her owner. Thus, slavery became hereditary. Although there was some division between slaves who served the owner's household and those who worked the land, most lived in wretched conditions. A common situation would find five or six slaves crowded into a one-room shack often without a wooden floor, window, stove, bed, or any basic necessity. The food provided by the owner was of such poor nutritional value that under-nutrition and malnutrition, combined with the unsanitary living conditions, frequently resulted in deaths related to malaria, pneumonia, yellow fever, cholera, and other diseases. Infant and maternal mortality were very high. Even the proclaiming of the concept of democracy in the two basic documents of the U.S. did not dissuade the practice of slavery. It was under such conditions that the African American lived in the South for two centuries.

Wilderness Road, blazed by Daniel Boone in 1775, through Cumberland Gap into Kentucky. The first stage in the development of America had ended and a second had begun.

The Treaty of Paris in 1783 settled the northern border of the United States with Britain from the Atlantic Ocean to the Lake of the Woods (Minnesota) and from there west to the supposed source of the Mississippi River (Figure 4.8). Also, Florida, which had been ceded by Spain to Britain in 1763, was returned to Spain. The southern border of the young nation was delineated along the 31st parallel and various rivers in the **Pinckney Treaty** with Spain in 1795. (This line formed the basis for most of the northern border of Florida.)

The first major territorial acquisition by the United States was the **Louisiana Purchase** (Figure 4.6). The Louisiana Territory, which encompassed 800,000 square miles (2.1 mil sq km), had been obtained from France by Spain in 1762, but Napoleon won it back in 1800. Three years later, the United States took advantage of France's need for money to pay her extensive war debts and purchased Louisiana from her, thus receiving all the lands west of the Mississippi River drained by it and its tributaries. This one acquisition roughly doubled the size of the young United States.

The southern border of the United States north of Spanish Florida was redefined three times within the decade of the 1810s. First, in 1810, **East Louisiana** was acquired from Spain. This area was between the Pearl and the Mississippi Rivers south of the 31st parallel and gave the nation access to the mouth of the Mississippi. Today it is the southeastern corner of Louisiana. During and after the War of 1812, the Seminole Indians in Florida had been crossing the border from Spanish-held territory and attacking American settlers in the South, but Spain would not or could not stop them. General Andrew Jackson attempted to stop Spanish gun-running in this area. In 1813, the U.S. obtained **West Florida** from Spain. This was the section south of the 31st parallel between the Pearl and the Peridido Rivers and today is the southern-most extensions of the states of Alabama and Mississippi. In 1819, Spain agreed to sell **Florida** to the United States. Thus, in 1821, Spain followed France in withdrawing its claim to any area that was not to the south and west of the Louisiana Territory.

In the **Adams-Onis Treaty** of 1819, Spain also ceded to the U.S. the land between the Red River of the South and the Sabine River, thus further defining the eastern border of Spanish territory to the west of Louisiana. (On today's map, the Sabine River marks most of the boundary between Louisiana and Texas.) The treaty also defined other parts of the borders between Spanish and American territory north of the Sabine along the 94th meridian to the Red River, up the Red River to the 100th meridian, then up the Arkansas River to the crest of the Rockies, then north to the 42nd parallel and from there west to the Pacific Ocean. (The western part of this boundary was to eventually become the northern border of the states of California, Nevada and most of Utah.)

The Spanish, who had established missions in the southwest at San Antonio (1718), San Francisco (1775), San Jose (1777) and Los Angeles (1781), had never established large-scale permanent settlement in North America. An independence movement in Mexico (including the present-day southwestern U.S.) arose in 1817 to overthrow Spanish rule, and in 1824, Mexico was granted its independence. But Americans were already moving into the area of Texas.

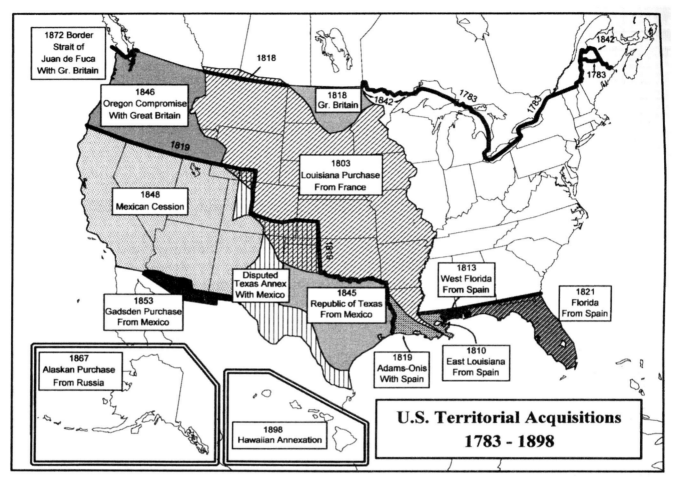

Figure 4.8 -- U.S. Territorial Delineation and Expansion

In 1836, the Americans in Texas declared independence from Mexico, leading to the defeat of the American settlers at the famous battle of the Alamo in San Antonio. However, within a year, the Mexicans had been driven out by a group of Americans led by Sam Houston. In 1837, **Texas** was granted its independence, and in 1845, the U.S. annexed it.

Also, in 1846, Mexico and the United States went to war over the refusal of Mexico to accept the Rio Grande as the border with the U.S. and Mexico's refusal to sell New Mexico and California to its northern neighbor. After two years of fighting and a change in the leadership of Mexico, the two countries agreed to settle these two disputes. In the resulting **Mexican Cession** (1848), Mexico sold the U.S. all the remaining southwest north of the Gila River. The United States could have taken more territory since its troops had captured much of Mexico, including its capital, in the Mexican-American War. The area acquired did include all of California, Nevada, and Utah, plus most of Arizona and New Mexico and part of Colorado.

Furthermore, in 1848, the California gold rush began creating a demand to build the Southern Pacific Railroad south of the Rockies and Gila River along the 32nd parallel. By 1853, the **Gadsden Purchase** from Mexico had added the final piece of the southwestern United States south of the Gila River. Two survey parties began on either end of the new border, one at the Pacific Ocean and one at the Rio Grande. They were supposed to meet, but the more rapidly moving team from the east reached the Colorado River about the same time as the western team which had had to traverse more rugged terrain; however, rather than meeting at the same location, they were nearly 20 miles apart; oops! Rather than survey the border again, they connected the two points using the Colorado River. Notice the southwestern corner of Arizona. These transfers established the current southern border of the U.S.

Resolution of the northern border required additional land purchases and treaties with Britain. The War of 1812 between Britain and the U.S. ended with the signing of the Treaty of 1818, which defined the border from the Lake of the Woods along the 49th parallel to the Continental Divide, a line which separates waters that flow into the Pacific from those which flow into the Gulf-Atlantic. By 1832, the Hudson's Bay Company dominated the northern fur trade and trapped in the area it claimed along the Rainy River and the Lake of the Woods. In 1842, Britain and the U.S. signed the **Webster-Ashburton Treaty**, which finalized two sections of the Canadian-United States border in northern New England and from Lake Superior to the Northwest Angle of the Lake of the Woods, thus confirming the 1818 treaty and assuring that Minnesota would be the northernmost of the 48 contiguous states, plus adding to the U.S. Aroostook County in Maine.

Meanwhile, in the Pacific Northwest, there had been several overlapping territorial claims. The Russians, who had discovered Alaska in 1741, had established the first white permanent settlement there by 1784 and had erected a fort just seventy miles north of San Francisco by 1812. The British explorer Cook sailed along the Alaskan coast as far as the Bering Strait in 1778 and Vancouver explored and mapped the coast in 1792. Americans landed on the Oregon coast in 1788 and sailed part of the way up the Columbia River in 1792. By 1805, Lewis and Clark reached the mouth of the Columbia River at the end of their overland journey. Early Spanish explorations also gave Spain claim to the region. In the Treaty of 1819 with the United States, the Spanish had agreed that the 42nd parallel would be its northern border in the west. In 1824 and 1825, Russia signed separate treaties with Great Britain and the United States relinquishing Russia's claims south of 54°40' North Latitude. This left Britain and the United States claiming the territory between the Russian and Spanish lands. This led to the **Oregon Compromise** of 1846, which set the 49th parallel as the border between Canada and the U.S. from the Rockies to the Pacific. The final piece of the northern border (the Strait of Juan de Fuca) was to come in 1872 more than 25 years later after the formation of the country of Canada. Today, the United States and Canada enjoy the world's longest friendly, if not undefended, border. Concerns due to smuggling and terrorism after the 9/11/01 attack have led to heightened border security between the United States and Canada.

U.S settlers migrating to the west coast before the completion of the transcontinental railroads had two choices. The first was to travel by ship from eastern seaports to Panama where they would have to disembark for the short railroad trip across the Isthmus of Panama. On the Pacific side they

BOX 4.2 -- Migrant Trails West

Between 1843 and 1869, nearly half a million migrants from the eastern U.S. utilized a network of wagon trails to settle lands in Oregon, California, and the Salt Lake Valley (Figure 4.13). While their importance diminished greatly with the completion of the transcontinental railroad in 1869, the trails were still utilized as recently as the first decade of the 20th century. Westward migration across these routes was spurred by the offer of free federal land in the Oregon Territory, the discovery of gold in California, and Mormons escaping religious persecution. The journeys were long, typically four to six months, and difficult. Disease was the greatest threat, but starvation, dehydration, accidents, and attack from hostile natives all took a toll. In all 50,000, or one out of ten, died along the way.

The trails began at one of the Missouri River ports, notably Independence and St. Joseph in Missouri and Council Bluffs in Iowa, which were connected by steamboat service to St. Louis and points east. The Oregon and Mormon Trails followed the Platte, North Platte, and then the Sweetwater River across Nebraska and through South Pass in Wyoming. In western Wyoming, the Mormon trail branched off at Ft. Bridger to the southwest and Salt Lake City, while the Oregon Trail continued to the Pacific following the Snake and Columbia Rivers. With the discovery of gold in California in 1848, the California Trail came into heavy use. The California Trail split off from the Oregon Trail in south central Idaho at Ft. Hall, headed southwest across Nevada, following the Humboldt River, until it reached the Sierra Nevada Range. Here the pioneers had several choices of routes across the mountains, all of which were extremely difficult. At times the wagons would have to be disassembled so they could be hoisted up sheer cliffs or trees would be felled to make ramps and multiple teams of horses or oxen would then drag the wagons over the cliffs. In 1846, the infamous Donner Party arrived on the east slope of the Sierra Nevada late in the season with draft animals in poor condition. In their attempt to cross the mountains they became stranded in early heavy snowfalls. The party ran out of food and many starved, with some resorting to cannibalism to survive. Of the 87 only 48 reached their destination in California.

The Santa Fe Trail started at either Independence or St. Joseph, Missouri and headed southwest across Kansas. Upon reaching the Arkansas River some followed the river westward to the Front Range of Colorado and then south to Santa Fe. This route was significantly longer than the choice of heading directly toward Santa Fe along the Cimarron Branch of the trail, but had the advantage of reliable water for the entire journey. The Santa Fe Trail was primarily a military and commercial freight route connecting the southwest to the eastern United States. From Santa Fe less well known trails continued to California, Mexico City and Salt Lake City.

The completion of the transcontinental railroad in 1869 led to a rapid decline in traffic on the trails as rail offered far safer and faster transport across the country. Railroads competing for the migrant trade offered low cost one way tickets westward, but no provision for a like fare eastward, which further doomed the viability of the wagon trails.

would board ship again for the voyage to Los Angeles or San Francisco. The other choice was to go by wagon overland following one of the great migrant trails. (See Box 4.2 for a discussion of the migrant trails).

In 1867, the United States purchased Alaska from Russia, thus leaving only a relatively small Pacific coast area between its territories. The final acquisition that was to become a U.S. state was Hawaii in 1898. In that year, the Philippines, Guam, Cuba, and Puerto Rico were taken from Spain as a result of the U.S. victory in the **Spanish-American War**. Later, numerous Pacific Islands, the Panama Canal Zone (1904), and the Virgin Islands (from Denmark in 1917) came under its control. Cuba was a protectorate of the U.S. until 1934; the Philippines gained independence in 1946; Puerto Rico became a U.S. Commonwealth in 1952; the Marshall Islands became free in 1986; and the Panama Canal Zone (leased from Panama in 1903 after helping them secede from Columbia) was transferred to Panama in 1979 and reverted to Panama at the end of the twentieth century. Guam and Midway are still under the control of the U.S.

The Birth and Territorial Expansion of Canada

British control of Canada was formulated with the 1763 Treaty of Paris, but French settlers were in the majority. The **Quebec Act of 1774** settled many of the differences between England and France and granted rights to the French settlers in what is now Canada. After the defeat of the British in the American Revolution, many loyalists moved north to New Brunswick and Ontario after the war. Nova Scotia (New Scotland) was created for the British loyalists and others. In 1791, most of what is now the eastern part of Canada was divided along the Ottawa River into a mainly English Protestant Upper Canada and a primarily French Catholic Lower Canada. Despite bitter opposition, a closer union of the two was created in 1840-1841.

In the U.S. in 1862, with southern Congressmen no longer present to continue blocking settlement in the Midwest--a region they had feared would be unlikely to use slaves or support slavery, the **Homestead Act** was passed. Thousands of settlers flooded into the prairies. When all the best land had been taken, many pushed north across the international border. This was paralleled by calls from some Americans for the annexation of Canada. Many of the British north of the 49th parallel were afraid that the people and the government of the United States would now turn to the north to further extend its "manifest destiny." This was a particular concern once the United States had resolved its internal conflict with the end of the Civil War in 1865 and purchased Alaska in 1867.

Britain believed that the United States would be less likely to annex an independent Canada than some loosely confederated North American colonies. Although ties between Britain and Canada were maintained to counter fears of U.S. aggression, the **British North America Act** established an independent Confederation of Canada in 1867. French Lower Canada and British Upper Canada became the Provinces of Quebec and Ontario, respectively, while Nova Scotia (which included the initial French settlement of Port Royal) and New Brunswick (with many French settlers) rounded out the original four provinces (Figure 4.7). The capital was placed at Ottawa on the Ottawa River between the two major provinces. The capital's interior location was chosen partly because it would be insulated from potential American invasion. The federalist system of government in Canada left many powers with the provincial legislatures, ensuring the continuation of separate cultural developments within each governmental unit, including education and language. French and English were declared equal languages.

After the **Treaty of 1871**, which settled many differences between Britain and the United States, the British withdrew troops from Canada, thus allaying American fears of invasion. The U.S. agreed not to interfere with Canadians settling the west north of the 49th parallel. However, Irish Finean raids across the border into the Prairies of Canada from the Red River Valley of the north continued until the end of 1871. French Canadians had opposed efforts by the U.S. to annex Canada because they feared a takeover by Irish Catholics and the resulting decline of French nationalism. Although President Grant supported the idea of the U.S. annexing Canada, in **1872**, the border between the two nations was extended along the **Strait of Juan de Fuca**, putting this issue to rest and completing the border between Canada and the United States.

At the time of Confederation, much of what is today's Canada remained British territory, including northern areas of Quebec and Ontario, Prince Edward Island, Newfoundland, Rupert's Land controlled by the Hudson Bay Company, British Columbia, the North Western Territory, and the Arctic Archipelago. But by 1880, all of the British territory in North America, except Newfoundland, had been transferred to Canadian control. Manitoba became a province in 1870, British Columbia in 1871, Prince Edward Island in 1873, Alberta and Saskatchewan in 1905, and Newfoundland and Labrador in 1949. (See Figure 4.7.) Canadian provinces, like states in the U.S., enjoy autonomy, rights and responsibilities granted to them in the Constitution Act of 1867. The North of Canada remains organized as territories under the authority of Ottawa. Canadian territories have only a degree of autonomy, rights and responsibilities as granted by the central government in Ottawa. The Northwest Territories were created in 1870, the Yukon in 1898, and Nunavut out of the Northwest Territories in 1999 as an Inuit homeland.

Early Immigration and Population Growth

Most authorities believe that people first came to America from Asia as early as 25,000 to 40,000 years ago by crossing the Bering Strait to Alaska. They were dependent on large game, including the mammoth, horse, camel, and bison. As many of these large herd animals were exterminated by over-hunting, alternative food supplies were needed. No longer tied to the range of the animal herds, the population spread throughout the North American continent in the search for food. With the rise of agriculture in this region around 750 A.D., nomadic bands began to settle, forming villages. By 1000 A.D., Cahokia, near modern-day St. Louis, could lay claim to the title of the first North American city, containing over 40,000 inhabitants.

When Europeans began exploring North America in the late fifteenth century, it is estimated that the indigenous population numbered more than 3.5 million. These Native Americans were spread

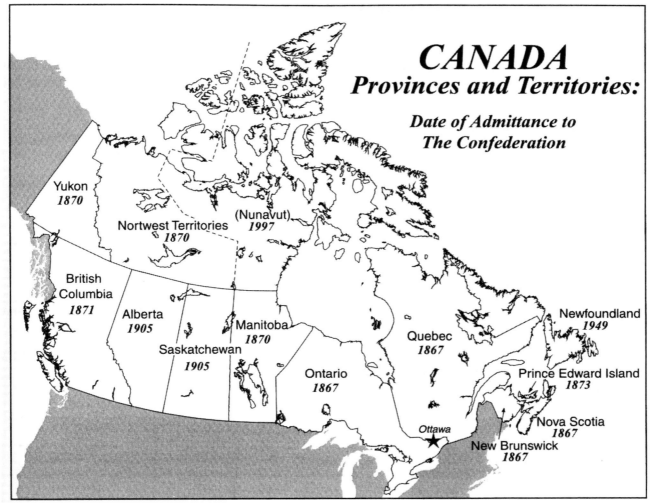

Figure 4.9 -- Canadian Territorial Development

widely throughout the continent. Contact with Europeans introduced a series of previously unknown diseases to Native Americans, including smallpox, measles, influenza, and mumps. Without the acquired immunities of the Europeans. The Native American population was decimated. By 1800, their number had declined to about one million. Most of those remaining were removed from their lands to reservations hundreds of miles away in completely different unfamiliar and less productive environments. (See Box 4.3 for a discussion of the expulsion of the Cherokees from western Georgia and North Carolina and their forced march to Oklahoma.)

Between 1500 and 1700, the European population increased very slowly in North America. By 1700, what is today Canada had about 20,000 people, about two-thirds of whom were French. The cities of Montreal and Quebec each had just under 2,000 residents in that year. With the fall of the city of Quebec to British forces and the subsequent signing of the Treaty of Paris in 1763, French

BOX 4.3 --The Trail of Tears

In 1783, early contact between the white settlers in the southeast and the Cherokees resulted in half dying from smallpox. During the mid-18th century, they fought the invading white settlers and later helped the British in the Revolutionary War.

But by the early 1800s, the Cherokees were again prosperous hunters and farmers living in the southern Appalachian mountains and foothills of Georgia. They began to incorporate the European economic and political systems. Not only did they operate individual small farms, but also large plantations with slaves. In 1821, one of them invented a special alphabet which enabled them to write their language. In 1827, they adopted a written constitution and set up a republican form of government with a legislature, court, and code of law. They called it the Cherokee Nation. They also set up schools and many adopted Christianity when the *New Testament* was translated using their new alphabet. However, the Georgia settlers demanded the Cherokees give up their land. In 1828-1829, the Georgia state legislature passed a law depriving the Cherokees of their rights. When the case went to the Supreme Court, Justice Marshall supported the Cherokees. However, President Jackson, who took office in 1829, supported the position of Georgia and a similar one by Mississippi. He sent special envoys to the leaders of the Cherokees, Choctaws, Creeks, and Chickasaws in an effort to sway them to sign an agreement to give up their land and move west of the Mississippi River. President Jackson also had bills submitted to Congress to remove the Indians from their land--with force if necessary. Removal of the Choctaws began immediately. The Cherokees resisted; but, in 1835, some tribal members signed an agreement with the U.S. government to move. After further opposition from most of the tribe, President Jackson sent the Army to forcefully remove them. During the winter of 1838-39, thousands were herded into stockades, where many died from disease and bad weather. Some escaped into the Smoky Mountains. When one Indian killed two soldiers and hid in the mountains, the government demanded he be executed in return for sparing the lives of the others. When he returned of his own accord, the government forced his own tribe to execute him, then, force-marched 15,000 a thousand miles to Oklahoma. Thousands died along the "Trail of Tears." Eventually, about a thousand stayed in the Smokies and were allowed to resettle there. The government in the late 1800s gave most of the Oklahoma Indian land to white settlers.

immigration to Canada effectively ended. Many Loyalists fleeing the Revolutionary War in the United States moved to Canada and additional immigration was actively encouraged by the British government. As a result, by 1800, English colonists outnumbered their French counterparts in a country of about 400,000 (Table 4.1). When Canada became independent in 1867, the population was only 3.5 million, slightly less than ten percent of that of the U.S. At this time, the British outnumbered the French three to two.

Canada, of course, has a more difficult environment than either most of the major European source areas or the alternative destinations in the United States, making it a less attractive destination, especially in the nineteenth century farming era. Natural population growth was the most important component of Canadian population growth before 1900. Between 1901 and 1931, however, immigrants accounted for 54 percent of Canada's population growth. These newcomers came mainly from Britain and Eastern Europe. After 1931, the Great Depression, World War II, and higher fertility after World War II made immigration a much smaller component of population growth in Canada.

Between 1500 and 1700, the **European** population increased very slowly in what is now the United States and, in 1700, there were only about 220,000 people in this area, mainly English, Scots-Irish, Welsh, Dutch, Swedes, and Germans. Most people lived on farms within a hundred miles of the coast. Few cities were in existence, the largest being Boston (7,000), New York (4,500), and Philadelphia (3,000). After the defeat of the British, American settlers began to cross the Appalachians into the interior. During the eighteenth century, the European population grew rapidly and, by 1790, the date of the first U.S. Census, the population in the United States was nearly four million, or about ten times that of the British territory to the north.

Table 4.1 Population and Percent Urban in Canada and the U.S., 1790-1950/51*

Year	The United States		Canada	
	Population	Percent Urban	Population	Percent Urban
1790	3,929,000	5.1%	400,000	NA
1850/51	23,192,000	15.4%	2,436,000	14.7%
1900/01	76,212,000	39.6%	5,371,000	37.5%
1950/51	151,326,000	59.6%	14,009,000	62.9%

Population Change in the U.S.

The word slave is a derivation of "Slav." During the Middle Ages, large numbers of Slavs from the Balkan Peninsula were abducted and forced to work on sugar plantations on islands in the Mediterranean Sea. With the introduction of sugar cultivation to islands of the Caribbean, **Africans** were imported to do the same work the earlier Slavs had done in Europe. Although Africans were brought to Florida by the French and Spanish by the early seventeenth century, they were introduced to the settlement of Jamestown in 1619 as indentured servants. However, by 1662, Virginia had declared them to be slaves. By 1700, their numbers had reached nearly 30,000 and soon after, in 1705, they were declared a form of property. In 1738, a group of black slaves had escaped from South Carolina to Spanish Florida, where they were given their freedom.

In 1790, the first U.S. Census estimated the number of African Americans in this country to be 750,000, or almost one-fifth of the population. (This was likely a conservative count because slaves were property on which taxes had to be paid, so owners did not admit to having any more than they felt they must.) About 95 percent of the slaves were held in the South, mainly laborers on plantations.

Stimulated by a demand for inexpensive labor by the California gold rush of 1848 and a few years later by the need for workers for the construction of the Central Pacific Railroad, large numbers of **Orientals** were imported into the western United States. As their numbers grew to about 300,000 by the 1860s, so did fear, resentment and hostility on the part of white workers in that area. In 1882, Chinese immigration was curtailed by the Oriental Exclusion Act. Japanese immigration to California and British Columbia via Hawaii in the late 1800s was also severely limited in 1907 and then eliminated completely in 1924.

Table 4.2. U.S. Population Change, 1790-1930

Year	Population	Increase During Preceding Ten-Year Period	
		Number	Percent
1790	3,929,214	--	--
1800	5,308,483	1,379,269	35.1
1810	7,239,881	1,931,398	36.4
1820	9,638,453	2,398,572	33.1
1830	12,866,020	3,227,567	33.5
1840	17,069,453	4,203,433	32.7
1850	23,191,876	6,122,423	35.9
1860	31,433,321	8,251,445	35.6
1870	38,558,371	7,115,050	22.6
1880	50,189,209	11,630,838	30.2
1890	62,979,766	12,790,557	25.5
1900	76,212,168	13,232,402	21.0
1910	92,228,496	16,016,328	21.0
1920	106,021,537	13,793,041	15.0
1930	123,202,624	17,181,087	16.2

Source: U.S. Census Bureau.

Between 1790 (the first census) and 1860 (the beginning of the Civil War), the population grew from less than four million to more than 31 million. The **decennial increment** increased from a little over one million in the 1790s to more than eight million by the 1850s, just prior to the Civil War. Even though the numerical growth was becoming greater and greater with each decade, the **rate of growth** remained between 33 percent and 36 percent because the number of people in the population was becoming larger (Table 4.2).

Political, economic and religious turmoil in Western Europe, such as the Irish potato famine of the mid-1840s, caused a sharp rise in immigrant numbers to the United States from about 150,000 in the 1820s to some 600,000 in the 1830s and 2,600,000 in the 1850s (Table 4.3). By 1860, Europeans, primarily from northwestern Europe, had surged to nearly 27 million in the United States. This was primarily due to the sharp rise in immigration after 1820. Even during this early period in U.S. history, the fertility rate was already beginning to decline.

Over a million immigrants entered the United States each decade from 1850 to 1890 and over 3.5 million entered every ten years from 1890 to 1930, when the Depression sharply curtailed immigration. Before 1890, over three-fourths came from the British Isles, Germany, Scandinavia, and Canada; but from 1890 to 1930, under half; with growing numbers from southern and eastern Europe, mainly Austria-Hungary, Italy and the Russian Ukraine. Immigration peaked between 1905 and 1914, after which it declined in most years because of World War I, immigration laws, the Great Depression, and World War II.

Table 4.3. Decennial Immigration into the United States, 1821-1930

Decade	Number of Immigrants
1821-1830	152,000
1831-1840	599,000
1841-1850	1,713,000
1851-1860	2,598,000
1861-1870	2,315,000
1871-1880	2,812,000
1881-1890	5,247,000
1891-1900	3,688,000
1901-1910	8,795,000
1911-1920	5,736,000
1921-1930	4,107,000

Source: U.S. Census Bureau.

Fertility in the United States declined from about seven children per woman in 1800 to just over five in 1860 to just over two in 1930 (Figure 4.10). As a result of this trend and increases in immigration, an increasing proportion of population growth was accounted for by people entering the country and a declining percentage from fertility. (A fertility rate of 2.1 is considered to be at replacement level, which means that a continuation of fertility at this rate would result in a failure of the population to grow after about 70 years, if there were not any net immigration during this time. The result, therefore, would be eventual zero population growth.)

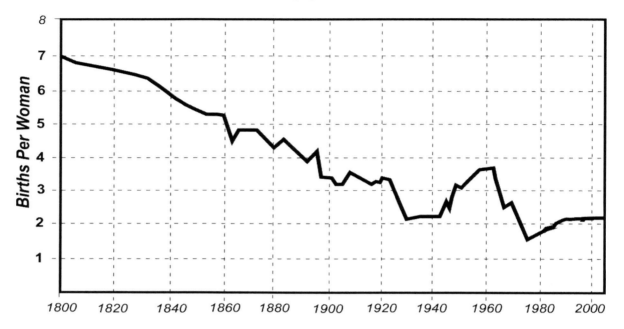

Figure 4.10 -- Fertility Change in the United States, 1800-2000. Data U.S. Census Bureau

While European immigration into the United States was rising rapidly, the importation of **Africans** nearly stopped after 1805, when slave trading was abolished. This was despite the fact that slavery had been given a major stimulus with the invention of the cotton gin in 1793, since many more acres of cotton could be processed in the same amount of time. A combination of great African immigration until the second decade of the 19th century and high fertility (partially offset by high infant and child mortality) increased the number of African Americans to over 4.4 million by 1860, with over 90 percent of them still living in the South (Table 4.4). However, they accounted for only 14 percent of the population because of the much greater European immigration. Although the Emancipation Proclamation had freed the slaves from legal bondage, they remained economically bound to the land by the sharecropper system. Nearly 50 years after the Civil War, almost 90 percent remained in the South mainly on farms. (See BOX 4.4 for a discussion of the life of African Americans in the late 19th century.)

Most of the immigrants not only arrived at large cities along the east coast but also remained in them. Thus, the percentage of the population living in **urban** places (8,000 or more till 1900) rose from five percent in 1790 to 20 percent in 1860 (Table 4.5). However, since most Africans had been brought into the southern part of colonial America and the young United States, where most were kept as slaves on large plantations in the rural areas, the percentage of this group living in urban areas was very small and increased little before the Civil War.

BOX 4.4 – African American Life in the Late 19th Century

In 1865, the home of the African American lay devastated and transport systems were inoperable. Since they were too poor to buy land or leave and knew little more than basic agricultural skills and since white planters had land but no workers, a system of mutual benefit was created whereby African Americans worked the white's land and paid for this by giving the owner a share of the crop (half or more). Thus, a **sharecropper system** began that included many whites and remains in parts of the South today. If one could save enough money, he could rent part of the farm for his own work. But the other half (or less) of his profit would have to be used to pay for food and other supplies obtained earlier. Few were thus able to become **tenant farmers** and even fewer could save enough money to buy land. Since few African Americans had the education or training to work in offices or factories, they were usually relegated to agricultural or to menial jobs in the towns. The **Reconstruction Era** after the Civil War gave good employment opportunities for only a minute portion of African Americans. Southern whites in local areas passed laws limiting newly won rights and state authorities did not prevent this. These "**black codes**" led to the passing of the 14th and 15th Amendments and the Civil Rights Act of 1875. In 1866, the Civil Rights Act, became the **14th Amendment**, after being passed over the veto of President Andrew Johnson, who succeeded President Lincoln after his assassination. It prohibited states from depriving anyone of life, liberty or property without due process of law and from denying anyone "equal protection of the laws." The **15th Amendment** (1870) assured all the right to vote. The **Civil Rights Act of 1875** prohibited anyone from being denied equal access to public transportation, lodging and amusement places. For five to ten years, African Americans made substantial strides in voter registration and school enrollment. But, rights guaranteed by the 14th and 15th Amendments depended on enforcement. Although African Americans had become important in the Republican Party, the federal government did not heed their call for enforcement of their rights and many left the party. By 1876, conservatives had enough power in the South to destroy Reconstruction in eight states. In 1877, a coalition of Republicans and southern Democrats in Congress voted to make Republican **Rutherford Hayes** President in return for ending federal support for African American rights and the return of state control over politics in the South. In 1883, the Civil Rights Act of 1875 was ruled unconstitutional by the **Supreme Court**. In 1896, it ruled that "separate but equal" facilities were constitutional. "**Jim Crow laws**" to promote segregation became the enforced law of the land. In the 1890s, "**Grandfather clauses**" were passed in many southern states limiting voting rights of African Americans. Ten southern states put a **poll tax** on voting, and lynchings and various torturous acts were used throughout the South as unofficial enforcements of the Jim Crow laws.

Table 4.4. The African American Population in the U. S., 1790-1930

Year	Number in U.S.	Percent of U.S Population	Number in The South	Percent in The South
1790	757,000	19.3	690,000	91
1800	1,002,000	18.9	918,000	92
1810	1,378,000	19.0	1,269,000	92
1820	1,772,000	18.4	1,643,000	93
1830	2,329,000	18.1	2,162,000	93
1840	2,874,000	16.8	2,642,000	92
1850	3,639,000	15.7	3,352,000	92
1860	4,442,000	14.1	4,097,000	92
1870	4,880,000	12.7	4,421,000	91
1880	6,581,000	13.1	5,954,000	90
1890	7,489,000	11.9	6,761,000	90
1900	8,834,000	11.6	7,923,000	90
1910	9,828,000	10.7	8,749,000	89
1920	10,463,000	9.9	8,912,000	85
1930	11,891,000	9.7	9,362,000	79

Source: U. S. Census Bureau.

After the defeat of the British and their Proclamation Line and with the founding of the new nation, the settlers began to follow Braddock's Road, Forbes' Road, Daniel Boone's Wilderness Road, and other trails west through the Appalachian Mountains to the interior. The **westward movement** of settlers resulted in a shift in the center of gravity (mean center) of the U.S. population from just east of Baltimore in 1790 to about 25 miles northeast of Portsmouth, Ohio in 1860 (Figure 4.11).

As westward expansion continued, the **center of gravity** of the population shifted from eastern Ohio to western Indiana--about 25 miles southeast of Terre Haute in 1930 (Figure 4.11). As cities continued to grow in number and size, the proportion of the population living in urban areas rose from 20 percent in 1860 to 51 percent in 1920 (urban being 2,500 or more since 1900) and 56 percent in 1930 (Table 4.5).

Despite higher fertility rates for **African Americans** than whites in the U.S., the massive European influx from 1860 to 1930 caused the proportion of African Americans to decline even more to a record low of under 10 percent in 1930 (Table 4.4). This was just half what it had been in 1790.

The proportion of **African Americans** living in urban areas jumped four times from 11 percent in 1860 to 44 percent in 1930, with over half of the gain coming after 1910 and being associated with new manufacturing job opportunities which began with World War I (Table 4.5). During the latter 20-year period, the share of African Americans living in the South suddenly declined from 89 percent to 79 percent as they moved to northern cities to take the new industrial jobs created there (Table 4.4).

Table 4.5. Percent Urban: 1830-1930

Year	Percent Urban Total Population	African Americans
1830	9	6
1840	11	8
1850	15	8
1860	20	11
1870	26	13
1880	28	14
1890	35	20
1900	40	23
1910	46	27
1920	51	34
1930	56	44

Source: U.S. Census Bureau

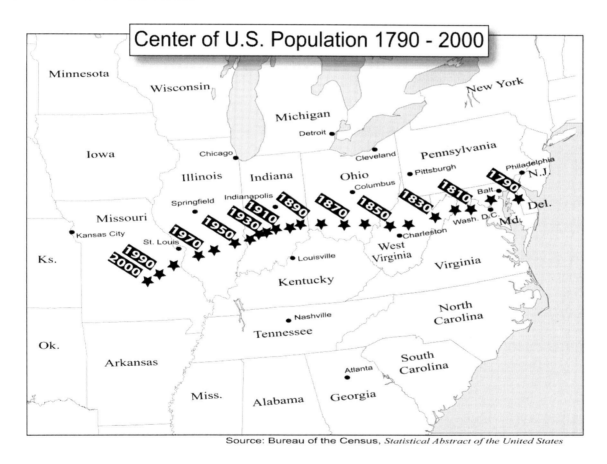

Figure 4.11 -- Center of Gravity of the U.S. Population, 1790-2000

Canadian Regionalism

Unlike the United States, where large numbers of Europeans arrived in a continuous and heavy stream beginning in the 1800s and continued until the Great Depression, Canada experienced only sporadic and scattered European settlement. Partly due to the harsh climate and the forbidding Canadian Shield (an area of bedrock covering half of Canada, unsuitable for farming), Europeans who arrived in Canada often chose homes far from any of the other groups who had preceded them. There was no Canadian "melting pot" because the groups were too far away from one another to even get "hot." The hodgepodge of European settlement began with the French in Atlantic Canada. This group was marginalized and eventually expelled by the British to be replaced by Scots and Irish from the British Isles. French settlement was more extensive in Quebec and remains the dominant culture there today, effectively splitting British, English-speaking Canada into to two parts. Atlantic Canada, but especially Ontario, received significant numbers of Loyalists who fled the United States during and after the Revolutionary War, forming a second concentration of English-speakers, this time west of Quebec. A mixed French-Indian people called the Metis was joined in what is today Manitoba by the first British islanders and in the 19th and 20th centuries by eastern Europeans creating an agricultural economy in the Great Plains. Far across the Rockies, British fur traders founded the British Columbia region. The far north of Canada remains an Inuit (Eskimo) homeland.

Widely scattered settlements promote regional, rather than national, identity. In his essay "Regionalism and the Canadian Archipelago," geographer Cole Harris describes strong regionalism present in today's Canada. "The political map of North America sustains the illusion that Canada is a continental giant spanning 70 degrees of longitude and some 40 degrees of latitude; whereas on any long, clear-night flight, this Canada dissolves into an oceanic darkness spotted by occasional islands of light. These lights mark the lived-in Canada, the Canadian ecumene, an island archipelago spread over 7200 east-west kilometers." Each of these "islands" tends to form a group consciousness, a sense of place, unique to their region of Canada. For example, in the north of Canada, the Inuit (Eskimos) share a common cultural identity and language, while the Quebec government to the south has taken a hard line to preserve French culture, legal systems, traditions, and language.

Robert Bone structures his book, *The Regional Geography of Canada*, around "faultlines" that have emerged in Canada through centuries of limited interaction among the islands of the Canadian archipelago. Bone's faultlines focus on these differences: French vs. English, Native vs. non-native, new immigrants vs. European heritage, the centralists who favor federal government control vs. regionalists who favor provincial authority. He divides Canada into six regions (Figure 4.12), which serve to illustrate his Canadian faultlines. The United States, of course, may also be divided into physical or cultural regions, but the sense of regionalism with faultlines is not so strong as in Canada. Beyond cultural regionalism, regional economies also differ and this serves to enhance regional identities. For example, the sparsely-populated, fertile prairies of Western Canada have produced an economy where agriculture is key; fishing has been the lifeblood of Atlantic Canada until recently; and British Columbia has been a resource hinterland for centuries. On the other hand, southern Ontario is the population, industrial, export, and high-technology core of Canada. (See Box 4.5 for a discussion of regional economic disparities of Canada.)

Figure 4.12 -- Canadian Regions (after Bone).

Intense regionalism led to calls for secession of the province of Quebec during the last decades of the 20th century, led by Jean Lesage and later Rene Levesque, who founded the Parti Quebecois (PQ) in 1968. In, 1969, Canada became officially bilingual. The PQ came to power in 1976 largely because of disenchantment with the ruling provincial government in Quebec and the promise to allow a referendum on separating Quebec from Canada politically but not economically. However, in 1980, 60 percent of Quebec's voters said **no**. In 1987, the Meech Lake Accord was proposed as a constitutional amendment to recognize the cultural distinctiveness of Quebec but was not ratified because the conservative provinces of Manitoba and Newfoundland and Labrador would not consent. As a result, many Quebecois increased demands for independence. In late 1992, a majority of voters in each province, including Quebec, rejected a variety of amendments, including separating Quebec from Canada, and in 1995, Quebec voters narrowly rejected a referendum on withdrawing from Canada.

BOX 4.5 — Heartland and Hinterland in Canada

The regional divide in Canada has been expressed in the terms "heartland" and "hinterland." also called core and periphery. The heartland, or core, is the most influential part of Canada, where the most people live, is highly urbanized, the location of the national government in Ottawa, the location of the headquarters of the most important corporations, contains the largest cities, and dominant culture(s), is where most manufacturing occurs, where the highest order of goods and services are available, and where growth and success lead to further growth. The hinterland, or periphery, is secondary in importance to the core and is characterized by resource extraction for core industry, branches of core businesses and industry, a smaller population, net out-migration of workers to the core, low levels of urbanism, and slow-growth or stagnant economics.

The pattern of core-periphery evolves over time. At first, Quebec and the Atlantic colonies were the core. Southern Ontario emerged as part of Canada's core in the late 1800s and has slowly overtaken southern Quebec in dominance since then. At the national scale today, southern Ontario and southern Quebec form the heartland of Canada. A secondary core is emerging in British Columbia and, perhaps, Alberta. Peripheral, or hinterland, Canada includes western Canada (Alberta, Manitoba and Saskatchewan), Atlantic Canada (Prince Edward Island, Nova Scotia, New Brunswick, and Newfoundland and Labrador), and the Territorial North (Northwest Territories, Yukon, and Nunavut).

The heartland-hinterland economic divide is illustrated by the distribution of Federal Transfer Payments to provinces and territories. The Canadian Constitution provides for the collection of money from the "have" provinces to be transferred to the "have-not" provinces for the provision of basic services. All provinces receive transfer payments to provide the government health care system to its citizens. Less wealthy provinces receive additional transfer payments to provide other services. The Territorial North and Atlantic Canada receive the most transfer money per capita from the federal government in Ottawa. One type of transfer payment is called Equalization. "Equalization is the Government of Canada's transfer program for addressing fiscal disparities among provinces. Equalization payments enable less prosperous provincial governments to provide their residents with public services that are reasonably comparable to those in other provinces, at reasonably comparable levels of taxation" (http://www.fin.gc.ca). In 2008-2009, six "have-not" provinces and all the territories received equalization payments for education, social programs, and infrastructure: Yukon, Nunavut, Northwest Territories, Newfoundland and Labrador, Prince Edward Island, Nova Scotia, New Brunswick, Quebec, and Manitoba. Such transfer payments identify them as hinterland areas. Ontario is the wealthiest province and provides the vast majority of funds to be transferred, making it perhaps "the" heartland province.

HISTORICAL GEOGRAPHY REVIEW

1. Describe the major food areas of Native Americans in the 15th century and locate each on a map.

2. Identify the route of exploration, in writing and on a map, of each of the following explorers: Cabot, Ponce de Leon, Pineda, Gordillo, Cartier, de Vaca, de Soto, Moscoso, Coronado, Cardenas, Cabrillo, Drake and Erickson.

3. What were the main geographical advantages/disadvantages of settlement at the following: Jamestown, Quebec, the 3 Dutch areas and Plymouth.

4. What were the European territorial claims in North America in 1660? What changes occurred in these claims in 1664? 1713? 1762? 1763?

5. Discuss life in the English colonies of New England, the South and mid-Atlantic regions.

6. What was the importance of portages and primarily to whom?

7. What are long lots and what is their purpose?

8. How did the British Proclamation of 1763 impinge upon the rights of the colonists?

9. What U.S. territorial acquisitions and alterations resulted from each of the following: (be specific and locate these on a map, such as: 1795--Pinckney Treaty--31st parallel established as southern border of U.S. east of the Mississippi River--with Spain--now much of northern Florida border.)

    1803--Louisiana Purchase
    1810--East Louisiana
    1813--West Florida
    1818--Treaty of 1818
    1819--Adams-Onis Treaty
    1819 (1821)--Florida Purchase
    1842--Webster-Ashburton Treaty
    1845--Texas
    1846--Oregon Compromise
    1848--Mexican Cession
    1853--Gadsden Purchase
    1867--Alaskan Purchase
    1872--Treaty of 1872
    1898--Hawaii

10. What circumstances led to the displacement of the Cherokees from their land? Where were most of them forced to move?

11. What was the Quebec Act of 1774 and the British North America Act of 1867?

12. What is the background and present status of the Quebec separatist movement?

13. What defines the heartland (core) and hinterland (periphery) of Canada? Which provinces make up each one?

HISTORICAL GEOGRAPHY EXERCISE

Below is a map showing the major overland migrant trails (Figure 4.13). Using it as a base, draw the Mormon, Oregon and California trails on the physiography map (Figure 4.14). Along which river valleys did each one follow and through which lowlands and passes did they go? At what specific points did one trail diverge from the other? Why do you think they followed these particular routes?

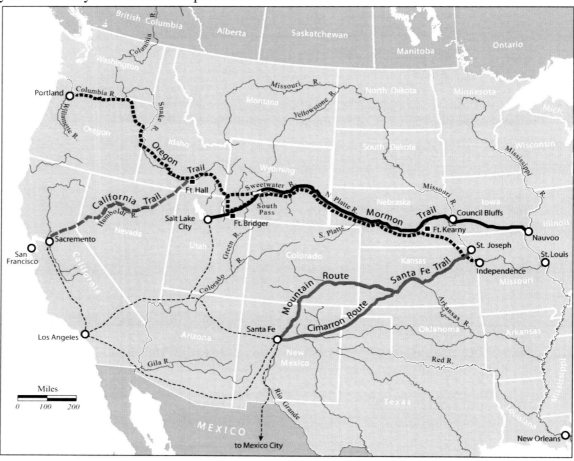

Figure 4.13 – Major overland wagon routes.

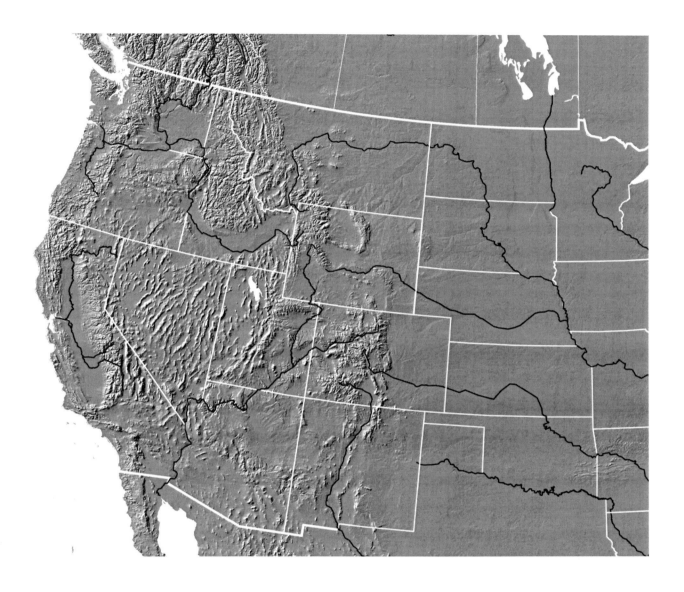

Figure 4.14 -- Physiography of the western U.S. for Historical Exercise

Figure 5.1 -- Ukrainian Church in Central Saskatchewan, Canada

CHAPTER FIVE

POPULATION AND CULTURE

Population Density

About 3.5 million aboriginals lived in what is today the United States and Canada when Europeans discovered the continent. Today, the population of the United States is over 310 million, ranking a distant third among the countries of the world, while Canada with about 33 million people ranks 35th. Thus, Canada has slightly more than 1/10 the population of the United States and this proportion has remained roughly the same during the last 200 years. Because Canada is slightly larger than the United States in land area, but has a much smaller population, its population density (number of people per square mile) is much lower. Whereas the Netherlands has an arithmetic density of about 1,000 per square mile and Japan about 900, the United States' density is only 81 and Canada just nine, while Australia's is seven. From a world perspective, Canada has a very low density, while the U.S. might be considered to be at a low-to-moderate level. However, a very large proportion of the land area of North America is nearly uninhabitable—rugged mountains, deserts, and the frigid north. A second, more meaningful gauge of population density—physiologic density—measures people per square mile of arable (farmable) land. Both Canada and the United States have large areas of arable land. Because of Canada's more limited growing season and smaller area of good soils, about ten percent of the country is arable, compared to 20 percent in the United States. Using this gauge, few countries of the world have lower physiologic densities than Canada (174 people per square mile of arable land) or the United States (384). In other words, both countries enjoy low populations relative to land area and farmland resources.

Population density is not the same as population distribution, however, since people are not spread evenly across the landscape. Population geography is a field of study that examines the nature of and reasons for the distribution of people. The clustering of North America's population is evident in Figure 5.1. About 80 percent of the people live in urbanized areas. At a glance, one can see that the eastern United States is more densely populated than the West and that large areas of Alaska, Hawaii, and the north of Canada are nearly empty. Areas in the East and Great Lakes region were settled early by Europeans, possessed abundant mineral and soil resources, were easily accessible by water, experienced the arrival of millions of immigrants in the nineteenth and twentieth centuries, industrialized first, and maintain higher population densities due to historical inertia and favorable climates. These processes are manifested in the list of the top ten states in population in the U.S. (Figure 5.2), many of which are found along the east coast or in the Great Lakes industrial region.

Along the northeastern seaboard of the United States (Figure 5.1) is a continuously urbanized area known as Megalopolis ("large city"). This string of connected coastal cities includes four of the

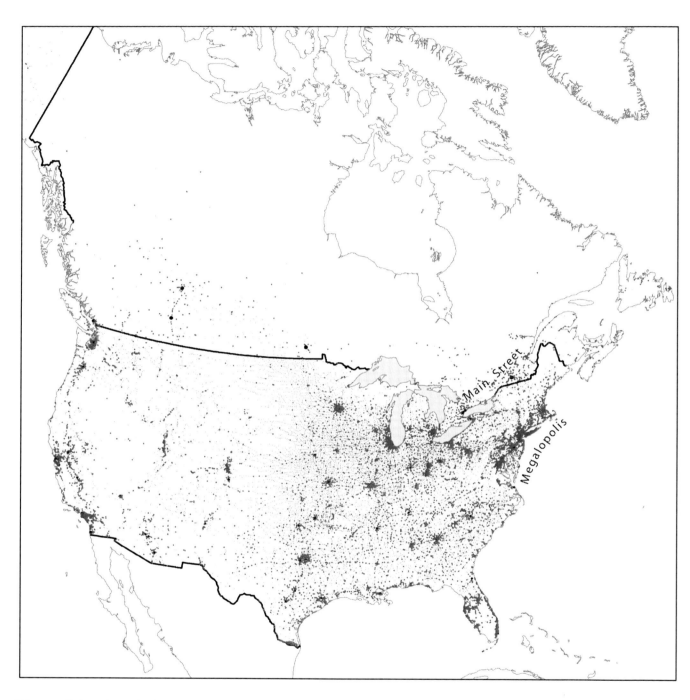

Figure 5.1 -- Population Density

ten largest U.S. cities—Boston, New York City, Philadelphia, and Washington, DC (Table 5.1) and contains about 20 percent of the population of the country. Rural regions in the arid West tend to have very low densities. Population density is also high along the west coast of the continent (Figure 5.1). After World War II, westward migration to California accounted for that state's rapid growth. In addition, California continues to be the recipient of a large proportion of both Hispanic and Asian immigrants to the United States (Figure 5.2), has more people than all of Canada, and would be among the ten largest economies of the world if it were independent from the United States.

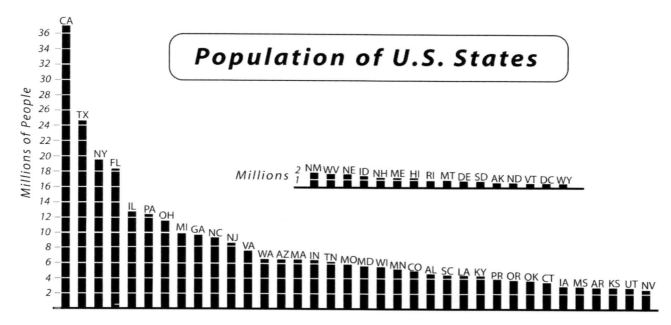

Figure 5.2 -- Rank of U.S. States including Puerto Rico and the District of Columbia. U.S. Census Bureau, 2009 estimate.

Table 5.1 Top Ten U.S. and Canadian Metropolitan Areas

U.S. Metropolitan Area	Population	Canadian Metropolitan Area	Population
New York, NY	18,800,000	Toronto, ON	5,100,000
Los Angeles, CA	12,900,000	Montreal, QC	3,600,000
Chicago, IL	9,500,000	Vancouver, BC	2,100,000
Dallas, TX	6,100,000	Ottawa, ON	1,100,000
Philadelphia, PA	5,800,000	Calgary, AB	1,100,000
Houston, TX	5,600,000	Edmonton, AB	1,100,000
Miami, FL	5,400,000	Quebec City, QC	700,000
Washington, DC	5,300,000	Winnepeg, MB	700,000
Atlanta, GA	5,300,000	Hamilton, ON	700,000
Boston, MA	4,400,000	London, ON	500,000

Sources: U.S. Census Bureau and Statistics Canada

In Canada, about 60 percent of the population is found in southern Quebec and southern Ontario near the St. Lawrence River, Great Lakes, and U.S. border, an area called "Main Street" Canada due to its central importance to Canada's population (Figure 5.1). Main Street also hosts six of Canada's ten largest cities—Toronto, ON, Montreal, QC, Quebec City, QC, Ottawa (the national capital), Hamilton, ON, and London, ON (Figure 5.1). The province of Quebec was the heart of early French settlement in Canada, while Ontario became the focus of English-speaking settlement after the American Revolution. Ontario, the most populous Canadian province today, has moderate climate and good soils, and generates about 40 percent of all Canadian gross domestic product (GDP). Westward movement and Asian immigration to Canada's British Columbia province, especially to the area of Vancouver, have made it the third most populous province after Ontario and Quebec (Figure 5.3). The Canadian north, comprised most notably of three territories (Yukon, Northwest and Nunavut), but also including the northern reaches of most other provinces, is sparsely settled.

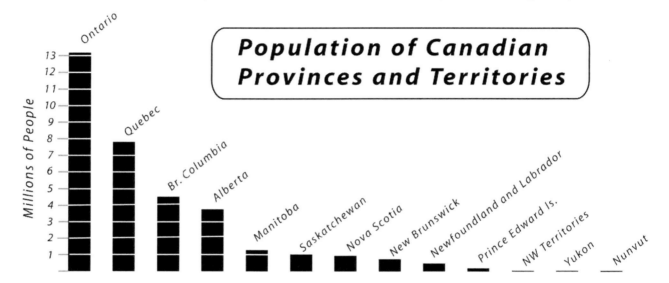

Figure 5.3 -- Population of Canadian Provinces and Territories. *Statistics Canada,* 2010 estimates.

Natural Increase

Both the United States and Canada have low rates of natural increase, the difference between the birth rate and death rate (Table 5.2). Low death rates are indicative of widely available, advanced medical care, sanitary sewer, and clean water. Low birth rates reflect a variety of cultural factors, such as widespread use of birth control, a significant percentage of women in the workforce, urbanization, and changes in economic activities. No longer are large families necessary to run the family farm or care for elderly parents. As both countries have urbanized, adopted government-provided care for the elderly, and had their populations leave the farm, first for the factory and then for the office, fertility rates have declined. Women today are better educated, delay marriage and childbearing, and enter the workforce younger and for a longer time, resulting in fewer births.

Indeed, the total fertility rate rose slowly at first after the Great Depression, then more quickly after World War II from 2.1 in the early-to-mid 1930s to 3.7 in the mid-to-late 1950s (a 75% gain), but then dropped sharply to 1.8 (a decline of more than half) by the mid-1970s. It stayed below replacement (2.05) till early in the new century, after which it leveled off. Canada's fertility followed a similar trend but at a lower level and its current rate of 1.58 children per woman is far below the replacement level. Notice in Table 5.2 that despite these numbers, the annual rate of natural increase is positive for women who are still of childbearing age (Figure 5.4). As these women have their children, population continues to grow. As time passes, without a change in fertility rates, the rates of natural increase will approach zero. Some writers have decried the low fertility, especially among the White (non-Hispanic) population of the United States, which is projected to be only 53 percent of the population in 2050. Among some religious groups, such as the Latter Day Saints, some ethnic groups, such as Hispanics, and recent immigrants, fertility is higher.

Table 5.2. Demographic Rates for the U.S. and Canada, 2009/2010

Characteristic	*United States*	*Canada*
Population, 2010	308,745,538	33,000,000
Number of Legal Immigrants, 2009	1,130,818	252,000
Total Fertility Rate	2.05	1.58
Birth Rate	13.8/1,000	10.3/1,000
Death (Mortality) Rate	8.4/1,000	7.7/1,000
Annual Rate of Natural Increase	0.54%	0.25%
Infant Mortality Rate	6.3/1,000	5.0/1,000
Annual Growth Rate from Immigration	0.43%	0.56%
Total Annual Growth Rate	0.97%	0.82%
Population Doubling Time	74 Years	87 Years
Life Expectancy	78.1 Years	81.2 Years
Percent Older than 65 Years	12.8%	15.2%

Source: U.S. Census Bureau

The annual rate of natural increase in the United States is 0.54 percent, which would result in a doubling time of 114 years, without considering immigration. Legal immigration raises the total annual growth rate to 0.97 percent, which yields a doubling time of 74 years (Table 5.2). Illegal immigration to the United States further increases annual growth probably to between 1.05 percent and 1.11 percent. Canada's total annual growth rate of 0.82 percent, with a doubling time of 87 years, reflects a lower rate of natural increase, but a higher rate of growth from legal immigration.

The mortality rate in Canada (0.77%) is somewhat lower than that of the United States (0.84%) largely because the United States has a higher infant mortality rate (infant deaths per 1,000 births) than Canada (6.3 vs. 5.0). This difference in infant mortality is largely attributable to the disproportionately high rates among African American, Native American and Hispanic minority groups. Inadequate prenatal health care and poor maternal and infant nutrition contribute to higher rates of infant mortality among these minorities. The African American infant mortality rate is nearly double the White rate in the United States. Similarly, the Canadian Native American infant mortality rate is three and a half times the rate for the rest of the country's population.

The demographic structure of a country can be visualized using an age-sex pyramid, which is a horizontal bar graph that shows the number or percent of males on the left and females on the right for each age group, called a cohort (Figures 5.4 and 5.5). Slightly more males than females are born, resulting in a higher percentage of males than females under five years of age. Since males have higher mortality rates throughout life (beginning at birth), there is a narrowing of the gap between the numbers of males and females until the early forties, when females become more numerous. By the age of eighty, females outnumber males by at least two to one. The disproportionately large numbers of both males and females ages 40 to 54 is the result of the baby boomers born between 1954 and 1968 and the tremendous number of young adult immigrants since 1990.

Immigration

After the historic low fertility and immigration levels of the years of the Great Depression (which coincided with the beginning of the implementation of the U.S. Quota Laws), fertility, immigration and population growth accelerated (Table 5.3). Since the mid-1960s, the numbers of immigrants soared, while the fertility rate declined to below replacement level. Whereas fertility accounted for nearly all growth during the 1930s and 1940s and most of the increase in the 1950s and 1960s, by the 1980s and 1990s, (legal and illegal) immigration was contributing 40 to 50 percent of the gains in population.

During the 1930s, the United States experienced the smallest population growth since the 1860s, as fertility dropped to replacement level and net migration was negligible. After the 1930s, numerical and percentage increases rebounded significantly, with the 1950s having record numerical gains and the highest rates of growth since the 1890-1910 period, as both fertility rates and immigration levels rose substantially during the 1940s and 1950s. But even continued rises in immigration could not offset the plunging fertility rates from the late 1960s to the mid-1970s and the continued low levels of the 1980s and 1990s. Numerical gains were considerably less in the 1960s and continued to lessen in the 1970s and 1980s as the population growth rate continued to drop; until in the 1980s, it was the lowest of any decade, except the 1930s.

The last decade of the twentieth century and the first one of the twenty-first century witnessed the surpassing of the immigration record of the first decade of the twentieth century, as the numbers of immigrants continued to rise. This helped to account for a record numerical gain in the 1990s and the highest rate of growth since the 1960s. But both numerical and relative growth dropped during the first decade of the twenty-first century as fertility and immigration declined with the "Great Recession" of 2008-2010.

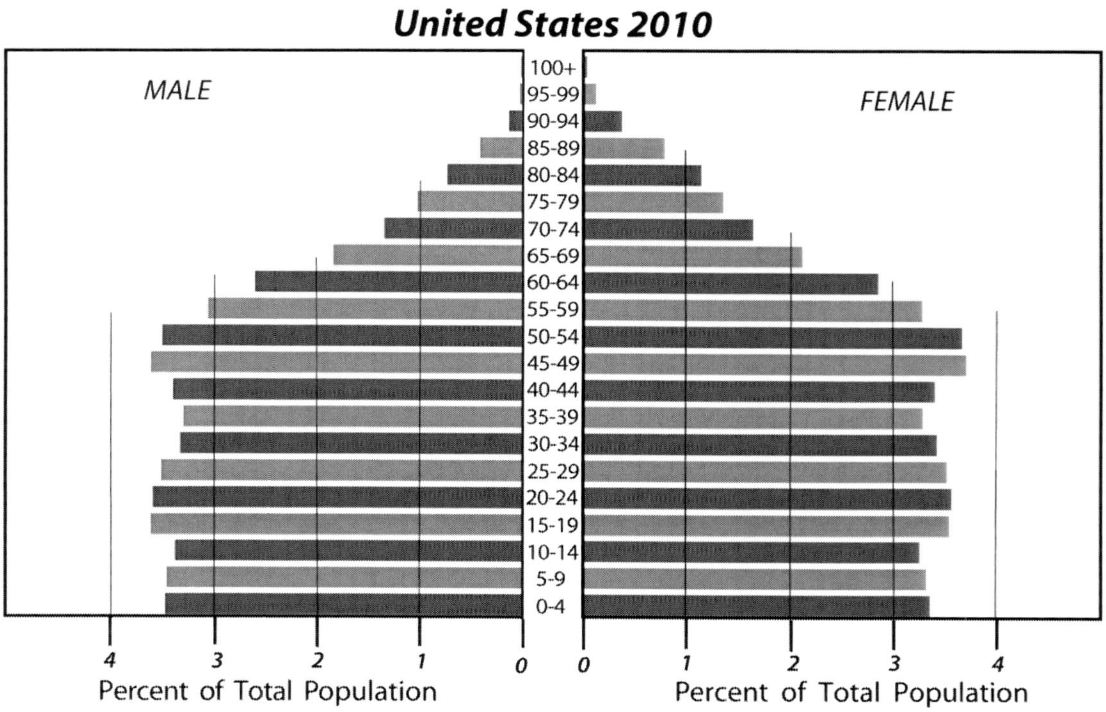

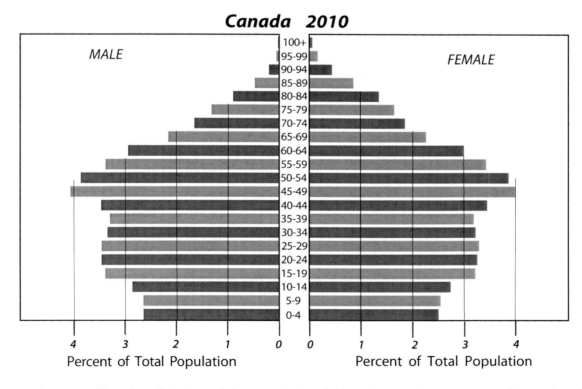

Figure 5.4 -- U.S. Age Structure Diagram.   Data – U.S. Census Bureau.

Figure 5.5 -- Canadian Age Structure Diagram.   Data–U.S. Census Bureau International Data Set.

Table 5.3 -- U.S. Population Change, 1930-2010

Year	Population	Increase in Last 10 Years Number	Percent	Number of Immigrants During Previous Decade	Total Fertility Rate
1930	123,202,624	17,181,087	16.2	4,107,000	2.60
1940	132,164,569	8,961,945	7.3	528,000	2.30
1950	151,325,798	19,161,229	14.5	1,035,000	3.09
1960	179,323,175	27,997,377	18.5	2,515,000	3.65
1970	203,211,926	23,888,751	13.3	2,948,000	2.48
1980	226,545,805	23,333,879	11.4	4,336,000	1.84
1990	248,709,873	22,164,068	9.8	7,338,000	2.08
2000	281,421,906	32,712,033	13.2	9,095,000	2.05
2010	308,745,538	27,323,632	9.7	10,800,000*	2.12**

*2001-2007 estimate.
**2001-2008 estimate.
Source: U.S. Census Bureau.

Mexican, other Latin American, and Asian immigrants to the United States have greatly increased (Figure 5.6). After the 1960s, Europeans accounted for under 20 percent of all immigrants, compared to about 60 percent or more prior to that decade. Latin America and Asia have been the source of increasing numbers and high proportions of all immigrants (85% in the 1980s and 79% in the 1990s) as wars, revolutions and overpopulation have pushed people toward greater opportunities in the United States. In addition, immigration policies that previously favored Europeans have been reformed to facilitate immigration from Latin America and Asia.

In 2007, nine of the top ten source countries for immigrants to the United States were either Latin American (Mexico, Colombia, Haiti, the Dominican Republic, and Cuba) or Asian (China, the Philippines, India, and Vietnam). See Table 5.4. In addition, one Department of Homeland Security report estimates that there are 12 million illegal immigrants in the United States, of which seven million are from Mexico. From 2001 through 2007, about nine million people obtained legal immigrant status in the United States, with about half going to the states of California and New York. Furthermore, immigration has accounted for a rising share of U.S. population growth, reaching 40 to 50 percent during the last two decades.

While Canada has also experienced a decline in the proportion of immigrants from Europe, Europeans still constitute the second largest group (but this is only 16% of the total, down from 62% in 1971, compared to 14-15% for the U.S. in the 2001-2007 period). See Figure 5.7. From 2001 to 2007, 1.7 million people entered Canada legally. More than 80 percent of them settled in the country's three most populous provinces (Ontario, Quebec and British Columbia). For the most part, they chose one of Canada's three largest cities (Toronto, Montreal and Vancouver) as home.

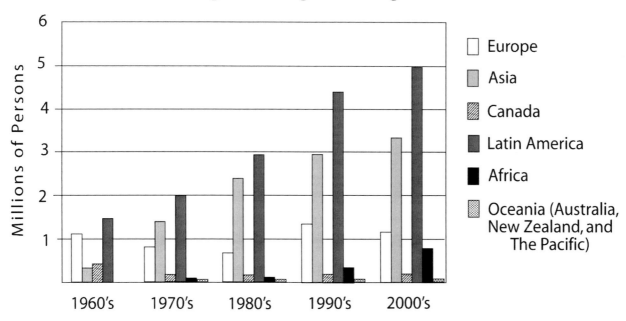

Figure 5.6 -- Major Source Regions of U.S. Immigrants. Source: U.S. Statistical Abstract 2011

Table 5.4. Major Source Countries and Number of Immigrants to the U.S., By Decade
(in thousands)

1951-1960		1971-1980		1981-1990		1991-2000		2001-2009	
Germany	345	Mexico	637	Mexico	1653	Mexico	2251	Mexico	1554
Mexico	319	Phil.	360	Phil.	495	China/T	531	India	593
Canada	274	Cuba	277	Vietnam	401	Phil.	506	China	592
U. K.	209	Korea	272	China/T	389	Vietnam	421	Phil.	529
Italy	188	China/T	203	Korea	339	India	383	Cuba	285
Poland	128	Vietnam	180	India	262	Dom.Rep.	341	Vietnam	276
Cuba	78	India	177	Dom.Rep	252	El Sal	217	Dom. Rep.	275
Hungary	65	Dom.Rep.	148	El Sal	215	Haiti	182	El Sal.	234
Ireland	64	Jamaica	142	Jamaica	214	Cuba	181	Columbia	229
Yugosla.	59	Italy	130	Cuba	159	Jamaica	174	S. Korea	199
All Cos	2516		4493		7338		9095		9458

Source: U. S. Census Bureau. *U. S. Statistical Abstract, 2011.*

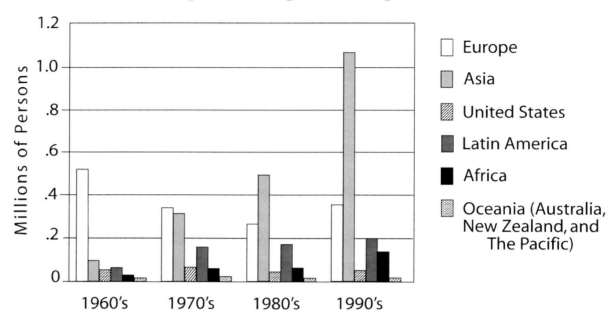

Figure 5.7 -- Source regions for legal immigrants to Canada

Immigration Policies in the United States and Canada

The cultures of both the United States and Canada have long been shaped by immigration. While various restrictions on immigration had been passed as early as 1790 in the U.S., it was largely unrestricted until the late 19th and early 20th centuries. The poem on the pedestal of the Statue of Liberty in New York harbor written by Emma Lazarus in 1883 conveys this open door spirit:

> *Give me your tired, your poor,*
> *Your huddled masses yearning to breathe free,*
> *The wretched refuse of your teeming shore.*
> *Send these, the homeless, tempest-tossed, to me:*
> *I left my lamp beside the golden door.*

Canada has also pursued pro-immigration policies. The Canadian government began encouraging southern and eastern Europeans to settle the prairie provinces (Manitoba, Saskatchewan and Alberta) in the mid-1800s, due in part to fear of U.S. annexation of western Canada. This policy to promote European settlement in the prairies continued until after World War I.

Significant restrictions on immigration began in the United States in 1885 with the Oriental Exclusion Act, which barred Chinese. The U.S. Quota Acts of 1921 and 1924 limited immigration from all regions except northern and western Europe. A backlog of immigrant demand from southeastern Europe and elsewhere built up, while quotas from many northwestern European countries went unfilled. Canada adopted similar policies restricting immigration from non-European countries. After World War II, a reversal in policy resulted in changes in immigration to both countries.

The U.S. Immigration Act of 1965 ended the use of national origins as quotas and abolished discrimination against Asians. Family members of U.S. citizens and those with highly valued skills were given priority. Although the countries of southern and eastern Europe were expected to gain the most from this change in the law, immigrants from Europe continued an earlier pattern of decline, while the numbers from Latin America and Asia increased rapidly. Due to concern over illegal immigration, the 1986 Immigration Reform and Control Act assessed fines against employers of illegal aliens, but granted amnesty and an opportunity for citizenship for many of them. The 1990 Immigration Act increased preferences for immigrants from Europe and other developed areas by favoring educated and skilled workers rather than relatives of U.S. citizens. In 2004, President George W. Bush endorsed legalizing all current illegal immigrants who had worked in America for a limited number of years. The U.S. Senate supported his plan, but the House rejected the idea and called for more severe penalties for illegal immigrants and for strengthened border enforcement.

Racial and ethnic restrictions for immigrants to Canada were eliminated beginning with the Immigration Act of 1976. Canadian immigration policy now defines three classes of immigrants: (1) family members of current Canadian citizens, (2) refugees and (3) the business class. Immigrants in the last group, who constitute the largest numbers of immigrants, are assigned priority based on education, age, job skills, and ability to speak English or French. The Canadian government sets a target for new immigrants at about one percent of the population. The current population of 33 million, then, results in about 330,000 new faces for Canada each year. This rate is about three times the rate of legal immigration in the U.S., where about a million immigrants arrive every year. Since September 11, 2001, Canada has increased border and immigration security at the urging of the U.S.

Internal Migration

The percentage of Americans moving each year decreased from nearly 20 percent in the 1970s to 14-17 percent in the 1990s to just 12 percent in 2008. Nevertheless, about a third of those in their twenties move each year. Nearly two-thirds move within the same county, a little over a sixth move to another county within the same state, and about a sixth move to another state. Hispanics move more than African Americans, and both move more than whites. This is because whites have higher incomes and are more often homeowners, who are less likely to move than lower income renters.

Westward and Sunbelt Migration

In addition to changes in racial and ethnic composition and fertility and immigration levels, the distribution of the population has also continually shifted in North America. Since European settlement began in the East, one principal direction of migration has been the redistribution of the population by movement westward. This is demonstrated by the shifting **center of gravity** of the population from 15 miles (24 km) west of Bloomington, IN in 1930 to 30 miles (48km) southeast of St. Louis in 1970 to 100 miles (62 km) southwest of St. Louis in 2000 (Figure 5.8).

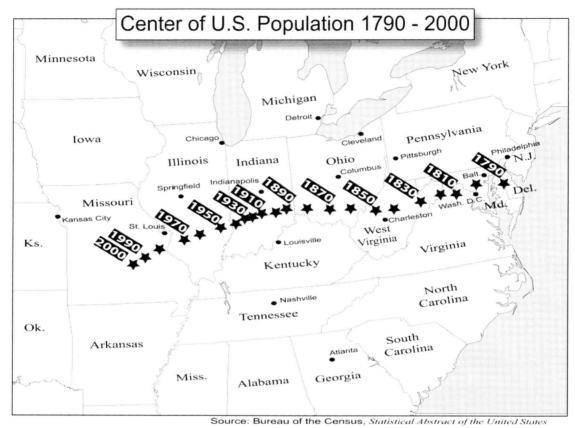

Figure 5.8. Center of Gravity of the U. S. Population, 1790-2000

Since World War II, a second major directional movement in the population has been from North to South. This movement has been termed "Sunbelt" migration, since it is frequently the result of the desire for warmer temperatures and amenities, such as year-round recreation, which is less available in northern states.

California has been the major receiver of the westward migration. During the 1950s, this state had almost three times the number of net in-migrants as the second-ranking one. The continuation of this trend in the 1960s resulted in California overtaking New York as the most populous state in the U.S. In the 1970s, California led the nation in net in-migration and Arizona was in the top ten. During the 1980s and 1990s, westward migration, plus immigration from Asia and Latin America to California and Texas, were major contributors to differential growth and redistribution of the national population.

Representation in the U.S. House of Representatives demonstrates population migration because the number of members from each state is proportional to the population. As a result of the 2000 Census, over half of the Congressional seats shifted to states in the Southwest (Figure 5.9). **Texas**, surpassed New York State during the early 1990s to become the nation's second most populous state, and it and Arizona gained two seats each, as did Florida and Georgia in the Southeast. The only states to add one seat were North Carolina (which also gained one in 1990-92), Colorado, Nevada, and California (which had gained 7 seats in 1990-92). The only two states to lose two seats in 2000-2002 were New York and Pennsylvania. In 2010-2012, Texas added four seats and Florida two, while one was added to Arizona, Nevada, Utah and Washington in the West and to Georgia and South Carolina in the Southeast. Both New York and Ohio lost two seats, while Massachusetts, New Jersey, Pennsylvania, and Illinois, Iowa, Michigan and Missouri lost one each.

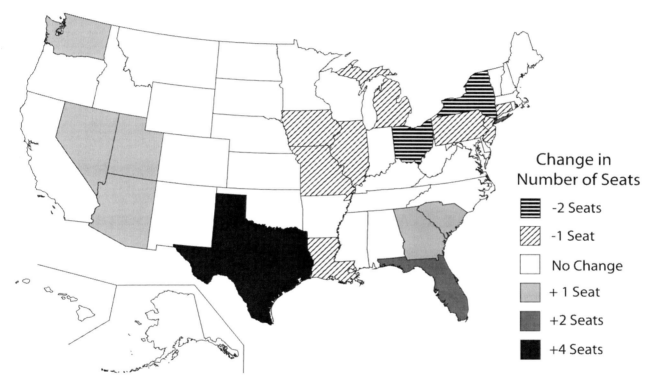

Figure 5.9 -- Change in Number of U.S. Congressional Seats, 2010-2012

The main direction of **migration in Canada** has also been west. Recently, even the "heartland" provinces of Quebec and Ontario have been losing migrants to western provinces (Figure 5.10). Most of the people have always lived within 150 miles (242 km) of the U.S. border where temperatures are warmer, the growing season is longer, and access to American markets is easier. Canada's "sunbelt" has traditionally been the United States. Since 1900, over 3.6 million Canadians (nearly 10% of the present population) have moved to the U.S.

The migration to the South and to the West was paralleled by movement from the farm to the city (which also involved movement from the South to the North during and after World Wars I and II)

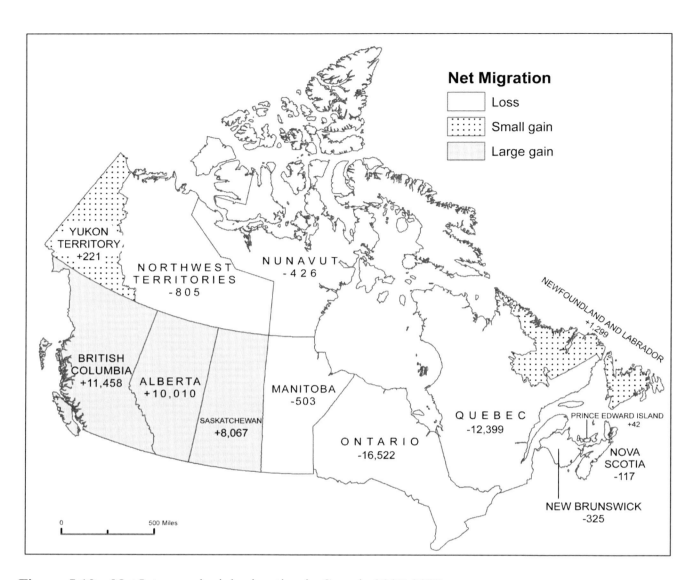

Figure 5.10 – Net Interprovincial migration in Canada 2007-2008

and from the city to the suburbs. Whereas the United States was only 40 percent urban (2,500 or more from 1900 to the present) in 1900, it reached 52 percent in 1920, 70 percent by 1960 and 79 percent in 2000 (Table 5.5). The urbanization trend, therefore, often paralleled the post-war movements to the North and West, but also included the movement to the South in the latter part of the 20th century (Figure 5.11). The movement to urban areas occurred in two phases: (1) the establishment of new towns and the growth of these and older ones and (2) the metropolitan explosion in and around the largest urban centers.

Table 5.5. Percent Urban: 1930-2000

	Percent Urban	
Year	Total Population	African Americans
1930	56	44
1940	57	49
1950	64	62
1960	70	73
1970	74	81
1980	74	85
1990	75	87
2000	79	90

Source: U.S. Census Bureau.

Figure 5.11 -- Atlanta night time skyline. Southern cities such as Atlanta have grown steadily since 1960. Photo by Chuck Koehler

Metropolitan areas are generally those counties with at least one city of 50,000 or more and counties adjacent to them which are economically interdependent—with a 25 percent commuting threshold--and which have a total of 100,000 or more people. The idea behind metropolitan areas is that "cities" serve as employment centers, social spaces and market places. Thus, cities are defined by the spatial interaction of people in a region focused on a place, or node. Because city legal boundaries rarely coincide with the actual area of spatial interaction, the statistical concept of "metropolitan area" better captures the size, importance and zone of interaction of "cities." These metropolitan areas approximate, though because of issues with the Census definitions do not coincide with, the hinterlands of the places which interact with the cities. Thus, the metropolitan regions might be considered to roughly approximate functional, or nodal, regions. (There are smaller functional regions of places for which there are no metropolitan areas, but rather micropolitan regions. Smaller places are not the center of either.)

The U.S. Census Bureau listed 280 metropolitan areas in 2000, of which 50 had at least one million people (more than twice the number of such large areas in 1960). In Canada, there were 27 metropolitan areas of a million or more in 2006 (compared to just two in 1960). The population of the city of New York is 8.2 million, but there are 18.8 million people in the New York-Northern New Jersey, Long Island, NY-NJ-PA metropolitan area. Thus, the number of people officially tied economically and socially to New York is much larger than the population within the city limits. In sparsely settled Canada, the threshold is even lower at 1,000 people. Officially defined urban areas might or might not have incorporated city limits or city government. Canada is now 80 percent urban. Growth rates have recently been highest among cities in the South and West in the United States. During the period 2000 to 2006, 49 of the 50 fastest growing metropolitan areas were in the West and South, with the Atlanta metropolitan area gaining the most people during that time period and the Dallas-Fort Worth metropolitan area adding the second largest number of new residents.

In 2000, although 55 percent of **African Americans** lived in the South (Table 5.6), there were more of them living in either the New York, Chicago, or Washington, D.C. urbanized areas than in the entire states of either Alabama, Arkansas, Mississippi, or South Carolina. The African Americans who left the South were better educated on the whole than those who remained behind. Thus, for decades the South was deprived of many of its more qualified citizens, especially among African Americans. Nevertheless, they still represented a poorer, less educated group than the residents of the cities into which they moved. (This was also true, but to a lesser extent, for the white migrants who moved from the South to the North.) The consequence of poor African Americans and whites moving into northern cities was the creation of ghettos and an increased demand for social services, especially for the former. The enormous movement of poor people to the cities of the North has resulted in some northern cities having more persons living in poverty than there are in some entire states in the South. Moreover, the "poverty gap"--the aggregate amount of money needed to raise all the poor above the poverty threshold--is greater in many northern cities than in some southern states.

African Americans had been only 23 percent urban in 1900 because most of the African Americans had remained in the rural South until after that date. But by 1960, the pull of economic opportunity in the cities--particularly in the North--and the push of discrimination and of mechanization off the farm had resulted in the percentage of them living in urban areas (73%) exceeding that of whites (70%). See Table 5.5. By 2000, 90 percent of all African Americans resided in urban areas.

Table 5.6. The African American Population in the U. S., 1930-2008

Year	Number in U.S.	Percent of U.S. Population	Number in The South	Percent in The South
1930	11,891,000	9.7	9,362,000	79
1940	12,866,000	9.8	9,905,000	76
1950	15,045,000	9.9	10,225,000	68
1960	18,872,000	10.5	11,312,000	60
1970	22,673,000	11.2	11,790,000	53
1980	26,495,000	11.7	14,048,000	53
1990	29,986,000	12.1	15,829,000	53
2000	34,658,000	12.3	20,030,000	58
2008	37,131,771	12.3	NA	NA

African American alone, plus as one of two or more races.
Source: U. S. Census Bureau.

Of course, both African Americans and whites with limited training filled low-level, but necessary, jobs during the industrial boom of the 1940s and early 1950s, when immigration had been curtailed and when those born in the U.S. entering the labor force were relatively small in number because of the lower fertility rates of the 1920s and 1930s. Recent studies have shown that while educational selectivity in migration to the North has not always occurred, migrants usually have been better educated than non-migrants of sending and often receiving communities. Thus, any period of large net out-migration from the South has been deleterious to that region, whereas the reverse has been advantageous to it. Conversely, the more recent trend of Sunbelt migration has benefited the South.

The migration of African Americans to the city occurred at about the same time as **metropolitan expansion and the movement to the suburbs**. However, the poorer members of this group moved mainly into the older central cities as the middle and upper income whites gathered their belongings and headed for the periphery and beyond. During the last six decades, the suburbs have grown faster than the central cities, and the gap has continued to widen. While suburban growth exceeded central city gains by only a third in the 1920s, the outlying areas grew nearly nine times faster than the cities during the 1960s. Moreover, all of the white increase in the metropolitan areas in the 1960s could be accounted for by the suburbs, but 80 percent of the black growth in the MSAs (Metropolitan Statistical Areas) was in the central cities. The movement **out of the central city**, especially among whites, became so great during the 1970s and 1980s that a large number of the central cities lost population. Both African Americans and whites had a considerable net movement into the suburbs.

By the **1970s**, two **migration reversals** had become important. One was a reversal of the South to North movement, even among African Americans, so that the **South (Sunbelt) became a net gainer** of both whites and African Americans. The South and West, in 1976, finally exceeded the

North in population. In the 1990s, the South had a net in-migration of African Americans from the Northeast, Midwest and West. Most of the metropolitan areas gaining the most African Americans were in the South, with Atlanta being the leader. The other reversal was a temporary interruption to metropolitan areas growing faster than nonmetropolitan regions. The more rapid growth of nonmetropolitan areas compared to metropolitan areas has often been termed **counter urbanization**. This is somewhat of a misnomer since it was more of a move to nonmetropolitan areas, including their urban places, than to completely rural sections. However, the most rapid gains were in those areas farthest from the metropolitan centers. Most of the movement to nonmetropolitan areas seems to have been related to amenity factors, especially on the part of the retiring elderly.

The return to a higher **metropolitan growth** rate in the 1980s and 1990s was partly a result of a surge of immigrants entering metropolitan areas, especially in California, Texas, Florida and other states in between. However, during the 1980s, the number of metropolitan areas losing population was more than double that of the 1970s, with most of the losers having a population of less than 500,000. Simultaneously, "edge cities," dominated by office/retail/hotel complexes, caused an explosion of suburban growth in many of the major metropolitan areas. With most of the nation's population already living in metro areas, most of the movement today is from one suburban area to another either within or between MSAs. During the 1990s, metro areas of a million or more doubled from 15 percent to 30 percent of the population, with the fastest-growing areas being in the one-to-five million category.

The urbanization and suburbanization of **Canada** has paralleled that of its neighbor to the south. This has been especially important in Quebec, where the movement from the farm to the city, together with the settling of recent immigrants in urban centers, have significantly altered other demographic characteristics of the province, especially the fertility rate, which has dropped sharply. But this rural-to-urban trend is also important in Ontario, the Prairie Provinces, and British Columbia. Today, more than three-fourths of the people live in urban areas, but this varies from just over a third in Prince Edward Island to about 80 percent in Alberta, British Columbia, Ontario, and Quebec. In 2000, about a third of the people in Canada were living in just the Montreal and Toronto metropolitan areas.

CULTURE

Culture consists of many elements, including art, heritage, food, resource use, economy, race, values, customs, politics, music, television programming, literature, and education. Among the most important indicators of culture are ethnicity, language, and religion.

Language

Although the United States was settled by large groups of English speakers, or Anglophones, people speaking many different languages have immigrated to the United States. In addition, a number of languages were spoken by the Native Americans before the arrival of European colonists. According to the 2000 U.S. Census, however, 82 percent of Americans (age 5 and over) spoke only English at home and about 11 percent spoke Spanish at home. The remaining seven percent spoke other languages, with Chinese being the most common (Figure 5.12). According to the U.S. Census Bureau, "Most people who reported speaking a language other than English at home also speak English." Thus, English is the overwhelmingly top language of the United States, although there is no official language. Some areas of the country, however, have significant numbers of people who use another language at home. As one might expect, Puerto Rico (85%) and areas in the South and Southwest with many Hispanic immigrants from Mexico and Latin America have the highest rates of non-English speakers (39.5%), while West Virginia has the lowest rate (2.7%). About nine percent of Americans are bilingual.

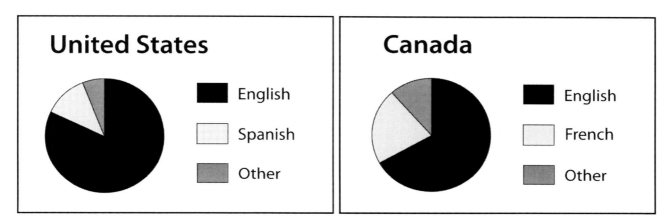

Figure 5.12 – Language groups in the United States and Canada. U.S. data provided by the U.S. Census Bureau. Canadian data provided by Statistics Canada.

Canada has two official national languages, English and French (Figure 5.12), although the provinces have the authority to adopt their own official languages for the province. There remains a strong link between historical settlement and current language preference. In other words, Canada can be divided into language regions based on settlement patterns. Canada was settled most heavily at first by French speakers, or Francophones, who still comprise about 22 percent of the population. French is the official language of the province of Quebec, where 82 percent are Francophones (Figure 5.13). New Brunswick, the only officially bilingual province, is about 33 percent Francophone. No other province or territory is even five percent Francophone.

After the French were defeated by the British in 1759 and after the American Revolution, there was a long period of settlement by English speakers from the United States, Scotland and England. Today, about 57 percent of Canada's population considers English their mother tongue (language of choice at home). The most strongly Anglophone provinces/territories (Figure 5.13) are Newfoundland and Labrador (98%), Prince Edward Island (94%) and Nova Scotia (93%). In Quebec, less than a tenth of the people are Anglophones, whereas in Ontario, nearly three-fourths are in this group. English is the primary language of business—at work, 85 percent of Canadians use English at least some of the time.

About 20 percent of Canadians are allophones, those who speak a mother tongue other than English or French. European languages, such as Italian, Spanish and German, are the mother tongues for about 2.8 million (8%) of Canadians. Significant numbers of allophones in the Prairies (Great Plains) of Canada (Figure 5.13) are descended from Europeans who migrated there in the nineteenth

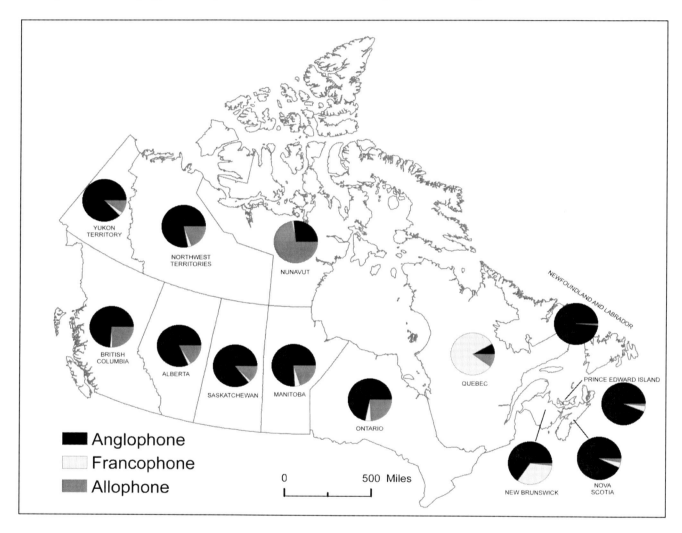

Figure 5.13 -- Portion of population whose mother tongue is English, French or a language. other than English or French by province or territory.

century to start farming. In the provinces of Manitoba, Saskatchewan and Alberta, where German is the second most common language after English, between 12 and 20 percent are allophones. In the territorial north, allophones are mostly native peoples who comprise 10 percent of the population of the Yukon Territory, 19 percent of the Northwest Territories and 72 percent of Nunavut. There are over 700,000 Canadians whose mother tongue is a language of India; they live mostly in cities. Chinese is a mother tongue to over a million Canadians, who also live mainly in cities. In the province of British Columbia, for example 25 percent of the population is allophone. In Vancouver, the largest city in British Columbia (and the third largest in Canada), Chinese and Punjabi (an Indian language) are the most common languages after English. These few statistics, however, cannot adequately convey the diversity of languages in Canada, which prides itself on being multicultural.

Immigrants who are allophones are the fastest growing language group in Canada. In some cases, this has political ramifications. In Quebec province, where preservation of French is an important provincial concern, immigrant allophones can get a mixed reception. Francophones may view allophones as a threat to French language preservation. By law, free public schools in the province of Quebec teach only in French. The disproportionate concentration of French-speaking people in Quebec led to an attempt to promote and preserve the French culture there and to an effort to separate the province from the rest of Canada. Separation referenda held in Quebec in 1980 and 1995 failed in each instance. See Box 4.2 in Chapter 4. Allophones were blamed by some Quebecois (French-speaking residents of the province) for the failure of the 1995 referendum vote to secede from Canada.

Race and Ethnicity

Ethnic and racial groups are complex and not easily distinguished. Both terms are social and cultural, not biological, and rely primarily on self identification (Table 5.7). In the United States, for example, Hispanics are an ethnic group that could belong to a number of different racial categories. Sammy Sosa, a famous U.S. baseball player from the Dominican Republic, would likely be identified as a Black racially, but Hispanic ethnically. "Asian" is a U.S. Census Bureau racial category, but includes such diverse ethnicities as Hindus from India, Buddhists from Vietnam, and Japanese Ainu. Similarly, while most Whites in the United States share a similar ethnicity, there is diversity here, too.

In Canada, "visible minority" is a race term that describes a person, such as Chinese or African, whose physical appearance is noticeably different from the Caucasians from Europe (Table 5.7). The Canadian government uses the distinction in race for "employment equity" similar to affirmative action quotas in the United States. Under this system, Francophones and Anglophones would, therefore, be of the same race but differ from each other ethnically. Allophones could be white or among the visible minorities. For example, an immigrant from Romania would be an allophone ethnically, but white racially, while an immigrant from Algeria would be a Francophone ethnically and a visible minority racially. Blacks in Canada are not called African-Canadians because many Blacks identify with their Caribbean heritage instead of Africa. Even "American Indian" is not a satisfactory racial/ethnic moniker, because natives of North America were and remain a diverse group of cultures. Canada officially recognizes three major groups of aboriginal peoples—North American Indian, Metis, and Inuit of the far north.

Table 5.7. Self-Identified Racial and Ethnic Groups in the United States and Canada

United States 2007		Canada 2006	
Single Race	**Percentage**	**Race**	**Percentage**
White	66	White	84
Black	12	Visible Minorities	16
Asian	4		
American Indian/Alaskan Native	<1		
Ethnicity	**Percentage**	**Single Ethnic Origin**	**Percentage**
Non-Hispanic	85	Canadian	31
Hispanic	15	English	7
		French	6
		Chinese	6

Sources: U.S. Census Bureau and Statistics Canada.

Canadians are asked on census questionnaires about their ethnic origins. Canadians may choose more than one ethnicity, so the total percentage of all ethnic groups adds to more than 100 percent. In 2006, nearly half of Canadians chose more than one ethnic group. Common responses were "Canadian and English" or "Canadian and French." Totaling all responses to the question about ethnic origin, the largest ethnic groups were English, French, Scottish, Irish, German, Italian, and Chinese. For those choosing a single ethnicity, the largest ethnic groups were Canadian, English, French, and Chinese (Table 5.7). Statistics Canada reports that most people who choose "Canadian" as their ethnicity are Anglophones or Francophones whose families have been in Canada for many generations.

In the United States, the only ethnicity options on the census form are Hispanic and non-Hispanic. Considering White (non-Hispanic) as the majority race/ethnicity, Hispanics are the largest minority group in the population, numbering 44 million, or 15 percent, and they continue to grow rapidly through both high natural increase and immigration rates, having increased by 60 percent during the 1990s. Most Hispanics are racially White or mixed White and Native American from many Latin American countries and only a small proportion are non-White. About 64 percent of Hispanics are Mexican, another nine percent are Puerto Rican, and three percent are Cuban. Although the primary concentrations of Hispanics in the United States are in the southern and western states (Figure 5.14), many communities throughout the country have a Hispanic presence. The rapid increase and concentration of Hispanics (over 80% being in the Southwest) have led to attempts to end bilingual education and public services and designate English as the official language of the nation. While the United States does not have an official language yet, many states have already adopted English as their official language.

African Americans are the third largest racial/ethnic group in the United States. In the 1990s, African Americans in the U.S. grew more rapidly than White non-Hispanics, but not as fast as Hispanics. As a consequence, by 2000, Hispanics outnumbered Blacks for the first time. Blacks now number 37 million and account for 12 percent of the population, their highest percentage since 1880. In 2007, 56 percent of Blacks lived in the South, the highest proportion since 1960.

Asians in the United States number over 13 million (4%), with most living in western states or in major cities elsewhere (Figure 5.14). Five centuries after Columbus discovered America, Native Americans in the United States number about two million, just over half their number in 1492. Most live on the western reservations to which their ancestors were sent (Figure 5.14). Native Americans have been given special flexibility for economic development on reservations. Many reservations have been found to contain valuable fish or petroleum resources. Some tribal governments have constructed casinos or other tourist attractions to raise funds needed to improve the plight of their constituents.

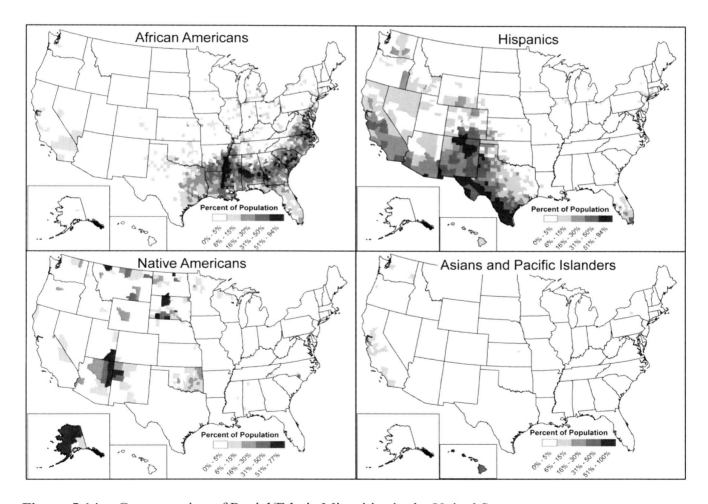

Figure 5.14 -- Concentration of Racial/Ethnic Minorities in the United States

Religion

The majority of North Americans identify themselves with some religious denomination, but adherence to organized religion might be on the decline in North America. In Canada, "according to GSS (General Social Survey) data, attendance at religious services has fallen dramatically across the country over the past 15 years. Nationally, only one-fifth of individuals age 15 and over attended religious services on a weekly basis in 2001, compared with 28 percent in 1986. In 2001, four in 10 adults reported that they had not attended religious services during the 12 months prior to the survey, compared with only 26 percent in 1986" (Statistics Canada, 2009). The decline of the importance of religion is also evident in the number of people who claim no religion. "Prior to 1971, fewer than one percent of the Canadian population reported having no religion. In 2001, that percentage had increased to 16 percent, or just under 4.8 million people." Statistics Canada provides the following data showing the largest religious denominations in the country (Table 5.8).

Table 5.8. Religious Preference in Canada.

Preference	Percentage
Roman Catholic	43.2%
Protestant	29.2%
Christian Orthodox	1.6%
Christian, not included elsewhere*	2.6%
Muslim	2.0%
Jewish	1.1%
Buddhist	1.0%
Hindu	1.0 %
Sikh	0.9%
No religion	16.2%

*Includes those who report Christian, Apostolic, Born-again Christian, and Evangelical.
Source: Statistics Canada, 2001 Census.

Since 1939, about 40 percent of Americans have responded "yes" to the yearly Gallop Poll question, "Did you attend church or synagogue this week"? Social scientists, however, by comparing church membership rolls with actual Sunday attendance have determined that people tend to overstate their actual attendance. The number of worshipers each week is probably about half the self-reported total. This rate is roughly equivalent to weekly attendance rates in Canada.

The U.S. Census Bureau does not collect statistics on religious affiliation; however, private groups, such as the Glenmary Research Center, attempt to obtain information from organized groups like the Roman Catholic Church or Southern Baptist Convention. Figure 5.15 shows the group with the highest percentage of followers in each U.S. county. Within each county, however, there can be a great deal of diversity. For example, even though Roman Catholics are the largest group in more counties than any other group, the United States remains mostly Protestant in religious affiliation because Protestants are spread among a number of denominations (Table 5.9). Among Protestant denominations, the largest numbers of adherents are Baptists (32%) and Methodists (12%). Roman Catholicism is the second most popular religion in the United States, while Judaism is a distant third.

Table 5.9. Religious Preference in the United States

Preference	Percentage
Protestant	51.9%
Roman Catholic	24.8%
Jewish	1.7%
None	16.5%
Other	5.0%

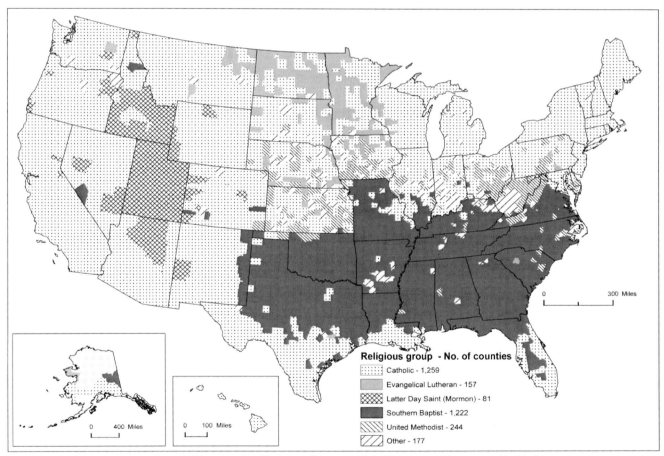

Figure 5.15 -- Largest Participating Religious Groups, by County. Source: Religious Congregations and Membership, 2000, a voluntary census of organized religious groups.

Poverty

Poverty is a relative, as well as an absolute, situation. When most people think of poverty, they imagine malnourished, homeless people with only the clothes on their backs. That picture is more typical of the absolute poverty in the developing world than the relative poverty in the United States and Canada. There is a clear discrepancy between the commonly held perception of poverty as absolute and the relative poverty experienced by some North Americans. During the last two decades, the living standards of most North Americans have risen. For example, during this time, median household income (adjusted for inflation) in the United States increased by more than $2,000. (However, males suffered a loss of $250 a year, while females gained nearly $5,000 in annual income. Moreover, after three years of gains, annual income declined by nearly $2,000 to $50,300 from 2007 to 2008.) With regard to income level and possessions, many of those classed as poor in North America might be considered relatively wealthy compared to most persons living in developing countries. For example, 46 percent of all poor households in the United States own (or are buying) their own home, 76 percent have air conditioning, about 75 percent own a car, and 97 percent have a color television set. Compared to all western Europeans (not just the poor), the poor in America enjoy more living space per person. Undernutrition (too few calories in the diet with impaired health due to chronic shortage of food) is practically absent from the United States and Canada. Despite overall high family income levels and impressive industrial and agricultural outputs, some families struggle to make ends meet. Short term hunger due to lack of money affects about 2.4 percent of Americans per year and many poor households have more difficulty paying rent (about 1% are evicted each year).

The poor in the U.S. might be considered to be those living at a low economic level compared to the rest of the population. Definitions of the cut-off level differ, but in order to be consistent, the U.S. Census Bureau's definitions and data will be used. As income, cost of living, and standard of living have risen, so has the **threshold** of poverty (from $6,200 in 1977 to $14,300 in 1994 to about $22,000 in 2008 for a family of four). The poverty line as a percentage of median family income has remained at about 40 percent since 1968.

After having declined during the early and mid-1960s, the number and percent in poverty fluctuated somewhat for a decade at levels near or below the 1968 levels, before the number and proportion rose sharply between 1978 and 1983, before declining slowly till 1989, then rising to pre-1968 levels by 1992. The percentage in poverty then fell again to the lowest rate in 27 years in 2000 (Figure 5.16 and Table 5.10). However, by 2008, nearly 40 million Americans were living in poverty, over 40 percent more than in 1978 and the most since 1960, though the percent in poverty (13.2%) was not as high as in the periods 1981-1987 and 1990-1997. Income is related to health care and nutrition and in 2008, 46 other countries had a lower infant mortality rate than the United States. In 2010, the Congress passed a sweeping national health care bill which should decrease both the more than 40 million without health insurance and the infant mortality rate.

Citing difficulty defining what it means to be poor, Canada does not have an official "poverty line," but Statistics Canada classified about 3.3 million individuals (10.5% of the population) as low income after taxes in 2006. Despite all the government programs designed to alleviate relative poverty, the percentage of people in poverty in the U.S. has exceeded 12 percent since 1980.

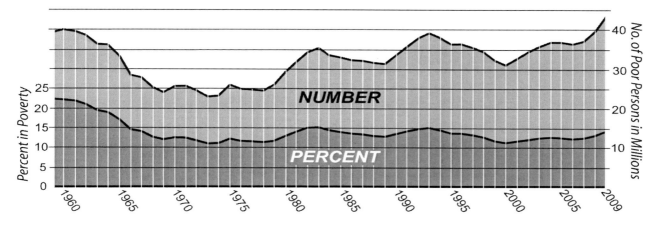

Figure 5.16 -- Number and Percent in Poverty in U. S., 1959-2009

Table 5.10 -- Poverty in the United States: 1977, 1994, and 2008

	1977	*1994*	*2008*
Percent of Population in Poverty	11.6%	14.5%	13.2%
Number of People in Poverty	24 mil	38 mil	39 mil
Percent of White/Non-Hispanic in Poverty	8.0%	9.4%	8.6%
Number of White/Non-Hispanic	14 mil	18 mil	17 mil
Percent of African Americans in Poverty	31.3%	30.6%	24.7%
Number of African Americans in Poverty	8 mil	10 mil	10 mil
Percent of Hispanics in Poverty	22.4%	30.7%	23.2%
Number of Hispanics in Poverty	3 mil	8 mil	11 mil
White/African Amer. Median Income Gap*	$14,200	$15,800	$18,100
White Non-Hisp/African Amer. Income Gap			$21,300

*1979, 1989, 2008   Source: U.S. Census Bureau

Where the Poor Live

The poor are found throughout all regions and come from many cultural groups. In the U.S., the South continues to have the greatest number and proportion of the poor. In 2008, the South led all regions in the incidence of poverty (>14%). The Northeast and North Central states were both below the U.S. average. The core U.S. states with the highest incidences of poverty (>15.6%) extended from New Mexico to Alabama, plus South Carolina, Kentucky and West Virginia (Figure 5.17).

In the South, most of those in poverty have usually lived in rural areas. The high levels of poverty have been long associated with three interrelated factors: the importance of agriculture, the emphasis upon a one-crop system, and the reliance upon a large supply of the cheapest possible hand labor. Other contributors to poverty here, as well as in many other sections of the nation, are low levels of education and training, discrimination, technological changes, personal and regional economic crises, and lack of adequate employment opportunities.

The proportion of the population of the South living in poverty has greatly declined during the last 30 years as education levels have risen and as more non-agricultural jobs have become available. However, technological and scientific developments in agriculture and farm subsidy programs have not generally benefited the rural poor. Instead, those who were already successful farmers and could afford the necessary purchases and were knowledgeable about government programs, plus many

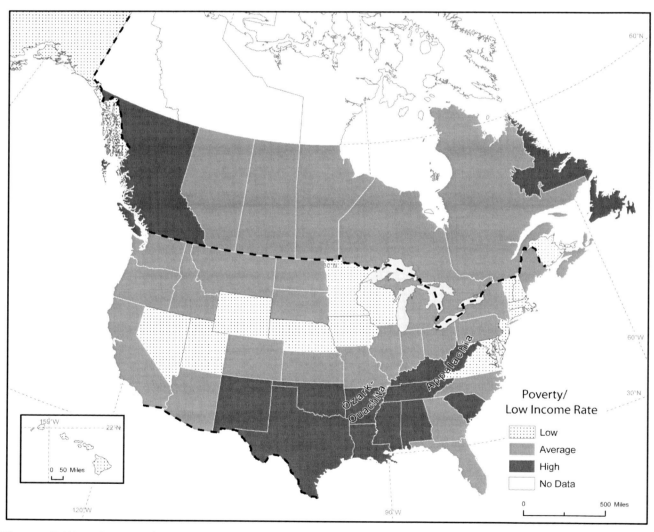

Figure 5.17 -- Percent in Poverty, by State or Province, 2008

absentee investors, have taken advantage of these benefits. Often, many of the poor farmers--owners, tenants, and sharecroppers--have been forced off the land because of not having enough capital to compete at a higher mechanized level and because of less demand for hand labor. The income gap between the rich and poor has widened in the South despite the decline in the percentage of Southerners in poverty.

Appalachia, which includes West Virginia and part of Kentucky, is found largely within the South and is a word that has become synonymous with poverty. Here, thin, stony soil and rugged topography throughout most of the area have combined to make farming difficult. The main economic activities of large numbers of people have been coal mining and subsistence farming. At one time, coal mining provided jobs for many more of the men than is the case today because the closing of some of the mines and the mechanization of others have led to chronic unemployment and low standards of living. In addition, the ravaged landscape--the legacy of strip mining--remains a symbol of the poverty of the area. Although more than two million persons have moved to other parts of the country in order to secure a better livelihood, millions of others have remained behind in poverty. Many of those who fled elsewhere simply increased the number of poor people where they settled. These individuals were largely too poorly educated and trained for the better jobs which were available.

The **Ozark-Ouachita area**, which includes parts of Arkansas and Oklahoma, is another poverty district within the South. It is similar to the Appalachians in the proportion of its people being of early Yankee origin, in its isolation from the changes which have occurred as part of the evolution of modern American society, in the significance of subsistence agriculture, and in the role of primary extractive industries. Although coal deposits are not important in this area, lumbering has continued as a source of income for many. Some mining of lead, zinc, and other minerals has occurred but has been concentrated in only a few centers.

The incidence of poverty is somewhat greater in nonmetropolitan than metropolitan areas. But central cities of metropolitan areas have the highest incidence of poverty and suburbs of metro areas have the lowest rates. However, even in the suburbs about one of every eleven people is poor. As those who could afford it left the inner cities, as did former downtown businesses and industries, they typically left behind the poor and many abandoned houses and buildings. Many of those in poverty are living in concentrated districts often referred to as **ghettos**, (neighborhoods of similar ethnic or racial background), but a large proportion of the urban poor live in small pockets in other sections of the city. The urban poor are both African American and white, young and old, male and female, worker and nonworker, educated and uneducated. A variety of circumstances have trapped them in poverty. Some were born poor; others joined late in life. In the city, little opportunity exists for the poor person to live in a single family residence, to grow part of his food, or to have surrounding fields for play and enjoyment, as might have been the case in a rural setting. In the city, those in poverty are most often--but not always--found in multi-family units in high-density neighborhoods. Since many cannot afford private transportation, they must depend on the slow public transit system to get them to work. This has become an increasing problem during the last two decades as more and more industries and businesses requiring unskilled or semi-skilled labor have moved to the peripheries of the cities or beyond.

By the year 2000 in Cuyahoga County (Cleveland, Ohio), for example, the number of high poverty census tracts (where at least 40 percent of the residents were below the poverty line) had doubled since 1970, while population density in high poverty tracts was half the 1970 density. The urban-to-suburban migration has produced a clear spatial divide between rich and poor (Figure 5.18). Census tracts of high poverty are clustered in the heart of central cities like Cleveland, while high income residents tend to live in nearby suburbs. Many cities have trouble providing adequate basic services, such as street paving and police protection, sue to the declining tax base.

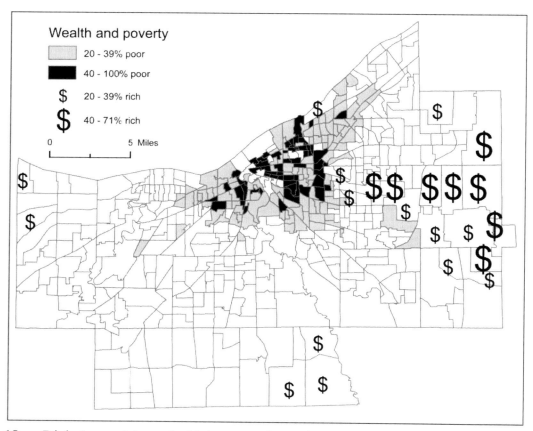

Figure 5.18 -- Rich (annual household income above $150,000) and Poor (individuals below the poverty level) by Census Tract in Cuyahoga County (Cleveland), Ohio.

Who the Poor Are

Minorities have higher rates of poverty in the United States and Canada. About a fourth of African Americans, Native Americans, and Hispanics in the U.S. are poor. In Canada the incidence of low income is highest (as high as 30%) among recent immigrants and aboriginals (American Indian, Inuit, and Metis). Among all ethnic and racial groups in North America, married-couple families have much lower rates of poverty than female head-of-household families.

White/Non-Hispanics

In the United States, the largest number of the poor are white/non-Hispanics, being over 17 million persons, or 43 percent of all the poor (Table 5.11). However, despite the high proportion of the poor in this category, less than nine percent of the white/non-Hispanic population is poor. Nearly two-fifths of poor white/non-Hispanics are outside the labor force age group. Many whites who live in poverty, therefore, are not personally capable of raising their economic level. They must depend on others to assure them of a decent standard of living at the younger and older stages in their lives. Between 1974 and 2003, the number of poor white/non-Hispanics increased by nearly 30 percent. However, during this time, the percentage of the poor being in this group decreased from 57 percent to 43 percent.

African Americans

Nearly 17 million white/non-Hispanics live in poverty and about 9.4 million African Americans do so (Table 5.11). However, it is important to note that a fourth of the poor in this nation is African American, which is twice their proportion of the population. Moreover, even in the prosperous 1990s, one out of every four African Americans was not able to rise above the poverty level and this is still the case. The great proportion of poor people among the African American population reflects their serious economic and social plight.

African Americans were long found primarily in the rural South. During the mid-twentieth century however, they joined--and sometimes surpassed--the whites in the exodus from the southern farms to the cities. The first stimulus to major African American and white movement to the urban

Table 5.11. Number and Percent of U. S. Poor, by Ethnicity and Age, 1974 and 2008

Ethnic and Age Group	1974 Number	Percent	2008 Number	Percent
White/Non-Hispanic	13.2 mil	57%	17.0 mil	43%
Under 18 Years of Age	4.8 mil	36%	4.4 mil	26%
18-64 Years of Age	6.1 mil	46%	10.4 mil	61%
Over 64 Years of Age	2.3 mil	17%	2.3 mil	13%
African American	7.2 mil	31%	9.4 mil	24%
Under 18 Years of Age	3.8 mil	53%	3.9 mil	41%
18-64 Years of Age	2.8 mil	39%	4.9 mil	52%
Over 64 Years of Age	0.6 mil	8%	0.6 mil	6%
Hispanic	2.6 mil	11%	11.0 mil	28%
Under 18 Years of Age	1.4 mil	54%	5.0 mil	45%
18-64 Years of Age	1.1 mil	42%	5.5 mil	50%
Over 64 Years of Age	0.1 mil	4%	0.5 mil	5%

Source: U.S. Census Bureau.

centers was the lure of higher paying industrial jobs in the North during the First and Second World Wars, especially the latter. Later, the mechanization of agriculture pushed others off the farm. Finally, the civil rights movement was successful in bringing more rights to them, which further increased their economic potential in cities, particularly in the North and West.

The percentage of poor African Americans being elderly is much lower than for white/non-Hispanics (6% and 13%, respectively), and the proportion being children is much greater (41% vs. 26%). The reasons for this are that higher African American fertility rates have resulted in very large numbers of poor youth and that the life expectancy at birth for this group is five years less than that of white/non-Hispanics. Nearly half of all poor African Americans is too young or too old to be employed full time in at least moderate wage positions.

Although African Americans made greater relative gains than whites in education and certain aspects of employment, they have not done so in income. African American family income as a percent of white family income has remained at about 60 percent since 1969; however, the absolute median family income differential has risen dramatically from $3,900 in 1969 to $14,200 in 1977 to $15,800 in 1994 to $18,100 in 2008—and $21,300 for white/non-Hispanics—as a result of larger gains in white incomes and inflation (Table 5.10). Thus, in absolute dollars, African Americans have lost considerable ground.

The African American infant mortality rate is still more than twice that of whites and higher than the overall rate of about 40 other countries and that, compared to whites, African Americans are still nearly three times as likely to live in poverty, more than twice as likely to be unemployed, and only three-fourths as likely to complete high school.

Hispanics

A third major group among the poor are the Hispanics. They are composed of whites, African Americans, and Orientals. Whereas the African American has skin color as a dominant factor barring his acceptance by the white community, the Hispanic has a language barrier, cultural influences, and a high illiteracy rate. The percentage of persons of Spanish origin living in poverty is nearly as high as that of African Americans, but the number and the proportion of all the poor being Hispanic are up sharply over the last three decades from 2.6 million to 11 million and from 11 percent to 28 percent of all the poor. Half of the poor Hispanics are under 18 years of age, but only five percent are elderly (Table 5.11). This distribution is indicative of the very young age structure of the Hispanic population, as a result of their high fertility and the recent large immigration of young adult Hispanics.

About half of the Hispanics are **Mexican Americans**. First, second, and third generation migrant farm laborers from Mexico are found from the Southeast to the Southwest, as well as elsewhere. These people have generally not been United States citizens and, therefore, have been accorded few rights. Although recent laws have improved the living conditions of many of the migrant laborers, many others usually sleep in unsanitary, overcrowded, substandard housing; eat high-caloric, low-protein food; and have few educational opportunities. Malnutrition is not uncommon. They make up about half of all migrant workers in the United States and spend their lives moving with the crop harvest. Many migrate from the early vegetable gardens of Texas in the winter through the Interior Lowlands to the cucumber and fruit fields of Michigan in late summer. Other migrants move from Arizona and California north into Oregon and Washington or from Florida along the east coast to the Delmarva Peninsula.

Native Americans

The Indian reservations, located in the Southwest, Southeast and Great Plains, contain the most dispossessed and neglected of all the poor. The annual income of the Native American is only about half the poverty threshold. Their rate of unemployment is several times the national average. Life expectancy is about twenty-five years less than for whites, and the infant death rate is twice the national average. One the whole, the Indian is the most segregated of all minorities. The political and economic power of the Native American people is, perhaps, less than that of any of the poor. Most of them live on reservations, and are thus out of the sight and the thoughts of the average American citizen. Many of the states with high incidences of poverty contain large numbers of Native Americans.

The Elderly

The aged have had the greatest improvement among the poor since 1974, with their rate of poverty being cut by a fourth to less than 10 percent in 2008. The median income of the elderly is only about three-fourths of that of the total population, but this is considerably higher than it was in 1974.

The rural elderly have much less income than those in urban areas. Many of the elderly poor have lived in poverty for most of their lives, but millions of others have been thrown helplessly into this predicament by a combination of high medical bills, low income, rising living costs, and lost jobs and medical benefits decimating a segment of the American people who have for a half century worked hard at being good citizens and building a prosperous and powerful nation for their descendants. For most of these persons, the latter years of life hold little more than pain, hunger and loneliness. Fortunately, federal medical aid and higher social security benefits have helped to lower the proportion of the elderly living in poverty.

Children

The proportion of children in poverty (19% in 2008) has declined since 1974 and was below 20 percent in 1998 for the first time since 1980. Moreover, the percentage of the poor being children, which had remained at about 40 percent for three decades dropped to 35 percent in 2008. The percentage of white/non-Hispanic children being in poverty (11%) is only a third that of African Americans (35%) and Hispanics (31%).

While yet unborn, many embryos and fetuses of poor pregnant women receive insufficient protein, vitamins, and minerals. At birth, these children are already behind others as a result of improper physical and mental development before birth. As children, food consumption often continues to be inadequate in quality and quantity. A high incidence of maternal and infant mortality exists. Illness is contracted more easily because an inferior diet provides less resistance. These factors, plus less encouragement at home, result in low educational achievement. The low educational levels prepare them for only low-paying jobs, which often lead to another generation to be reared in poverty.

The Working Poor

The proportion of the poor in the working ages rose by more than a sixth since 1974 and the percentage of Americans working full time but earning less than poverty-threshold wages rose by half since 1978. The problem is even greater among those full-time workers 18 to 24 years of age, for which poverty-level wages more than doubled to nearly half of all those in this age group. Only two wage-earner families kept a larger number and proportion of families from being in the poverty category.

Possibilities of Reducing Poverty

Many of the poor lack proper nutrition and, thus, are unable to reach their educational and working potentials and are more susceptible to disease. The poor lose more work days because of illness than do persons with higher incomes. They also visit doctors less often. Many, therefore, find it difficult to climb out of poverty. Only a very small percentage of all the poor are men who are capable of working, but who do not.

Most authorities agree that the present welfare program does not meet the needs of the poor. Certainly, many alternatives have been offered. So far, changes in the welfare system have done little to help most of the poor move out of poverty. In 2007, Congress raised the minimum wage from $5.15 to $7 an hour, or $14,872 a year for someone working 40 hours a week for all 52 weeks a year, which is more than $4,500 below the poverty level for a family of four. During the 10 years since the last increase in the minimum wage, the Congress voted themselves increases of more than $30,000 a year.

The question of providing the poor female householder with young children a job sufficient to offset her public assistance will prove difficult, since low-cost day care will be necessary for many. But such an arrangement could prove beneficial to mother and child. Finally, most of the elderly poor will have to receive public assistance.

POPULATION REVIEW

1. Discuss the difference between population (arithmetic) density and physiologic density. Roughly, what is the ratio of the former and the latter for the U.S. compared to Canada?

2. Explain what is meant by the term "megalopolis."

3. Where is Canada's "main street"?

4. How did the total fertility rate change in the U.S. from the Depression to the late 1950s, from then till the mid-1970s, and since the mid-1970s?

5. Compare the demographic rates of Canada and the U.S.

6. Discuss the age-sex structure of the U.S. population.

7. Compare the age-sex structure of the U.S. to that of Canada.

8. Discuss changing immigration patterns (number and origin) during the 20th century and their impact on the distribution of the population and on particular ethnic groups.

9. Explain how the source regions for Canada's immigrants differ from those of the U.S. in recent decades.

10. Explain how immigration laws (policies) changed in the U.S. since 1921.

11. Discuss how U.S. internal migration rates have change since the 1970s, where most moves occur and who moves more often.

12. Give the major regional migration patterns in the U.S. since 1900 and the impact of the recent patterns on state representation in Congress.

13. What were the major regional migration patterns in Canada during the twentieth century?

14. How does the U.S. Census Bureau define "urban" and "metropolitan" and how did the percentages for the overall population and African Americans in urban areas change since 1900?

15. How did the percent of African Americans living in the South change since 1900?

16. Discuss the changes in the proportion of the U.S. population being African American prior to 1930 and since 1930 and the reasons for these changes.

17. Discuss changes in the numerical increases and rates of growth in the U.S. for the decades since 1930.

18. What were the two migration reversals of the 1970s? Which one has continued to the present and which one ended by the mid-1980s?

19. What are the main language groups in Canada and where are they located?

20. Explain the differences in the concepts of racial and ethnic groups in the U.S. and Canada? What are the main racial and ethnic groups in each country?

21. In 2008, median household income was about $_____, while the poverty threshold was about $_____.

22. In 2008, the number and percentage of people in the U.S. in poverty was _____ and _____%.

23. What region and what states have the highest poverty rates in the U.S.?

24. What percentage of poor is in the child category? What percentage of poor is in the elderly category?

25. What percentage of children is poor? What percentage of the elderly is poor?

26. What percent of white/non-Hispanics, African Americans and Hispanics were poor in 2008?

27. How does life expectancy and infant mortality for Native Americans and African Americans compare to whites in the U.S.?

28. What groups in Canada have the highest incidences of poverty?

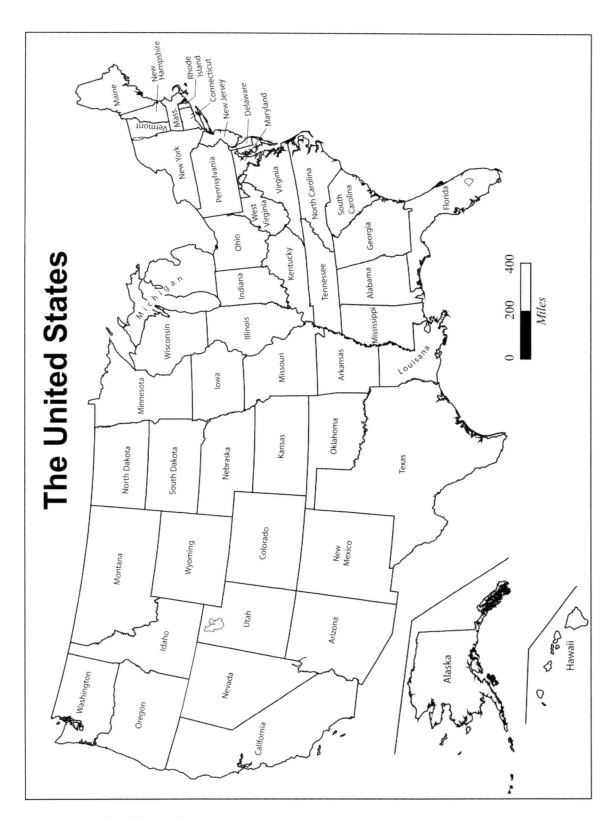

Figure 5.19 -- The United States

POPULATION EXERCISE

Table 5.12. 2009 U.S. Immigrants for Top 15 States for Six Main Source Countries

STATE	TOTAL	MEXICO	CHINA	PHILIPP.	INDIA	DOM-REP	VIET.	COLOM	S. KOR
CA	227876	59814	17139	24937	12826		10280		IRAN* 11227
NY	150722		19921		4410	23793	BANG* 8529	JAMAI* 7104	PAKIS* 4798
FL	127006		CUBA* 31928		HAITI* 13403	GUYA* 13403	JAMAI* 6655	11139	VENEZ* 6381
TX	95384	38597	2616	2797	4716		3361		ELSAL* 2632
NJ	58879			2509	7080	7445	PERU* 2352	2867	ECUA* 2330
IL	41889	9202	1739	2902	3946			PERU* 2553	PAKIS* 1389
MA	32607		2202		1666	4048	HAITI* 1948	CAP V* 1654	BRAZ.* 2025
VA	29825			1503	1944	PAKIS* 1514	EL SAL* 1646	ETHIO* 1302	1446
GA	28396	3325			1856	Nigeria 1176*	1011	1009	1350
WA	27562	2710	1474	2169	1670		1539	UKRAI* 1540	
MD	26722		1195		1518	Nigeria 1878*	EL SAL* 1635	ETHIO* 1440	CAME* 1158
PA	24105	794	1620		2142	1848	816	EGYPT* 1277	
AZ	20997	9168	499	877	553			IRAQ* 751	SOMAL* 509
MI	18919	1168			1294	YEME* 805	BANG* 908	IRAQ* 2691	LEBN* 829
NC	18562	2923	709		1026		1158	575	BURM* 508
Total	1130818	164920	64238	60029	57304	49414	29234	27849	25859

*"Other" main source countries that are not one of eight top source countries for the U.S.
SOURCE: Dept. of Homeland Security.
(http://www.dhs.gov/files/statistics/publications/LPR09.shtm)

*TOTALS FOR "OTHER" COUNTRIES: Bangladesh, 16,651; Brazil, 14,701; Burma, 13,621; Cameroon, 3,463; Cape Verde, 2,238; Cuba, 38,954; Ecuador, 12,128; Egypt, 8,844; El Salvador, 19,909; Ethiopia, 15,462; Guyana, 6,670; Haiti, 24,280; Iran, 18,553; Iraq, 12,110; Jamaica, 21,783; Lebanon, 3,831; Nigeria, 15,253; Pakistan, 21,555; Peru, 16,957; Somalia, 13,390; Ukraine, 11,223; Venezuela, 11,154; and Yemen, 3,134.

The only additional countries to contribute more than 11,000 U.S. immigrants were Canada (16,140), Guatemala (12,187), and the United Kingdom (15,478). Two of these three countries were one of the top eight sending countries to either Arizona (C), Michigan (C) or North Carolina (UK).

In 2009, 1,130,818 immigrants entered the U.S. <u>Fifty-eight</u> percent of them settled in just five states. (Shade these black with pencil on your map.) Another five states (ranked 6th-10th) accounted for an additional <u>14</u> percent of the immigrants. (Draw a diagonal criss-cross pattern for these states on your map.) An additional five states brought the total to <u>82</u> percent of all immigrants. (Draw one-way diagonal lines in these five states.) What pattern do you notice about the location of these 15 states?

_____

_____

In 2009, over 40 percent of the U.S. immigrants were from just the eight main countries of birth. 82 percent of the immigrants from one country, _____, went to just one state, _____, and that country accounted for a fourth of that state's immigrants.

Why? _____

_____

Also, 60 percent of the immigrants from _____ went to just _____ and _____, and this country accounted for over 40 percent of those going to _____ and over a fourth of the ones to _____. Although less than six percent of the legal immigrants from this same country went to this state _____, this country accounted for 44 percent of all its legal immigrants. Why do these three states account for 2/3 of all immigrants from this country?

_____

_____

Five countries that are one of the six main sources for a state but contributed far fewer immigrants than the leading eight countries for the U.S. are _____, _____, _____, _____, and _____.

Nearly 3/4 of the immigrants from _____ settled in _____ and almost 2/3 of those from _____ moved to _____ . These are two exaggerated examples of the channelization of migration.

List below the **four** main receiving states (in declining order) for each country and indicate after each state the percent of all immigrants to that state coming from that country. Then indicate the percent of all migrants from that country accounted for by that state.

Mexico: CA (26%; 36%), _____.

China: _____.

Philippines: _____

India: _____.

Dominican Republic: _____.

Vietnam: _____.

Colombia: _____

South Korea: _____.

Senator Phil Gram ringing the opening bell of the NY Stock Exchange. (Dept. of Commerce)

Aluminium Can Manufacturing Plant (Dept. of Commerce)

Loading grain on a ship in Superior, WI. (U.S. Corps of Engineers)

Technician inspects a valve at the Strategic Petroleum Reserve - Freeport, TX. (Dept. of Energy)

Figure 6.1 – Economic Activities

CHAPTER SIX

THE ECONOMIC BASE

Categories of Economic Activities

Economic activities can be categorized as primary, secondary, tertiary, quaternary, and quinary. Raw material extraction comprises the primary sector of the economy. It includes such jobs as gold mining, oil drilling, cattle raising, corn farming, cod fishing, and logging. The secondary sector consists of manufacturing and construction. In essence, the secondary sector processes the raw materials from the primary sector into finished goods. Primary and secondary activities together comprise the goods-producing sector of the economy: the final product is a tangible object.

The tertiary sector originally included all the rest of the economy—services. The tertiary sector includes a vast array of low paying jobs, such as retail sales, auto mechanics and barbers, to high-skill, high-wage careers, such as computer programmers, dentists and doctors. The large scope of the tertiary sector and the growth of new economic activities, such as information technology and government services, have given rise to the quaternary/quinary categories. Since the economic activities included in the last two sectors are not fully agreed upon, they will be combined here and are generally defined as information industries, such as education, research and information technology, and activities often equated with non-profit or government services. Tertiary, quaternary and quinary activities combined provide the services-producing sector of the economy: the product is a non-tangible service.

In 2008, four percent of Canadians were employed in the primary sector, 18 percent in the secondary sector and 78 percent in the services sectors; for the United States in 2008, the rates were two percent in primary, 15 percent in secondary and 83 percent in services. These proportions are typical for developed countries. Developing countries tend to have a much larger percentage of the workforce employed in primary activities like subsistence farming (growing food that the farmer eats).

A geographer's interest lies primarily in the distribution (where?) and locational processes (why there?) of economic activities. For example, agriculture is limited by climate, availability of water, flat land, and good soils, while corporate headquarters tend to be concentrated in large urban centers like New York City and Toronto. Gas stations and grocery stores, however, are ubiquitous. This chapter will focus largely on the spatial distribution and locational factors of the three main categories of economic activities: agriculture, manufacturing and services.

Agriculture

The Europeans, who largely developed American and Canadian agriculture, came upon a large area with the best combination of soils, climate, and landforms for farming anywhere on earth. (See Chapters 2 and 3.) Although agriculture in the United States and Canada has declined significantly in terms of the number of farms and workers, the average acreage in farms and the total value and volume of agricultural goods produced and exported rose during the last two decades. While crop yields per acre are not as high as in more intensively farmed countries, such as Japan, capital/technology inputs, such as hybrid seeds, herbicides, fertilizers, and even GPS-guided tractors, allow productivity (output per worker and per hour worked) in the U.S. and Canada to far exceed that of almost any other nation. Even where farming conditions are less than ideal, American and Canadian farmers have adapted. For example, in dry climate zones of the U.S., center pivot irrigation is common (Figure 6.2). In the cool Canadian climate, farmers maximize productivity using crops like spring wheat, rapeseed (used to make canola oil) and hybrid corn.

Figure 6.2 -- Satellite image of center pivot irrigation in central Kansas. Water, fertilizers and herbicides/pesticides are pumped underground to the center of the field and dispensed from the device as it slowly rotates on its pivot, creating a circular pattern of growth. Image courtesy of NASA.

International Trade in Agriculture

The United States and Canada are the first and fourth leading agricultural exporting nations in the world. (The value of the major export crops is shown in Table 6.1.) Thus, they specialize in the export of grains, such as wheat and corn. Half of all countries require outside food aid, although many of these might be net exporters of one or more individual grains or other cash crops. Thus, while farmers in developing countries cannot feed their populations, the average farmer in the U.S. produces enough for about 130 people.

Table 6.1. World, U.S. and Canadian exports of selected agricultural products and ranks.

Commodity	Total World Exports	U.S. Exports	U.S. % of World Total	U.S. Rank in World	Canadian Exports	Canadian % of World Total	Canadian Rank in World
Wheat	117.2 million metric tons	34.4 mmt	20%	First	6.8 mmt	6%	Second
Coarse grains -- (corn/sorghum/ barley/oats/rye)	127.2 mmt	69.9 mmt	55%	First	24.0 mmt	19%	Second
Corn only	98.6 mmt	61.9 mmt	58%	First	(not a major producer)		
Cotton	38.3 million 480 lb bales	13.6 mb	36%	First	(not a major producer)		
Soybeans	79.5 mmt	31.5 mmt	40%	First	(not a major producer)		

Source: USDA World Agricultural Supply and Demand Estimates 2007/2008, 2009.

Food aid sent to the needy abroad under a variety of slogans, such as "Food for Peace," obviously scored political points for any administration. Most of the food has often gone to less than a half dozen carefully chosen political friends (countries) the U.S. government would like to influence rather than to those nations where the problems of hunger were the most severe. Moreover, the major **food recipients** from the United States in 2008 were neighboring countries and those that could afford to buy the food, with nearly 60 percent of U.S. food exports going to Canada, Mexico, Japan, China (the country which lately has been financing the greatest increase of U.S. debt), and countries of the European Union. Moreover, since Japan and Western Europe are the customers for more than one out of every five dollars of farm exports from the U.S., any legislation in this country restricting Japanese or European imports could lead to trade reprisals and prove devastating to the agricultural economy.

In economies often beset by trade deficits, agricultural exports provide trade surpluses for this sector of the economy in both the U.S. and Canada. According to the U.S. Department of Agriculture, the United States exported $115 billion in agricultural products and imported $79 billion of such goods in 2008, leaving a trade surplus of $36 billion. In 2007, Canada exported $32 billion and imported $26 billion of farm goods, for a $6 billion trade surplus.

The United States is the world's leading exporter of food. It remains an important part of the **export** segment of the economy. In 1970, agriculture accounted for 17 percent of all exports by value; it rose to 18 percent in 1980, but dropped to 10 percent in 1991, then to seven to nine percent from 1997 to 2007, before rebounding to 10 percent in 2008. Although the value of all agricultural exports rose till 1996, it declined during the latter part of that decade, but then rose again, with 2004 exceeding the 1996 previous record high and then almost doubling again by 2008 and increasing by nearly a fifth from 2009 through 2010.

Between 1970 and 1986, agricultural **imports** rose steadily, after which they leveled off for a few years, while farm exports continued to rise, with the **balance** increasing from $1 billion in 1970 to $24 billion in 1980, before declining to $5 billion in 1986, then rising again to $27 billion in 1996, before declining once again to $11 to $14 billion from 1998 to 2003 then to four to seven billion dollars from 2004 to 2006, after which it rose spectacularly to $18 billion in 2007 and $35 billion in 2008 (Figure 6.3). Even though all agricultural imports, except sugar, rose slowly most years from 1970 to 2000, they doubled between 2001 and 2008. Agricultural imports declined as a percentage of all imports from 15 percent to seven percent in 1990 and then four percent from 1993 through 2008. Grains, fruits and vegetables tripled their value of imports between 1970 and 2003, then doubled again by 2008, with these products having the greatest gains in the shares of imports, while the shares for beef/veal and pork became smaller, although the amounts rebounded by roughly doubling from 1990 to 2008.

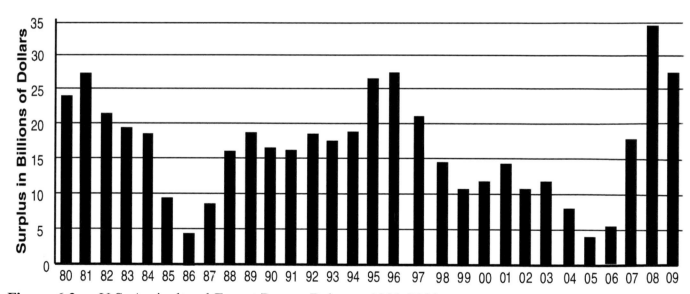

Figure 6.3 -- U.S. Agricultural Export/Import Balance, 1980-2009

Farmers and Farm Size and Ownership

The development of agriculture has generally followed the pattern of settlement and population growth throughout the U.S. and Canada. Continued residential, industrial, and commercial expansion, together with transportation uses, have reduced the amount of farm land by more than seven percent in the last 20 years--and it has often been among the most fertile. Canadian and American agriculture originally developed as small-scale, family-farm operations and still remains largely a family business, with 98 percent of all farms in the U.S. being family owned. Similarly, only two percent of Canadian farms are owned by "non-family corporations." Ninety-one percent of all U.S. farms are "small family farms," which are defined by the USDA as farms selling less than $250,000 annually. However, large family farms account for almost 60 percent of production.

Since the end of World War II, there have been a steady decrease in the number of farms and farmers and an increase in the size of individual farms. The decline in the U.S. **farm population** has been underway for at least half a century. Although many thought it could not drop much more, the number declined by nearly five million, or by more than half, between 1970 and 1990. (Indeed, such a small percentage of the population lived on farms by 2000--1.9%--that the Census Bureau dropped the farm residence question from its "Current Population Survey.) Canada, which still tracks the farm population, has only two percent of the population living on farms. Several reasons account for the declining numbers of farmers. First, productivity rises continually, so fewer farmers operating larger farms are more efficient. Second, as urban sprawl continues, some farmers can sell their prime flat agricultural land for urban development in exchange for an easier lifestyle. Third, small farmers might find it difficult to compete against larger farms. Those remaining on the farm have increasingly supplemented their incomes with off-the-farm jobs in services and manufacturing, increasing from about a fourth to about a third of farmers having second jobs during the last two decades. In 2007, only 45 percent of U.S. farm operators reported farming as their primary occupation. In addition, some former urban dwellers have been moving onto farms and keeping their jobs, while only pursuing farming as a hobby. About a fourth of farm operators live off the farm and commute to work.

The **number of farms** in the U.S. dropped by about a fifth between 1970 and 1990. But between 1997 and 2007, the number of farms increased slightly. In Canada, the number of farms declined from 575,000 in 1956 to about 230,000 (60%) in 2008. Since many smaller farms were incorporated into larger ones, the **average size** of farms in the U.S. increased by about a hundred acres (39ha), or about a third, to about 440 acres (178 ha) by 2002. However, during the next five years, the average size declined to 418 acres (169 ha). In Canada, farm size more than doubled from 301 acres (122 ha) in 1956 to 729 acres (295 ha) in 2006.

The farmer has experienced numerous financial difficulties. The plight of the small-to-middle size farm operation became precarious during the early 1980s. Bankruptcy auctions became a common sight in rural America during the 1980s. The **average value of U.S. farm land** per acre grew more than three times between 1970 and 1982, dropped by about a fourth between 1982 and 1987, then rose again by a seventh to pre-1980 levels by the early 1990s and then nearly doubled by 2007. Likewise, the **value of farm assets** grew nearly two and a half times between 1970 and 1982, only to decline by about a fifth within the next four years, before rising again to pre-1980 values in the early 1990s and then doubling by 2007.

Ironically, these financial difficulties were occurring at the same time that the farmer was increasing his productivity and the yields, value, and volume of farm commodities. Nevertheless, gains made after the early 1980s were not as great as those of the 1970s. The more rapid growth in the cost of farm inputs than the prices received for farm products has hurt the farmers' net income. Fortunately, higher **yields** allowed the net income of farm operators to more than triple between 1970 and the mid-1990s. Between 1997 and 2007, the average value of agricultural products sold per farm rose by nearly half.

There has been considerable concern in the United States about the rise of **corporate farming** and agribusiness. Although insurance, petroleum and other companies have moved increasingly into agriculture during the last three decades, over 90 percent of U.S. corporate farms continue to be owned by fewer than ten shareholders, indicating that they represent family controls. The vertical integration of corporations, or **agribusiness**, presents a more serious problem as companies produce and sell many of the agricultural inputs, purchase farm products in advance at fixed prices, then process and transport these items to their own stores where the finished products are sold to the consumer. Thus, they control the entire process from the planting of the seed to the checking out of the groceries at the counter. Eventually, this could lead to a lack of competition and to a significant rise in the prices of many food items. At present, most such ventures are limited to a small number of specialized goods, but already less than ten percent of the farmers are producing well over half of all farm sales and the practice of vertical integration within corporate farming could spread.

Another related concern of many Americans is the increase in the **foreign ownership of farm land** in this country. Although the number of acres owned by persons from other countries, either directly or through U.S. corporations, more than doubled since 1980, they still account for only about two percent of all farm land. Even at present rates of growth, foreign ownership of U.S. farm land probably will not be a serious problem for many years.

Wheat and corn production in the United States roughly doubled after 1970 before peaking in 1984. However, corn production increased by about half between 1990 and 2008, while wheat production declined till 2005, then returned to the level of the early 1990s by 2008. The U.S. share of world wheat production declined to 11-12 percent in the 1990s and to ten percent by 2008, while its share of world exports declined from a third to a fifth. The U.S. share of world corn production is nearly two-fifths, with less than 20 percent being exported, but still accounting for two-thirds of world exports until 2008 when it dropped to 58 percent. The U.S. share of the world's production of soybeans, tobacco, rice, cotton, and vegetable oils all dropped significantly. The U.S. still accounts for over a third of the world's production of soybeans and nearly a fifth of the cotton. The U.S. is still the leading exporter of raw cotton accounting for over one-third of the global trade and of soybeans where U.S. farmers account for more than two-fifths of world exports.

Agricultural Regions

The products which account for 89 percent of agricultural marketing in the U.S. are corn, cattle, dairy products, soybeans, broilers, fruits and nuts, wheat, greenhouse plants, hogs, eggs, hay, cotton, turkeys, potatoes, and rice. (See Table 6.2 for the leading agricultural commodities.) In 2007, the ten leading agricultural-producing states were California, Texas, Iowa, Nebraska, Minnesota, Kansas, Illinois, Florida, Wisconsin, North Carolina, and Indiana. These states accounted for 53 percent of all farm marketing income (Table 6.3).

Farmers tend to specialize in the most profitable crops or livestock given their local geographic conditions: climate, soils, landforms, and distance to and size of markets. Some areas have ideal conditions for dairy cows, while other places have climates suitable for citrus fruit. By specializing, farmers make more money individually and produce more of all agricultural goods as a group. Regions where certain types of farming dominate are sometimes labeled "belts," such as the Dairy Belt of the Great Lakes region or the Winter Wheat Belt of the Great Plains. Notice the strong relationship between corn, soybeans and hogs. The leading producers of the major farm products give an indication of the broad agricultural regions of the United States and Canada (Figure 6.4).

In 2008, the three leading agricultural provinces of Canada were Ontario, Alberta and Saskatchewan (Table 6.4). They accounted for 65 percent of the value of agricultural production in the country.

Several of the major agricultural regions are associated with climate, soil, and physiographic regions. For instance, the **Corn (feed corn)/Livestock, Soybean Belt** is situated primarily in the Humid Continental, Long Summer Climate region of the gently rolling Central Lowlands, where the Alfisols and Mollisols are the most common soil types. Here, glaciation also played an important role smoothing the landscape while laying down fertile deposits of soil. The leading corn-producing states are Iowa, Illinois, Nebraska, Minnesota, Indiana, and South Dakota--all of which are largely or partly within this agricultural region. Most of these are also the leading soybean-producing states and most of these states are also among the leaders in the production of **hogs**. Soybean-corn crop rotation methods of this region have numerous advantages for farmers. Soybeans add nitrogen to the soil, which corn needs, lowering fertilizer costs and increasing corn yields. Soybean-corn rotation reduces pest build-up in the soil, benefiting both crops. Because corn and soybeans are planted and harvested at different times of the year, farmers can spread their workload over a longer period of time. Erosion is reduced by crop rotation. Because corn is used for feed for livestock, the leading states in the production of hogs, with the exception of North Carolina, are located in this belt. North Carolina now out produces all of them, except Iowa. However, the rise of North Carolina from sixth to second place in hog production in three years, combined with the state's weak environmental regulations for hog farms, resulted in the environmental deterioration of soil, rivers and estuaries in parts of the Coastal Plain and coast, where fishing and tourism are threatened. In Canada, southern Ontario shows a similar corn-soybeans-hogs relationship. They are also produced in the St. Lawrence Valley of southern Quebec, as well as also being important in southern Manitoba.

Table 6.2. Major Agricultural Commodities by Value and Major Producing States, 2008

Commodity	Value($Billions) 2008	Change in $ Billion 1994-2002	Change in $ Billion 2002-2008	Major Producing States
Corn	$51.6	+3.9	+33.7	Iowa, Illinois, Nebraska, Minnesota Indiana, South Dakota
Cattle	$48.2	-2.0	+10.2	Nebraska, Texas, Kansas, Colorado Iowa, Oklahoma
Dairy	$34.8	+1.2	+19.3	California, Wisconsin, New York, Pennsylvania, Idaho, Minnesota
Soybeans	$29.1	+3.2	+15.3	Iowa, Illinois, Minnesota, Indiana Nebraska, Ohio, Missouri
Broilers	$23.1	+3.0	+9.7	Georgia, Arkansas, North Carolina Alabama, Mississippi, Texas
Fruits/Nuts	$18.9	+2.7	+6.3	California, Washington, Florida
Wheat	$17.4	-2.1	+11.5	North Dakota, Kansas, South Dakota, Montana, Oklahoma, Washington
Greenhouse	$16.1	+5.8	+0.9	California, Florida, Texas, Oregon North Carolina, Michigan
Hogs/Pigs	$16.1	-1.3	+6.5	Iowa, North Carolina, Minnesota Illinois, Indiana, Nebraska
Eggs	$8.2	+0.4	+4.0	Iowa, Ohio, Georgia, Indiana Pennsylvania, Texas
Hay	$7.4	+1.4	+2.8	California, Idaho, Washington Texas, Colorado, Oregon
Cotton	$5.7	-5.2	+2.3	Texas, California, Georgia Arkansas, Mississippi, Missouri
Turkeys	$4.5	+0.1	+1.9	Minnesota, North Carolina, Missouri, Arkansas, Mississippi, Virginia
Potatoes	$3.7	+0.6	+0.8	Idaho, Washington, Wisconsin, Colorado, Oregon, California
Rice	$3.2	NA	NA	Arkansas, California, Louisiana

Source: U. S. Census Bureau. *U. S. Statistical Abstract, 1999, 2004, 2010;* ERS, USDA, 2010.

Table 6.3. Leading Agricultural States in the U.S., by Farm Marketing Income and Major Farm Commodities, 2007

State	Farm Income 2007 ($ Billions)	Farm Income Change ($ Billions) 1994-2002	2002-2007	Major Farm Commodities
California	26.1	+7.2	+9.5	Dairy products, greenhouse, grapes, lettuce
Texas	19.1	+1.2	+6.4	Cattle, cotton, greenhouse, dairy products
Iowa	19.0	+0.4	+8.2	Corn, hogs/pigs, soybeans, cattle
Nebraska	14.6	+0.8	+5.0	Cattle, corn, soybeans, hogs/pigs
Minnesota	12.5	+0.5	+5.0	Corn, soybeans, hogs/pigs, dairy
Kansas	11.7	+0.1	+3.8	Cattle, wheat, corn, soybeans
Illinois	11.7	-0.1	+4.2	Corn, soybeans, hogs/pigs, cattle
Wisconsin	8.9	0	+3.6	Dairy, corn, cattle, soybeans
North Carolina	8.7	+1.4	+2.1	Broilers, hogs/pigs, greenhouse, tobacco
Indiana	7.8	NA	NA	Corn, soybeans, hogs/pigs, dairy

Source: U. S. Census Bureau. *U. S. Statistical Abstract, 1999, 2004, 2010.*

Table 6.4. Leading Agricultural Provinces in Canada, by Farm Cash Receipts and Major Farm Commodities, 2008.

Province	Farm Cash Receipts ($ Billions)	Major Farm Commodities by Farm Cash Receipts
Ontario	10.3	Grains (canola, wheat), dairy, cattle, hogs/pigs
Alberta	10.0	Dairy, cattle, hogs/pigs, grains (corn, soybeans, wheat)
Saskatchewan	9.4	Grains (canola, wheat), cattle

Source: Statistics Canada, Agriculture Economic Statistics, 2008.

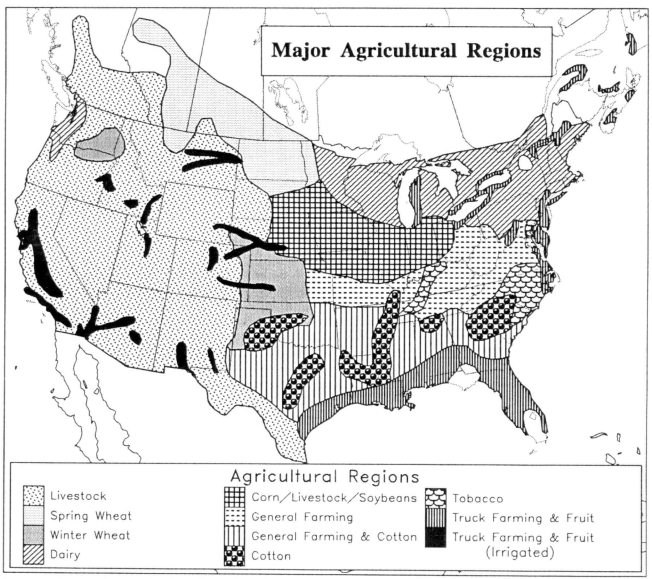

Figure 6.4 -- Major Agricultural Regions in the U.S. and Canada

Cattle are produced somewhat farther west in the Great Plains, with the leading U.S. producers being Nebraska, Texas, Kansas, Colorado, and Oklahoma. In these areas, drier climates have led to a more dispersed human settlement, which leaves large tracts of grassland open for grazing cattle. The Great Plains also benefited from proximity to areas where hay and other crops are grown for silage (animal feed). In the western Great Plains states, such as Colorado, drier conditions produce sparse grassland vegetation; very large ranches prevail here because a single animal requires many acres to have enough grass to survive. An important trend of the 1990s was the sharp concentration of the industry among the leading meat packers, from a third to over three-fourths of meat production. Coincidentally, the price paid to farmers/ranchers for cattle dropped greatly during this period, whereas beef prices to the consumer rose slightly. In Canada, beef cattle production is important in the Quebec-Ontario heartland, in the Great Plains, and in British Columbia. Additional beef cattle production (Figure 6.5) is scattered across the United States and Canada, where smaller areas of grazing land are supplemented by the growth of silage crops.

Milk cow production of the **Dairy Belt** is located just north of the Corn Belt around the Great Lakes, including Quebec and Ontario, the top producing provinces in Canada. This agricultural region is mainly in the Humid Continental, Short Summer Climate of the Central Lowlands and their Alfisols and the northern Appalachians, where poorer Spodosols, rougher terrain and cooler temperatures inhibit productive field cropping. As new hybrid strains of corn allow the maturing of corn farther north, the Corn Belt has been pushing into the southern margins of the Dairy Belt. Four of the six leading milk-producing states are within this belt, including Wisconsin, New York, Pennsylvania, and Minnesota. Farmers who are closer to large population centers focus on liquid milk, which is perishable and expensive to transport long distances, while farmers farther from the markets produce more processed milk products, such as butter (Minnesota) and cheese (Wisconsin). A secondary concentration of dairy cows is found in central California, the U.S. leader in milk production, and in Idaho, which ranks fifth.

Broilers are chickens raised for meat (Figure 6.5) and are in high demand. Americans consume an estimated 91 pounds per person per year on average; Canadians average 25 pounds per person. The Broiler Belt of the United States lies in the Southeast, stretching in a crescent from Texas and Oklahoma to the Delmarva Peninsula and Pennsylvania. The leading producers are Georgia, Arkansas, North Carolina, Alabama, Mississippi, and Texas, although of the ten leading agricultural states, broilers rank first only in North Carolina. Smaller production zones exist in several other states and in Ontario, Quebec and British Columbia, which are the leading provinces in Canada.

Both the **Spring/Durum Wheat Belt** and the **Winter Wheat Belt** (Figures 6.6) are found in the Steppe Climate of the Great Plains and in the Columbia Plateau, where Mollisols (the most fertile soils for grain production) are common. Longer, colder winters in the northern United States and Canada necessitate the growing of spring and durum wheat, which is planted in the spring and harvested in the late summer. The leading spring/durum wheat producers are Saskatchewan, North Dakota, Alberta, Manitoba, South Dakota, and Montana.

Winter wheat, which is planted in the fall, lies dormant in winter and is harvested in the spring, is grown farther south, where seedlings can survive the milder winter. Kansas, Oklahoma, and Montana are the leading winter wheat states in harvested acres. Corn, which is used mainly for livestock feed, would be grown farther west into the Winter Wheat Belt if there were greater precipitation there or if a hybrid could mature under the drier conditions because corn gives a much higher return on investment than wheat. Because wheat yields less per acre than corn, wheat farms tend to be larger and highly mechanized. For over a century, companies that specialized in wheat harvesting using large mechanical harvesters have hired temporary workers who have followed the ripening wheat from the south to the north. Many wheat farmers save money on the high cost of specialized equipment by contracting their harvests out to such companies.

Fruit is grown throughout much of the United States. Apples are produced in 36 states--mainly in Washington, New York and Michigan, whereas peaches are grown in 31 states--especially California, Georgia and South Carolina. Blueberries are raised primarily in Michigan, New Jersey, Oregon, Georgia, North Carolina, and Washington and grapes in 13 states, with most from

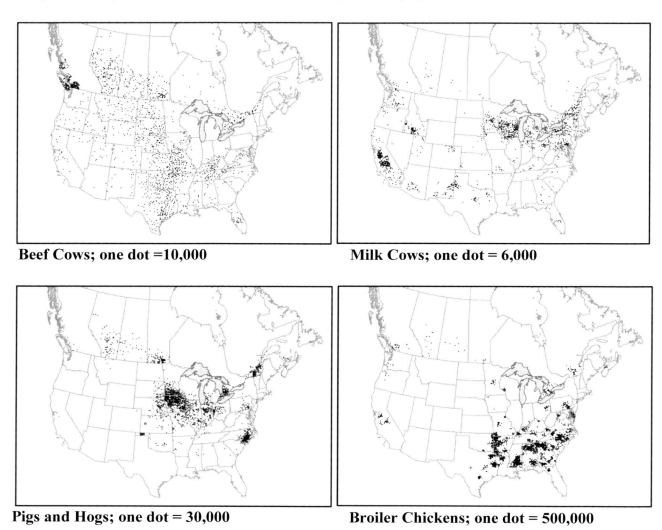

Figure 6.5 – Livestock products. Sources: USDA Census of Agriculture, 2007; Statistics Canada Census of Agriculture, 2006.

California, Washington and New York. **Tropical fruits and nuts** are found largely in California, which ranks first in walnuts, almonds, dates, pistachios, kiwi, nectarines, and lemons (Arizona second), plus figs and olives. The major producers of oranges and tangerines are Florida, California, Arizona, and Texas. Tangelos and limes are grown only in Florida; pineapples, papayas, bananas, and macadamia nuts are raised in Hawaii; and hazelnuts are produced in Oregon and Washington. **Cotton** (Figure 6.6) needs a 200-day growing season and 30 to 50 inches (76-127 cm) of rain in the early and middle stages of growth, so production is concentrated in the southern United States. Although cotton was king for a time in the Southeast, today most cotton is grown under irrigation in California, Texas and the states between them, as well as along the lower Mississippi River. However, because cotton cannot survive heavy rains during the late growing season and the harvesting period, the Mississippi River producing region is found at least 100 miles (160 km) inland from the Gulf coast to protect the plants from hurricane-induced heavy rain. Because of cotton's sensitivity to late heavy rain, production moved into the drier Southwest, where irrigation is supplied from underground water-bearing rock layers called aquifers.

Other crops, such as wheat and vegetables, are also produced in the dry western states using water from aquifers. This has led to concerns about exhausting this resource, which was built up over thousands of years and which only slowly replenishes itself. **Livestock ranching** is found in the Steppe and Desert Climates of the West, where Aridisols predominate. **Beef cattle** are also important in Florida and Alabama

Tobacco, once king in the Carolinas, is still grown in the Humid Subtropical Climate on the Piedmont and Coastal Plain sections of the southeastern United States, while it is also produced in the Interior Low Plateaus of Tennessee and Kentucky, where there are ultisols. Although tobacco is produced in several states (primarily North Carolina, Kentucky, Tennessee, Virginia, South Carolina, and Georgia), it is grown in only one of the 10 top agricultural states, North Carolina, where it declined from the leading to the fourth-ranking agricultural product in only ten years. The growing assault on this product because of health concerns and the recent increases in tobacco imports by major manufacturers led to this decline, severely damaging the agricultural and overall economy of the state of North Carolina, which long depended heavily on this product. Tobacco is no longer one of the top 15 agricultural products in the United States.

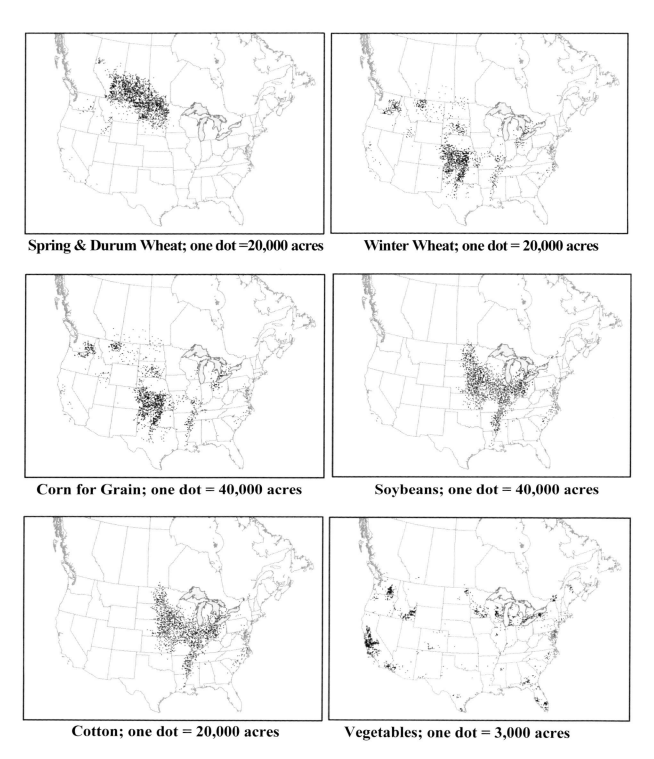

Figure 6.6 – Harvested Acres. Sources: USDA Census of Agriculture, 2007; Statistics Canada Census of Agriculture, 2006.

Manufacturing

Manufacturing Employment Since World War II

During the mid-to-late twentieth century, manufacturing had become the economic mainstay of any powerful, advanced country. The United States and Canada emerged from World War II as the two leading industrial countries of the world, as most of the European and East Asian manufacturing plants lay in ruin devastated by the war. Both countries remain world leaders in manufacturing. The protective military shield of the United States allowed the countries of Japan and Western Europe to direct their resources and industrial development to consumer goods. Also, American aid via the Marshall Plan and military protection stimulated economic recovery, making it possible for those defeated militarily to use their ingenuity and perseverance to rapidly close the manufacturing gap and to even surpass the United States and Canada in various types of industrial production, such as cars. The U.S. International Trade Administration affirms, however, that the United States' manufacturing sector retains greater worker productivity than Western Europe and that U.S. manufacturing output by itself would rank as the fifth largest economy in the world.

Although American supremacy in manufacturing was challenged, the number of industrial workers in the United States increased from 14 million in 1950 to a peak of 20 million in 1979. By this time, there had also been a considerable shift in the types of products Americans produced, as more emphasis was placed on higher skilled jobs. Mechanization, changing consumer preferences, new products, the rising value of the dollar, and increased foreign competition all played a role in this process. Between 1979 and 2007, the number of employees in manufacturing declined by 30 percent to the 1950 level of 14 million, which was 11 percent of all employees in the United States. Manufacturing had accounted for 27 percent of U.S. gross domestic product (GDP) in 1950, but only 11 percent in 2008, with over half the value from food products, chemicals, computers and electronics, motor vehicles, and fabricated metals. (U.S. Bureau of Economic Analysis). The decline of manufacturing in Canada has not been as severe. Statistics Canada shows that Canada has experienced a sight growth trend in manufacturing employment from 1.3 million in 1951, when manufacturing comprised about one-fourth of the workforce, to 1.7 million by 2006, representing only 12 percent of the workforce. Canadian manufacturing accounted for 14 percent of Canadian GDP in 2006.

During the 1970s in the United States, the **number of workers** in tobacco, textile, apparel, leather goods, paper, and chemical industries had already begun to decline. During the 1980s, workers in all these industries, except paper, continued to decline and losses were also suffered in petroleum and coal; stone, clay and glass; primary metals; fabricated metals; industrial machinery; electronics; and instruments. A decline in jobs often meant greater productivity (production per person). During the 1990s, all these industries, except stone, clay and glass products and fabricated metals, continued to decline. However, furniture, plastics and rubber products, fabricated metals, machinery, and food all increased the number of workers substantially. Unfortunately, after 2000, all major manufacturing sectors lost jobs. Especially hard-hit were apparel, leather, textiles, computers and electronics, primary metals, electrical equipment, and machinery. Most of these jobs were lost to foreign competitors after trade tariffs were substantially reduced or eliminated.

From 1977 to 1989, the **value of manufactured products** (in constant 1982 dollars) increased in most categories, but dropped for motor vehicles, primary metals, textiles, leather goods, and tobacco products. During the 1990s, the value of manufactured goods grew by nearly a third (in constant dollars), with major gains in electronics/electrical equipment, industrial machinery, motor vehicles and equipment, rubber and plastics, petroleum and coal products, and to a lesser extent in furniture, chemicals, and fabricated metals. However, large declines occurred in tobacco products and in transportation equipment other than motor vehicles (especially in guided missiles, etc.) and in instruments. From 1999 till the economic recession of the late 2010s, the value of manufactured goods continued to grow overall (in constant dollars), but every category of nondurable goods, except chemicals, declined. Most of the gain for durable goods was accounted for by the computer/electronics sector and nearly all the remaining increase was from motor vehicles.

International trade was a factor in manufacturing employment and production in the United States. During the 1980s, this country's share of world **exports** declined, as did employment related to exports. Jobs related to exports grew from the mid-1980s into the early 2000s, as the value of manufacturing doubled and the percent of manufactured goods exported rose from 30 percent to over 40 percent of the total. The greatest number of jobs related to exports were in fabricated metals, transportation equipment, computers and electronics, food, and machinery. In fact, over a third of all jobs in primary metals and computers/electronics were due to exports, as were over a fourth in machinery, electrical equipment, chemicals, and textiles. However, by value, the leading export industries were computers and electronics, transportation equipment, and chemicals.

During the first half of the 1980s, domestic **imports** of manufactured products increased in all categories, except tobacco, with the greatest proportional gains being in furniture, apparel, electric and electronic equipment, leather goods, machinery, and transportation equipment. But between 1985 and 1992, food products and minerals (except fuels), had import declines, while tobacco imports nearly quadrupled. During the 1990s, the value of manufactured imports at least doubled for apparel, lumber, furniture, chemicals, rubber and plastics, both electrical and non-electrical machinery, and instruments.

Although mechanization has occurred and **worker productivity** has increased in United States and Canadian industries since 1970, output per man hour worked has risen much more in several other industrial countries, especially Japan. Japanese productivity was only about 80-85 percent of that of the United States and Canada in 1970, but Japan surpassed them both during the late 1970s, and by the mid-1990s, exceeded the U.S. by over two-thirds and Canada by more than a third. During the 1970s, hourly worker compensation grew faster in the United States and Canada than in Japan, thus further improving the competitive position of the latter. However, between 1990 and 1996, productivity in the U.S. grew faster than it did in Japan and Canada. Since 1980, total manufacturing employment in the United States has declined by 23 percent and in Canada by more than four percent, but in Japan it has risen by five percent—though it peaked there in 1994.

Between 2000 and 2008, the annual average percent change in labor productivity was 2.1 percent in the United States, compared to 1.7 percent for Japan and 1.4 percent for Canada.

Industrial Location Factors

Manufacturing plants are not distributed equally across the United States and Canada, but are concentrated in manufacturing regions and centers, each of which tends to specialize in the production of goods different from other regions and centers (Figure 6.7 and Table 6.5). A number of geographic factors work together to create these specialized regions of manufacturing, including the source of raw materials, transportation costs, markets for finished goods, quality and cost of labor, proximity to other manufacturing plants, and the "business climate," including amenities which are available for plant managers and workers, unionization, government incentives such as local tax breaks, and legal impediments such as environmental laws. While production could theoretically take place anywhere, these location factors limit the possible locations where a firm can operate profitably. Savings resulting from favorable plant location, called economies of place, reduce the cost of production and thereby increase profits.

Because manufacturing was at first primarily an urban function, cities developed largely where industry could best locate. Since people and goods traveled most easily and cheaply by water, cities were often located on waterways. The transfer of goods from one carrier to another (e.g. from ocean vessel to river boat, or boat to wagon) provided an excellent opportunity for processing a raw material or semi-finished item into a finished product. Early large industrial cities were situated at such **bulk-breaking points** along the north Atlantic coast, where they had the best access to markets, raw materials, and skilled labor from Europe. Urban centers developed along waterways, especially where overland wagon routes intersected them. In the latter nineteenth and early twentieth centuries, other towns evolved and many earlier ones grew larger where rail lines intersected or crossed rivers or roads.

The location of manufacturing plants normally is based on minimizing the cost of production, especially for transportation. Each industrialist has had to consider **accessibility** to labor, market, raw materials, and energy and water needs when locating his plant. Accessibility focused on the availability and cost of transporting all the production ingredients. If the bulk or weight of the **raw material** used were diminished greatly during processing (e.g. ore refining) or if it were susceptible to rapid deterioration (e.g. fresh vegetables for canning), the factory would need to be located near that source. On the other hand, if great bulk or weight were added during manufacturing (e.g. farm machinery) or if the finished product were likely to become less desirable with an elapse of time (e.g. doughnuts or the local newspaper), the plant would be better placed near the **market**. Whichever might be the case, the need for efficient **transportation** is important. Heavy or bulky goods (e.g. iron ore) would more likely need access to water or rail transport, whereas raw materials or products of limited weight or size (e.g. clothing) could travel easily by truck. Perishable goods (e.g. fresh milk) often need rapid ground transfer, so the speed of the carrier becomes important. Light, highly valuable items (e.g. watches) will more easily withstand high cost air transport.

Figure 6.7 – U.S. and Canadian manufacturing regions.

The **labor** supply is also critical in manufacturing, since this is the major input cost of most finished items. If the product can be made by many people of reasonable skill (e.g. textiles), the industrialist might seek the lowest cost labor supply available within the needs of raw material, market, and transportation, plus any special requirement. This tendency has resulted in the movement of certain types of manufacturing from developed countries with relatively high wages, such as the United States and Canada, to low-wage countries, such as China. Clothing can be made and imported more cost effectively due to lower labor cost abroad. However, if the item demands considerable skill in its production (such as cutting-edge electronics), the manufacturer will probably look for higher skilled labor and pay the higher wages. Furthermore, market-oriented industries, such as medical equipment, are likely to be made in the United States and Canada. Foreign manufacturers have made significant direct investment in the U.S. and Canada, building factories here, despite higher labor costs, in order to serve these lucrative markets.

Table 6.5 Regional Manufacturing Centers and Specialty Industries

Manufacturing Center/Region	Specialty Industries
Boston/New England	Computers/electronics, industrial machinery, pharmaceuticals
New York	Pharmaceuticals, computers/electronics, apparel, metals printing, plastics, furniture
Philadelphia/Mid-Atlantic	Pharmaceuticals, navigational/medical/control instruments, animal processing
Montreal/St. Lawrence Valley	Aerospace parts, apparel, pharmaceuticals, printing
Toronto/Golden Horseshoe	Motor Vehicles and parts, plastics, furniture, printing
Pittsburgh - Cleveland	Iron and Steel, metalworking machinery, motor vehicle parts
Cincinnati - Indianapolis	Motor vehicle parts, aerospace parts, general purpose machinery, animal processing
St. Louis	Motor vehicles and parts, structural metals, pharmaceuticals, HVAC, refrigeration machinery
Detroit	Motor vehicles, metalworking machinery, plastics
Chicago - Milwaukee	Forging/stamping metals, animal processing, general purpose/metalworking machinery, plastics
Minneapolis	Navigational/medical/control instruments, general purpose/metalworking machinery, medical equipment and supplies
Kansas City	General purpose/industrial machinery, motor vehicles, printing
Atlanta/Southeast	Animal processing, plastics, aircraft, motor vehicle parts
Florida	Medical equipment, printing
Dallas	Aerospace parts, semiconductors, animal processing
Houston	Chemicals, synthetics, oil/gas/mining, navigational/medical/control instruments, electrical
Portland-Seattle-Vancouver	Aircraft, navigational/medical/control instruments, semiconductors, seafood packing, printing
San Francisco - San Jose (Silicon Valley)	Semiconductors, navigational/medical/control instruments, mobile phones, aerospace/space vehicle parts
Los Angeles/Southern California	Apparel, semiconductors, navigational/medical/control instruments, radio and TV equipment, aerospace/aircraft parts

Source: U.S. Census Bureau, County Business Patterns, 2007; Statistics Canada, Census 2006.

Savings that result from manufacturers locating near one another are called agglomeration economies. Parts suppliers that locate close to an assembly plant allow the assembly plant to request small batches of parts just-in-time for final assembly. This process contributes to quality control and eliminates large stockpiles of parts, while also reducing transportation costs to the assembly plant. A second assembly plant, perhaps a competitor to the first, can also reap savings by locating nearby and using the same plant suppliers. In addition, transporting a finished product to the market may require specialized packaging, so two plants producing similar products stand to benefit from the same transportation services. When manufacturers agglomerate, a specialized labor pool begins to develop because local institutions, such as technical colleges or unions, will train workers from the industry. This can result in further growth in the industry, creating a specialized region for that product. For example, furniture manufacturers clustering in Piedmont North Carolina benefit from agglomeration economies.

Energy supply is sometimes a major expense in the making of a product. Some industries must locate adjacent to major power sources, especially hydroelectric sites (e. g. aluminum producers), while others must be near power supplies, such as oil or coal fields or refineries (e. g. petrochemical industries). See Figure 6.8. Other industries use only small amounts of energy compared to total production costs (e. g. apparel makers), so they can locate without regard to the lowest cost energy or power sources. However, the availability of large quantities of highly reliable energy at a reasonable cost can also be a major location factor, as occurred with the expansion of the textile industry in the Carolina Piedmont in the 1960s and is now important in the continued attraction of major credit data centers in the same region.

In addition to the use of water for cheap power, some industries have sought **clean water** for rinsing or some other purpose in the manufacturing process (e.g. textiles). The great problem of industrial water pollution, which has endangered people living in many parts of America, has been brought under control in most areas, but not until federal legislation was passed. The use of rivers as sewers in manufacturing is no longer tolerated.

More and more communities and states are using the lure of land or buildings for industrial sites and special tax **incentives** to attract industries to areas which might not otherwise have been seriously considered. A court decision in North Carolina ruled that public money could be used for this purpose. If all other factors are generally equal for two competing locales, a financial inducement can make the difference. The Toyota automobile assembly plant in Georgetown (near Lexington), Kentucky was lured with an offer that cost the state of Kentucky about $150 million. By 2008, however, the plant had generated over $1 billion in revenues for the state. But some industries that move for these reasons are "**footloose**," so that once an advantage is gone, so are they. (Note the announcement of the closing of the 750,000 square foot Dell desktop computer manufacturing plant in Winston-Salem, NC just four years after having received nearly $300 million in incentives and tax breaks from state and local governments--the largest financial incentive package in state history. Since nearly 1,000 people lost their job, Dell returned about ten percent of the incentive package, though the agreement specified returning the entire amount.)

Figure 6.8 – Grand Coulee Dam on the Columbia River in Washington State. Hydroelectric power produces nearly one-fifth of the world's electricity. China, Canada, Brazil, the United States and Russia are the five largest producers of hydropower. Photo courtesy of the Bureau of Land Reclamation.

Prospective industrialists are increasingly concerned about **amenities**, especially for their executives and highly-skilled employees. The availability of parks, golf courses, coliseums and convention centers and the quality of the public schools which will educate the children of management are important factors. The availability of technical/community colleges and universities, which might be called on to train needed additional workers or to give expert advice on issues concerning the company, is also important. More recently, the importance of a thriving downtown with considerable emphasis on the arts and restaurants has been emphasized.

Changes in Manufacturing Employment and Location

By 1900, the core of North American manufacturing had been established in New England, the Great Lakes states and adjacent areas in Canada. The Manufacturing Belt (Figure 6.9) had early advantages in all major industrial location factors. Immigrants flooded into eastern cities, creating abundant, cheap labor. Population was concentrated (and continues to be concentrated) in the region, securing a market for finished goods. Access to nearby raw materials, such as iron ore from Pennsylvania, Minnesota and Ontario, and timber and coal from Appalachia was facilitated by low transportation costs. Major waterways, such as the Atlantic Ocean, Great Lakes, St. Lawrence River, Hudson River, and Ohio River, were the most economical routes for transporting bulky raw materials necessary for early manufacturing. Railroads and then roads were also first built in this area.

The Manufacturing Belt continues to enjoy many of these advantages, as well as a large pool of skilled labor, necessary for today's high-tech manufacturing. It remains the primary concentration of manufacturing in North America, although its dominance has declined since World War II. Manufacturing has spread west and south in the U.S. and west in Canada (Figure 6.9). Nearly all of the traditional Manufacturing Belt states account for a smaller percentage of U.S. manufacturing employment today than in 1950. The states with the most significant gains in terms of share of manufacturing employment since 1950 have been Texas, California and Florida. The provinces of Alberta and British Columbia experienced the greatest relative gains in Canada. The U.S. states that lost the largest share of national employment in manufacturing have been New York, Pennsylvania and other large Manufacturing Belt states. The provinces of Quebec and Ontario have had the greatest relative losses in Canada. These gains and losses reflect similar shifts in national population distribution, the attraction of cheaper labor in the southern United States and weaker unionization in the South.

Canadian manufacturing faced early disadvantages due to the presence of large U.S. manufacturers that dominated the continental market and American tariffs (taxes) on Canadian imports. To encourage the development of domestic manufacturing, Canada enacted the National Policy in 1876. The National Policy erected tariffs on imported goods from the United States. This meant that new Canadian manufacturing plants could start operating and survive in a protected environment, but cost Canadian consumers more. Creative U.S. industrialists skirted the Policy by opening branch plants in Canada. As a result, a close link developed between Canadian and American manufacturing that persists today. Tariffs on manufacturing goods have been gradually phased out by the Canadian government.

By the latter half of the twentieth century, the truck and automobile had led to a suburbanization of the commercial and residential sectors. Soon new and relocated manufacturing plants joined the move to the suburbs. The truck was replacing the barge and railroad as the main carrier of raw materials and finished products for a growing number of industries. Cramped quarters in congested downtown locations were often at a serious disadvantage to spacious, easily accessible suburban sites.

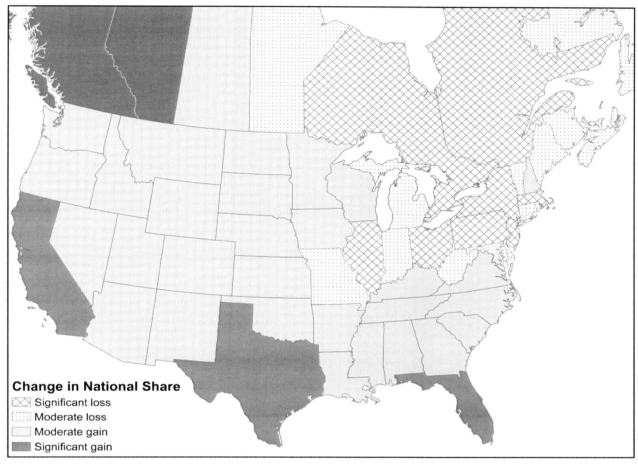

Source: U.S. Census Bureau, 1950 Census and American Community Survey, 2005-2007 estimate; Statistics Canada, 1951 Census and 2006 Census.

Figure 6.9 -- Change in Manufacturing Employment, by State or Province as a Percentage of National Share in the United States, 1950-2007, and Canada, 1951-2006.

While manufacturers avoid inner-city locations, suburban or metropolitan locations provide many of the benefits of cities—access to transportation and producer services, such as research and development activities, accountants, lawyers, and advertising firms.

Research and development were the hallmarks of industrial growth in the 1980s and early 1990s. Within the Manufacturing Belt, Route 128 around Boston is considered the leading research and development center. But the West and South have developed several such centers: Silicon Valley in California, the Research Triangle in North Carolina, central Texas, and the Huntsville, Alabama area (Figure 6.10).

Figure 6.10 -- Selected Research and Development Centers in the U.S.

Services

The most rapid increases in employment during the last two decades have been in the services sector. They are composed of the **tertiary** sector of transportation and public utilities; the **quaternary** sector, of wholesale and retail trade, finance, insurance and real estate; and the **quinary** sector of personal, professional, and business services. The continual relative decline in manufacturing jobs since 1960 by over half, or 21 percentage points, (from 31% to 10% of non-farm jobs) has been mirrored by the relative growth in non-governmental quinary services by 30 percentage points (from under 14% to 44%). (See Table 6.6.) During this period, tertiary employment dropped almost four points, while quaternary services dropped by more than four points. By 1982, employment in the non-governmental quinary services outnumbered jobs in manufacturing for the first time and, by 2000, was more than double the secondary sector. By 2008, quinary positions outnumbered manufacturing jobs by more than four to one.

Table 6.6. **Percent Distribution of Employees in Nonagricultural Establishments in U.S.: 1960-2008**

Type of Establishment	Percent of Employment					
	1960	1970	1980	1990	2000	2008
Mining	1.3	0.9	1.1	0.5	0.4	0.6
Construction	5.4	5.1	4.8	4.3	5.1	5.3
Manufacturing	31.0	27.3	22.4	15.9	14.0	10.0
Subtotal	37.7	33.3	28.4	20.8	19.5	15.9
Transportation/Utilities	7.4	6.4	5.7	5.2	5.3	3.7
Wholesale Trade	5.8	5.6	5.8	5.3	5.3	4.4
Retail Trade	15.2	15.6	16.6	17.9	17.7	11.2
Finance/Insur./Real Estate	4.9	5.1	5.7	6.0	5.8	5.9
Services	13.6	16.3	19.8	28.0	30.7	43.7
Government	15.4	17.7	18.0	16.8	15.7	16.4
Subtotal	**62.3**	**66.7**	**71.6**	**79.2**	**80.5**	**85.3**

Source: U.S. Census Bureau. *U. S. Statistical Abstract, 2010.*

In addition to the changes in job types and in regional employment patterns, shifts in metropolitan/nonmetropolitan shares will also continue to occur. Not only have residential and manufacturing patterns been undergoing suburbanization, but so too has employment in services. Office and hotel complexes are now following the residential areas, shopping centers, and the manufacturing plants to the suburbs. The rise of these so-called "urban villages," or **edge cities**, on peripheral beltways far out in the suburbs are anchored by hotel and office complexes and indicate a continued decentralization of American working patterns.

The services sector now accounts for 85 percent of the non-farm jobs in the United States (Figure 6.11). Services display primarily market-orientation because they are often made and consumed at the same location and require few, if any, raw materials. For example, a barber provides a haircut to the customer in the salon, food is prepared and consumed at a restaurant, surgery occurs in the hospital, and teaching takes place in the classroom. Services, then, are concentrated in cities and towns, where most of the customers live (about 79% of Americans and Canadians live in urban locations) or can easily access them (Figure 6.12).

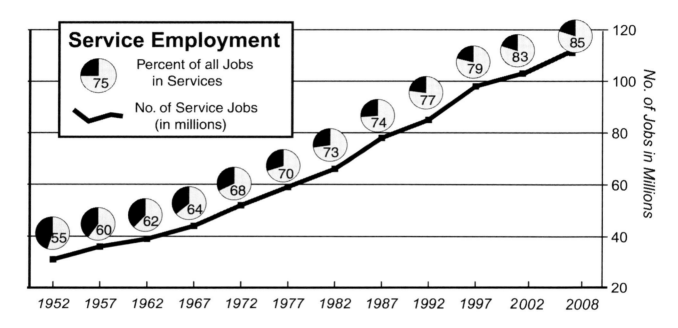

Figure 6.11 -- Growth of the Services Sector, 1952-2008.

Towns and cities can be thought of as "central places" where goods and services are made available to consumers. Thus, a map of services in the United States and Canada would resemble a map of cities. Larger cities offer more and a broader variety of goods and services, while smaller cities offer fewer and a smaller variety of goods and services. People who live in small towns might be frustrated that certain goods and services are not available nearby. While there might be a gas station, post office, church and grocery store in the vicinity, there might not be a movie theater or new car dealer. People there would assume correctly that new car dealerships and movie theaters cannot exist in a small town because there are not enough customers close enough in order for these businesses to operate profitably. They might have to drive past other small towns to a larger central place to see a movie or to buy a new car.

Each service or good for sale has its own range (the distance consumers will drive to get it) and threshold (minimum number of customers required to sell the good or service profitably). Range and threshold define the market area for each good (Figure 6.12). The map in Figure 6.13 shows the distribution of three goods or services that have different ranges and thresholds. Goods or services that require a large base of customers have larger market areas. For example, air travel is used infrequently by most people and tends to be expensive; thus airports require a large base of customers (large threshold). At the same time, passengers will often have to travel a long distance to get the flight they need (long range). Such goods or services are called higher order. Goods and services that are inexpensive and are purchased or used more frequently and by more people have shorter ranges, smaller thresholds (with many repeat customers) and smaller trade areas. These are lower order goods and services. Other goods and services, such as dry cleaning, fall somewhere in between. Bread and milk cost little but are needed on a weekly basis. Consumers are unwilling to travel long distances frequently to obtain these lower order items. Similarly driving a long distance to buy gasoline makes little sense. Gas stations or clusters of gas stations and stores that sell milk and bread, therefore, tend to be closely spaced on the landscape.

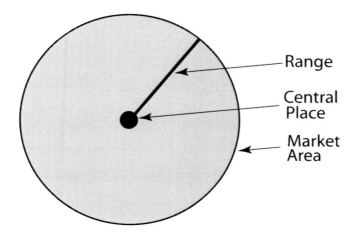

Figure 6.12 -- Relationship between Central Place, Range of Good or Service, and Trade (Market) Area

One can imagine a continuum of goods in a hierarchy from low to high order with each having its own range, threshold, price, and frequency of purchase. These factors create a geography of central places in their own hierarchy. Places offering only low order goods are spaced more closely together on the landscape, since numerous customers require proximity for the frequent purchase of these inexpensive items or services. Places offering higher order goods are spaced farther apart because these items and services are purchased less frequently, customers are willing to travel farther for the fewer number of transactions, thus resulting in the need for a larger customer base (larger trade area). In theory, a regular spacing of places emerges on the landscape. In practice, however, variations in population density, rivers and mountains, availability of roads, and other factors alter this optimal placement. Central places can be ranked from high order to low order according to the orders of goods and services that they provide. Small, low-order central places provide the basics, such as groceries, churches, elementary schools, and post offices. Mid-size central places additionally host such goods

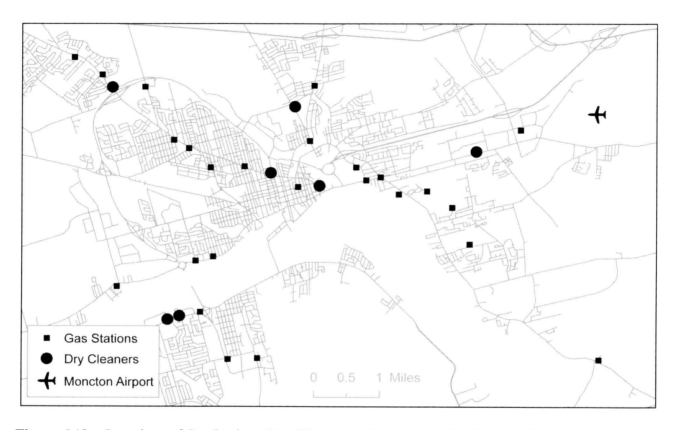

Figure 6.13 -- Locations of Gas Stations, Dry Cleaners and the Airport in Moncton, New Brunswick.

and services as television stations, newspapers, specialized medical services, and universities. Only the very largest cities offer professional sporting events, designer clothing stores, or Broadway productions in addition to all the goods and services offered by the mid-size and low-order central places.

ECONOMIC BASE

One of the many ways to understand the geography of local economies is the economic base model. The economic base model describes and measures development by dividing local activities into basic and non-basic sectors. Goods and services that are produced for markets outside the local region or are consumed by outsiders are called "basic" products. They are basic in the sense that they bring in money from outside to the local economy. For example, a regional cancer center would attract patients from a long distance and would produce revenue for a local community. An aircraft manufacturing plant ships planes all over the United States and world; local workers and managers share in the profits derived from sales outside the community. Goods and services that are consumed locally are termed "non-basic." They do not generate new money; rather, they circulate money generated by basic equivalent activities. When a person visits the family doctor or beautician, the money spent stays in the community. Note that geographic scale is a key consideration for basic and non-basic activities. Goods and services that are basic to a city may be non-basic for a region and goods and services that are basic to a region may be non-basic for the entire country. Products exported outside the United States and Canada would be basic for each country. Economic activities often fill both a basic and non-basic need. A farmer may sell produce at the local farmer's market, a non-basic activity, while at the same time selling bulk quantities to a food processing plant, a basic activity.

The economic base model assumes that basic industries are the engines of local economies and cause a "multiplier effect" in non-basic industries. The direct effect of basic industries is the wages and benefits paid to those directly employed by the basic industry. The multiplier effect measures further impact in the local economy on businesses that support the basic industry, such as parts suppliers, and on businesses, such as restaurants, that exist because of spending by the workers from the basic industry. Consider coal mining in West Virginia. Coal is used to generate electricity within the state, but is also sold outside the region, including overseas. The direct effects of coal mining are the jobs in the local economy (the miners who extract the coal) and the tax revenue generated for the state and local communities. The multiplier effects of coal mining include local companies that make and maintain mining equipment and places where miners spend their money. An Appalachian Regional Commission study estimated that the multiplier effect of coal mining in West Virginia was about 3.5 times the direct effect. That means that for every mining job, an additional 3.5 jobs were generated in the non-basic support industries.

One method to measure economic base is the use of location quotients. Location quotients compare the percentage of employees for an industry in a local area to the percentage in that industry in the entire country. The location quotient for a local area is calculated as follows:

$$LQ = \frac{\textit{Percent employed in an industry in a local area}}{\textit{Percent employed in an industry in the country}}$$

If the percentages are the same, the location quotient (LQ) equals 1.0. Such a result implies that the local area is producing about what is needed for local demand. If the percentage in a local area is higher than the percentage in the country, the LQ will be more than 1.0. This would indicate that the local economy is specialized in that economic activity and producing more than is needed for local demand. The excess production will be exported or consumed by those outside the local economy, making this a basic activity. For example, 4.9 percent of workers in Nebraska are employed in agriculture compared to 1.4 percent employed in agriculture in the United States, yielding a LQ of 3.5. Agriculture is a basic activity for Nebraska. If the LQ is less than 1.0, the local economy is probably not meeting demand and that product or service will need to be imported. For example, the LQ for health care and social assistance for Washington, DC is only 0.8. Thus, some residents of the city need to travel to the nearby states of Virginia and Maryland for their health care.

Changes in the American Economy

Between mid-1982 and late 1987 the value of the **stock market** nearly tripled, before dropping by nearly a third in one week in October, after which it fully recovered by late 1989. It then went on to add another 40 percent and set record-breaking highs above 11,700 in January 2000, before declining nearly 40 percent to below 7,300 in October 2002, then oscillating between that level and nearly 11,000 till early 2006, after which it rose to around 14,000 by late 2007. It then dropped to a monthly average in early 2009 of under 7100 (below the October 2002 level), after which it regained much of its loss reaching over 12,000 in early 2011. See Figure 6.14.

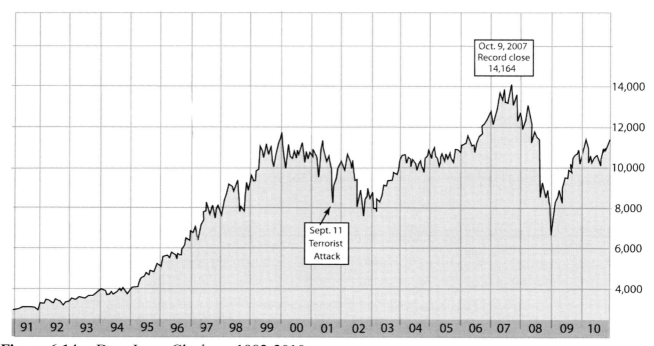

Figure 6.14 -- Dow Jones Closings, 1982-2010

Between 1981 and 1998, the **price of petroleum** fluctuated in a downward trend dropping by nearly two-thirds from $32 a barrel to $11.50, after which it rose to the 1980 level by 2004; it then surged upward to nearly $60 a barrel in April 2005 and over $90 a barrel by early 2008, an increase of about 1100 percent in four years. The price then plummeted to below $50 a barrel within two years (Figure 6.15). The **prime interest rate** was cut in half between 1981 and 1986, after which it fluctuated between six and 9.5 percent until 2002, then dipped again to below five percent, where it stayed until late 2004, after which it rose steadily to over 8 percent in mid-2006, but then dropped to 3.5 percent from mid-2009 to late 2010 (Figure 6.15).

Both the declines in the price of petroleum and in the prime interest rate acted as major factors slowing inflation and keeping it low. The annual rate of **inflation** for consumer goods fell from 10.3

percent in 1981 to under two percent in 1986, after which it fluctuated between 3.1 and 5.4 percent till 1992, when it stabilized at or below three percent. It then dropped to 1.6 percent in 1998 and oscillating between that level and 3.85 percent through 2008, before plummeting to a negative .34 percent for 2009 during the deepest recession since the Great Depression of the 1930s (Figure 6.16). Meanwhile, **unemployment**, which skyrocketed by more than two-thirds from 1979 to 1982, declined to its 1979 level by 1986 and still further by 1989, before rising again to reach 1984 levels by 1992. It then gradually dropped by nearly half to a 30-year low of four percent in 2000, before increasing again to six percent in 2003 and surging to ten percent in the last quarter of 2009 (Figure 6.16).

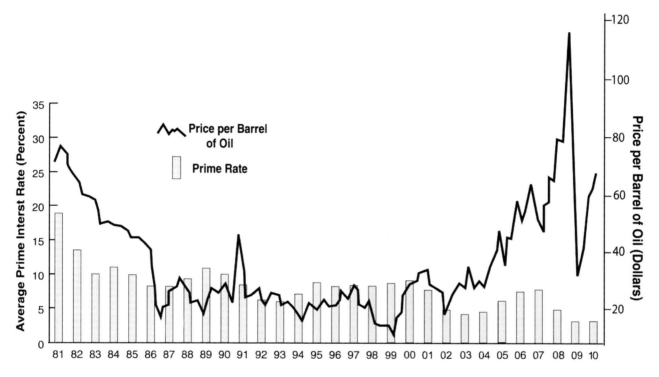

Figure 6.15 -- Petroleum Price and U.S. Prime Interest Rate, 1981-2010

Massive **job losses** in manufacturing in the 1980s were followed by less severe layoffs in the services industries during the latter 1980s and early 1990s. Part of the reason for the latter trend was the rash of corporate mergers. The number of manufacturing jobs bottomed out in 1993 and rose by a modest four percent by the late 1990s, after which it declined by about 20 percent by 2010. However, services-providing jobs have steadily increased since the early 1980s, have accounted for nine-tenths of all new jobs, and now represent over 80 percent of all non-farm employment. See Figure 6.11.

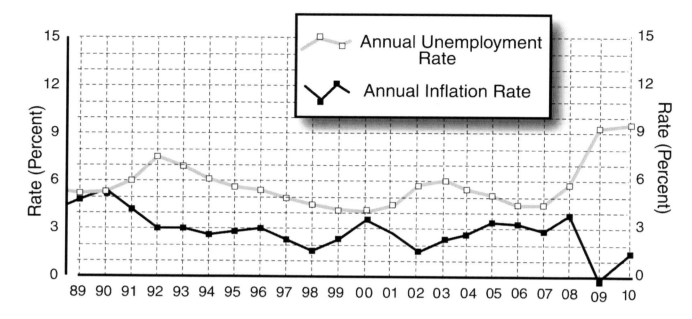

Figure 6.16 -- U.S. Annual Inflation Rate and Unemployment Rate, 1989-2010

As personally destructive as job losses were, they were not as ominous as the huge **budget deficits** which led the U.S. to unprecedented debtor status in the world. Before 1998, the last budget surplus had been in 1969, and the lowest budget deficit since 1974 and 1997 occurred in 1979. Between 1974 and 1986, the deficit rose about 600 percent. Although the deficit was reduced in 1987 to its lowest level in five years, it began to climb again and exceeded the 1986 high point after 1990, peaking in 1992. After three decades, budget surpluses finally occurred again from 1998 to 2001. However, a large tax cut for the highest income earners, plus the soaring costs of a prolonged war in Iraq, brought a surge in deficit spending. This resulted in a reversal from a $127 billion dollar surplus in 2001 to a deficit of $413 billion in 2004. Declines in annual deficits to $162 billion by 2007 were, unfortunately, only a lull before the catastrophic economic disaster which unfolded in December 2007 and lasted into 2010. These events brought the need for several federal programs to rescue banks and other businesses, plus provide stimulus money to save and create jobs in the economy. This, plus a new federal health plan, led to a 2010 deficit of three to four times the 2004 record (Figure 6.17).

By 1999, **the federal debt,** (the annual accumulation of annual budget deficits, plus interest) was six times the 1980 amount just two decades earlier (Figure 6.18). The yearly interest payment on the debt more than quadrupled, rising from nine percent to 15 percent of the federal budget, compared to under one percent for foreign assistance. About three-fourths of this debt is owed to U.S. individuals and institutions, but increasingly the deficit is being financed by China, Japan and Middle Eastern oil countries, who could at any moment withdraw their investments and cause economic calamity to the U.S. economy. Foreign governments now control 25 percent of U.S. debt, compared to just 13 percent 20 years ago. China, Japan and oil exporters to the U.S. now hold half of that foreign debt.

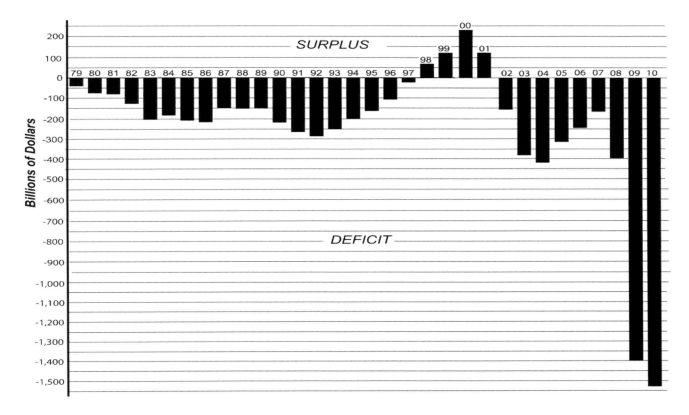

Figure 6.17 -- U.S. Budget Deficit, 1979-2010

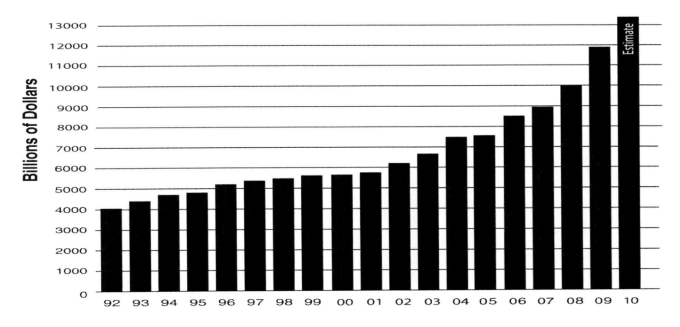

Figure 6.18 -- U.S. Federal Debt, 1992-2010

Exports from the United States last exceeded imports to it, giving it a positive **trade balance**, in 1975. Between 1977 and 1982, exports of goods exceeded imports by $24-$32 billion each year, but this imbalance then rose 400 percent in just four years, reaching $152-$153 billion by 1986 and 1987. It fell below $100 billion in 1991 and 1992 for the first time in nearly a decade as exports rose faster than imports. The deficit then increased to 1986 and 1987 levels by 1994 and went on to surpass these levels reaching $174 billion in 1995, then doubling to $336 billion in 1999. By 2004, the goods trade deficit had reached $666 billion, or four times what it had been just ten years earlier, a result of a surge in imports during prosperous times and a decline in exports. The deficit continued to rise till it reached $835 billion in 2008, but plunged to the lowest level since 2001 in 2009 ($507 billion) as the recession sharply curtailed the international trade of goods (Figure 6.19). Over half of the goods trade deficit in 2009 was tied to petroleum-related products. Another fourth of the goods trade deficit was tied to consumer goods, such as pharmaceuticals, electronics, clothing, furniture, and other household goods. Most of the rest of the deficit was related to cars, trucks and automotive parts. U.S. imports declined twice as much as its exports, but a 40 percent decline in the value of the Euro was not able to sustain its exports, which peaked in mid-2008. This is undoubtedly because as a result of the North American Free Trade Agreement (NAFTA) and other trade agreements; the major U.S. trading partners today are no longer primarily European countries, but rather Canada, Mexico, China and Japan. The U.S. now exports about a third of its goods to its neighbors to the north and south and another seventh to Japan, China and Great Britain. It gets about a third of its imports from Canada and China and another fifth from Mexico, Japan and Germany.

The surge in the trade deficit was largely accounted for both by the unprecedented job and income booms of the 1990s and the dropping of most tariff barriers, which resulted in much greater demand for imported goods. Between 1992 and 2008, imports of goods tripled while exports did not quite double. Although the addition of the exchange of the value of services is often touted as a great boon to U.S. international exchange (and in 2008, the export of services did exceed their import by $136 billion), during this period imports of services has risen by about 230 percent, while services exports have grown by only about 200 percent during this time. The economic recovery of 2010 was indicated by the surge of both U.S. exports and even more so imports. The negative trade balance of goods rose once again reaching $647 billion. A record surplus in services trade of $149 billion however, reduced the overall trade deficit to just under $500 billion. China accounted for over half of the U.S. trade deficit for 2010 because of its record exports to the U.S.

The large and often rising trade deficits were largely responsible for the changes in the international economic position of the United States from the world's largest creditor in 1982 to the world's greatest debtor by 1987, with a higher debt than the three largest debtor developing countries combined: Brazil, Mexico, and Argentina. By the mid-1980s, foreigners owned more of the United States than American citizens own of the rest of the world, and the situation has worsened since then. Between 1980 and 1993, there was a $950 billion shift from U.S. net assets to U.S. net liabilities. By the late 1990s, the United States had finally begun to get its debt under control, but the 2001-2009 period brought rising U.S. debt once again.

Japan has now replaced the U.S. as the world's greatest creditor. Ironically, the U.S. government has been using largely surplus foreign funds stemming from its negative trade balance to help finance the budget deficit. If it were not for the heavy influx of foreign capital and the falling oil prices of the 1980s, the budget deficit would have driven up interest rates and inflation would have been higher.

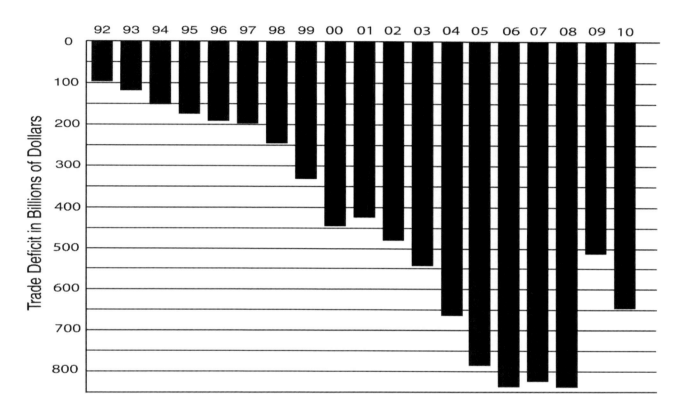

Figure 6.19 -- U.S. Net Goods Trade Balance, 1992-2010

ECONOMIC BASE REVIEW

1. What percent of the U.S. population and the Canadian population are employed in the primary sector? the secondary sector? and the services sector?

2. What factors have played a role in the great agricultural productivity of the U.S. and Canada?

3. What countries received most of U.S. agricultural exports in 2008?

4. How have each of the following changed since 1970: agricultural exports as a share of all U.S. exports? agricultural imports as a share of all U.S. imports? agricultural exports? agricultural imports? net agricultural trade? the kind of food imports?

5. Give the specific changes in each of the following: U.S. farm population, number of U.S. farms, average size of U.S. farms, percentage of U.S. farm population supplementing income from off-the-farm jobs, Canadian farm population, number of Canadian farms, average size of Canadian farms.

6. How has each of the following changed since 1970: the average value of U.S. farm land per acre? the value of farm assets?

7. During the late 20th century, how did each of the following change: bankruptcies? output per hour of livestock? output per hour for crops? use of fertilizer? use of pesticides? mechanization? irrigated acreage?

8. What is the degree of importance of each of the following: corporate farms? agribusiness? foreign ownership of farm land?

9. Since 1970, how have each of the following changed: U.S. corn and wheat production? U.S. share of world production of corn? wheat? soybeans? cotton? rice? vegetable oils? U.S. share of world exports of soybeans? cotton? corn? wheat?

10. What are the top five agricultural products by value in the U.S.?

11. Give the general areas of the U.S. that lead in the production of the following: corn, cattle, dairy, soybeans, hogs, broilers, winter wheat, spring wheat, cotton, turkeys, potatoes, rice.

12. Associate the following major agricultural regions of the U.S. and Canada with the major physiographic, climate and soil regions: corn/livestock/soybean belt, dairy belt, spring wheat belt, winter wheat belt, tobacco, cotton, livestock ranching.

13. What are the three leading Canadian provinces in agriculture? and their main products?

14. When did manufacturing employment peak and when did exports last exceed imports in the U.S.? How has manufacturing employment in Canada changed since 1951?

15. What factors have affected manufacturing employment in the U.S.?

16. How has the value of U.S. manufactured products changed since 1999?

17. What changes occurred in U.S. manufacturing employment in the 1970s? 1980s? 1990s? 2000s?

18. In the 1990s and 2000s, the major rates of decline were in which industries?

19. What role has the export market played in manufacturing in the last 20 years?

20. Since 1980, how has manufacturing employment changed in the U.S. compared to Canada and Japan?

21. What types of industries locate largely because of raw materials used? market for the product? skilled labor? cheap labor? major energy requirements?

22. What is the role of bulk-breaking points in industrial location?

23. What is the role of incentives in industrial location?

24. How has the regional location of industry changed in the U.S. and Canada since 1950?

25. How has the location of industry in metro areas shifted since 1980?

26. Since 1960, the greatest relative gain in employment was in what sector of the economy?

27. What percentage of non-farm jobs is now in the services-providing sector?

28. Discuss how the central place theory is related to the location of various services and goods.

29. Explain the use of the location quotient in measuring the economic base of an area. Distinguish between basic and non-basic goods.

30. How has the U.S. changed in its creditor/debtor status?

31. How has the U.S. budget deficit changed since 1980?

32. How has the U.S. goods trade balance changed since 1980?

33. How has foreign ownership of the U.S. changed compared to U.S. ownership in other countries since 1979?

ECONOMIC BASE EXERCISE
MAPPING LOCATION QUOTIENTS

Part I—Calculating Location Quotients for Canada

Mapping location quotients by states, provinces and territories permits geographic analysis of economic specialization and economic base in the United States and Canada. To determine a location quotient for a province/territory in Canada, divide the percentage for an industry in a province/territory by the percentage for that industry in Canada. For example, divide percent employed in Health Care and Social Assistance in Manitoba, 12.7%, by percent employed in Health Care and Social Assistance in Canada, 10.4%, to obtain the ratio 1.2. The result is the location quotient, a ratio comparing the province/territory to the entire country. LQs greater than 1.0 indicate that the province or territory specializes in the industry, that the industry is a basic activity for that province/territory.

Using the percentages in Table 6, calculate the LQs for the selected industries listed for Canada's provinces and territories. Record your results in Table 6.8. Round to one decimal place. LQs for the selected industries for the U.S. states have already been calculated in Table 6.9.

Table 6.7. Percent Employed in Selected Economic Activities in Canada and its Provinces and Territories. Totals do not equal 100%.

Political Area	Agriculture, Forestry Fishing & Hunting	Mining and Oil & Gas Extraction	Manufacturing	Information and Cultural Industries	Professional, Scientific & Technical Services	Health Care and Social Assistance	Accommodation & Food Services
Canada	3.0%	1.4%	11.8%	2.5%	6.7%	10.4%	6.5%
Nunavut	0.6%	1.1%	1.2%	2.0%	2.2%	9.4%	4.1%
Yukon Territory	0.9%	1.8%	1.9%	3.1%	4.6%	9.5%	7.7%
Northwest Terr.	0.8%	2.5%	1.9%	2.8%	4.2%	9.4%	6.9%
Prince Edward Is.	11.5%	2.0%	9.5%	1.7%	4.1%	10.2%	7.6%
Newfoundland and Labrador	4.9%	1.3%	8.2%	2.1%	3.8%	14.1%	6.1%
New Brunswick	4.1%	1.1%	8.3%	1.9%	4.1%	12.0%	6.6%
Nova Scotia	4.2%	1.0%	8.4%	2.3%	4.2%	12.2%	6.5%
Saskatchewan	7.1%	1.3%	7.6%	2.3%	4.4%	11.5%	6.4%
Manitoba	10.2%	2.7%	10.4%	2.1%	4.3%	12.7%	6.4%
Alberta	3.6%	0.9%	7.2%	1.9%	7.6%	9.2%	6.5%
British Columbia	3.6%	0.9%	8.6%	2.7%	7.5%	9.9%	8.1%
Quebec	2.3%	0.6%	14.5%	2.5%	6.4%	11.6%	6.1%
Ontario	1.8%	2.1%	13.9%	2.7%	7.3%	9.6%	6.2%

Source: Statistics Canada, 2006 Census

Table 6.8 Location Quotients for Canadian Provinces and Territories

Political Area	Agriculture, Forestry Fishing & Hunting	Mining and Oil & Gas Extraction	Manufacturing	Information and Cultural Industries	Professional, Scientific & Technical Services	Health Care and Social Assistance	Accomodation & Food Services
Nunavut							
Yukon Territory							
Northwest Terr.							
Prince Edward Is.							
Newfoundland and Labrador							
New Brunswick							
Nova Scotia							
Saskatchewan							
Manitoba							
Alberta							
British Columbia							
Quebec							
Ontario							

Source: Statistics Canada, 2006 Census

Table 6.9 Location Quotients for U.S. States and Washington D.C

Political Area	Agriculture, Forestry Fishing & Hunting	Mining and Oil & Gas Extraction	Manufacturing	Information and Cultural Industries	Professional, Scientific & Technical Services	Health Care and Social Assistance	Accomadation & Food Services
Alabama	1.0	1.3	1.3	0.8	0.8	1.0	0.9
Alaska	1.4	6.3	0.3	0.9	0.8	1.0	1.0
Arizona	0.6	1.0	0.7	0.8	0.9	0.9	1.1
Arkansas	2.1	1.0	1.4	0.8	0.5	1.2	0.9
California	1.3	0.3	0.9	1.2	1.2	0.8	1.0
Colorado	1.0	1.8	0.6	1.4	1.3	0.9	1.1
Connecticutt	0.2	0.3	1.1	1.1	1.1	1.4	0.8
Delaware	0.8	0.0	0.9	0.7	0.9	0.9	0.9
Florida	0.6	0.3	0.5	1.0	1.0	1.2	1.2
Georgia	0.8	0.3	1.0	1.1	1.0	0.9	1.0
Hawaii	1.1	0.0	0.3	0.8	0.8	1.0	1.9
Idaho	3.6	1.0	0.9	0.8	0.9	1.1	1.0
Illinois	0.6	0.5	1.2	1.0	1.0	1.1	1.0
Indiana	0.8	0.5	1.8	0.8	0.6	1.0	1.0
Iowa	2.8	0.3	1.4	0.9	0.6	1.1	0.8
Kansas	2.1	1.8	1.2	1.2	0.8	0.9	0.9
Kentucky	1.4	3.0	1.3	0.8	0.6	1.0	0.9
Louisiana	0.9	7.5	0.8	0.7	0.8	1.0	1.1
Maine	1.7	0.3	0.9	0.8	0.8	0.8	1.0
Maryland	0.4	0.3	0.5	1.1	1.7	0.8	0.9
Mass.	0.3	0.0	0.9	1.2	1.4	1.2	0.9
Michigan	0.7	0.5	1.7	0.8	0.8	0.9	1.0
Minnesota	1.5	0.5	1.3	0.9	0.9	1.1	0.9
Mississippi	1.4	2.3	1.3	0.7	0.6	0.9	0.9
Missouri	1.1	0.5	1.1	1.0	0.8	1.0	1.0
Montana	4.2	3.8	0.4	0.8	0.8	1.0	1.2
Nebraska	3.5	0.3	1.0	0.8	0.7	1.0	0.9
Nevada	0.4	2.3	0.4	0.7	0.8	0.6	2.2
New Hamp.	0.5	0.3	1.2	1.0	1.0	1.6	0.9
New Jersey	0.2	0.0	0.8	1.3	1.3	1.0	0.8
New Mexico	1.3	5.3	0.5	0.8	1.2	1.0	1.2
New York	0.4	0.3	0.7	1.4	1.1	1.3	0.9
N. Carolina	1.0	0.3	1.2	0.8	0.8	0.9	1.0
North Dakota	4.9	4.3	0.7	0.8	0.6	1.2	0.9
Ohio	0.6	0.5	1.5	0.8	0.8	0.9	1.0
Oklahoma	1.4	6.0	0.9	1.0	0.7	0.9	1.0
Oregon	2.4	0.3	1.1	0.8	0.9	0.9	1.0
Pennsylvania	0.6	0.8	1.2	0.8	0.9	1.3	0.9
Rhode Island	0.3	0.0	1.1	0.8	0.9	1.0	1.1
S. Carolina	0.6	0.3	1.3	0.7	0.7	0.8	1.1
Tennessee	0.7	0.3	1.3	0.8	0.7	0.9	1.0
Texas	0.8	4.0	0.9	0.9	1.0	0.8	1.0
Utah	0.6	2.3	1.0	1.0	1.0	0.9	1.0
Vermont	1.6	0.5	1.0	0.9	0.9	1.4	1.1
Virginia	0.6	0.8	0.7	1.1	1.6	0.9	0.9
Washington	1.7	0.3	1.0	1.2	1.1	1.1	0.9
W. Virginia	0.8	8.8	0.8	0.7	0.6	1.3	1.0
Wisconsin	1.7	0.3	1.7	0.8	0.7	0.9	0.9
Wyoming	2.6	18.8	0.4	0.6	0.6	0.9	1.2
Wash. D.C.	0.2	0.0	0.1	2.0	2.7	0.8	1.0

Source: U.S. Census Bureau. 2005-2007 American Community Survey, 3-Year Estimates of Employment.

Part 2—Mapping the LQs

Using colored pencils, the LQs and the blank maps below, map the LQs for the selected economic activities following the example in Figure 6.20. Because a value greater than 1.0 indicates a basic activity, two categories (above and below 1.0) work well for the maps. Use two colors, one color for values below the break point and another for the values above it. Create a legend to explain your categories and colors.

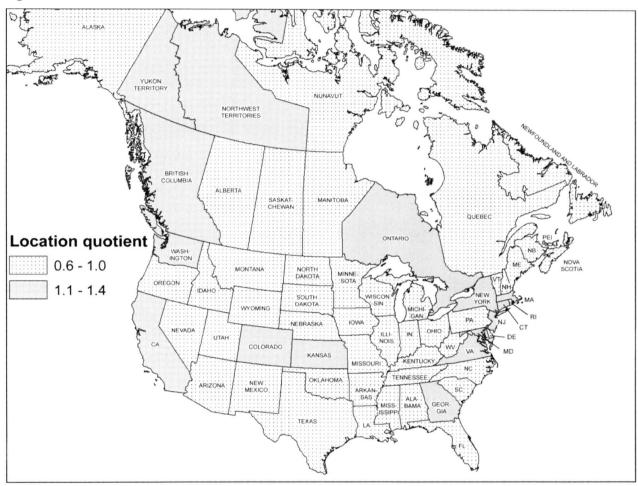

Figure 6.20 -- Location Quotients by State, Province, Territory and Washington DC for Information and Cultural Industries.

Part 3—Interpreting the Maps

1. Begin by describing and defining location quotients.

2. Visit the website http://www.census.gov/cgi-bin/sssd/naics/naicsrch?chart=2007 to get an idea of what occupations are included for each of the economic sectors in Tables 6.7-6.9.

3. Choose one of the maps that you created and describe the mapped information. Use geographic terms, such as north, southern region, or eastern states, instead of terms like above, below, left, or right. Which regions, states, provinces, or territories have the lowest LQs? Name them and their values. Can you detect regions or agglomeration of economic activities?

4. Next, choose one state, province or territory to investigate in more detail. Look at all the maps of economic activities for the state or province/territory you chose. Are they part of regions with high or low LQs for certain economic activities? Use the internet or other sources to see if you can find out why this area has high LQs in some economic activities and why it has low LQs in some industries. Perhaps, some large companies employ large numbers of workers in a particular industry. Perhaps physical geography renders some economic activities non-viable. Perhaps historical reasons play a role. Be sure to cite the sources for your information.

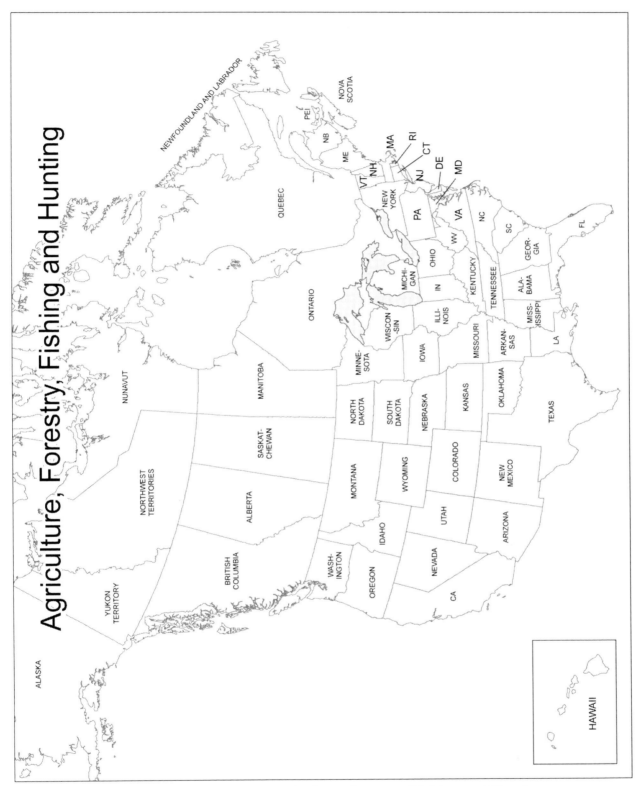

Figure 6.21 -- Location Quotients for Agriculture, Forestry, Fishing and Hunting.

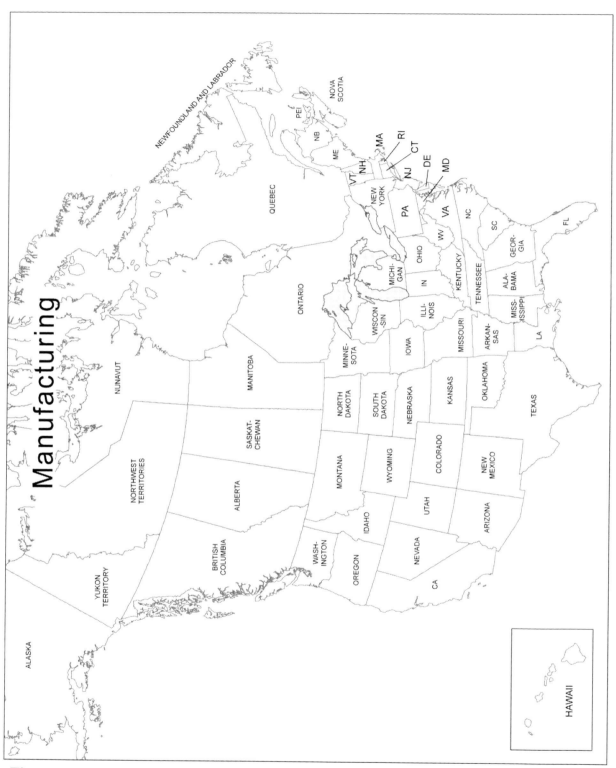

Figure 6.22 -- Location Quotients for Manufacturing.

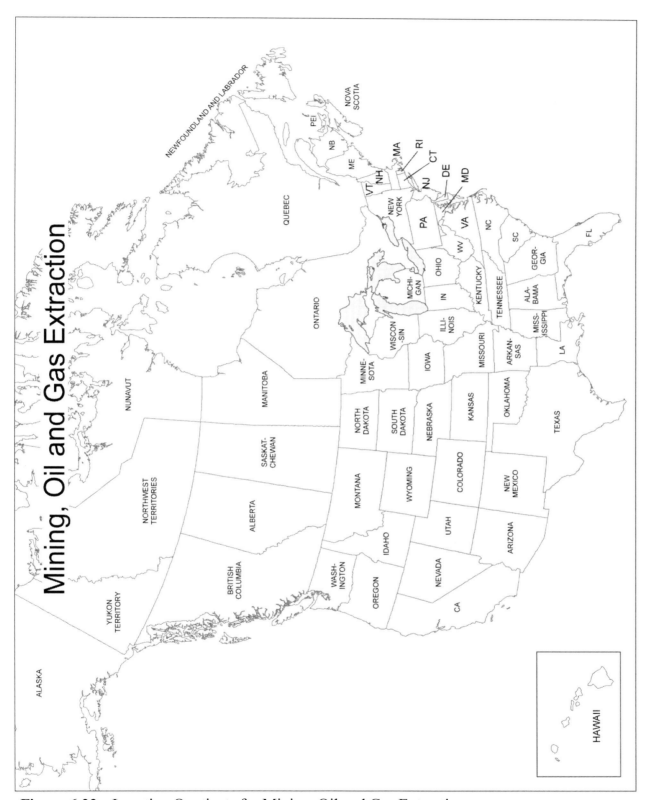

Figure 6.23-- Location Quotients for Mining, Oil and Gas Extraction.

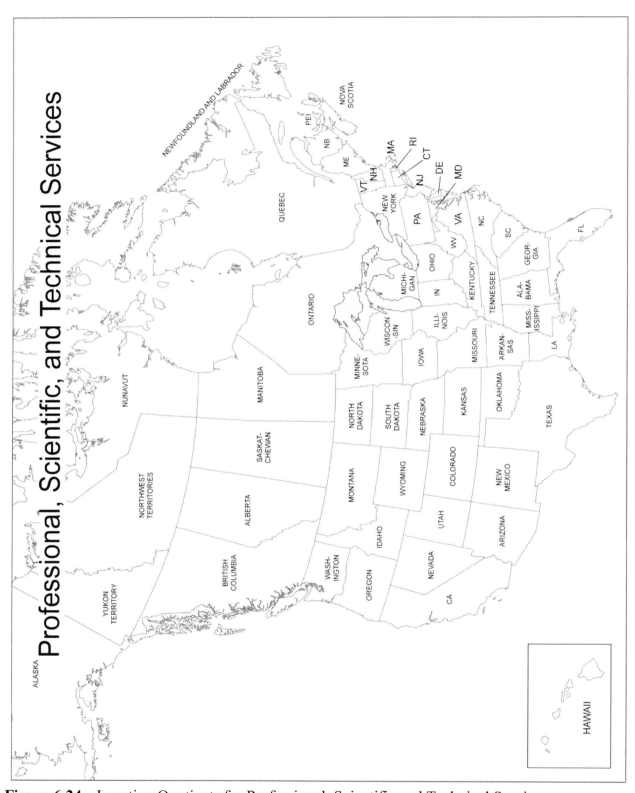

Figure 6.24-- Location Quotients for Professional, Scientific and Technical Services.

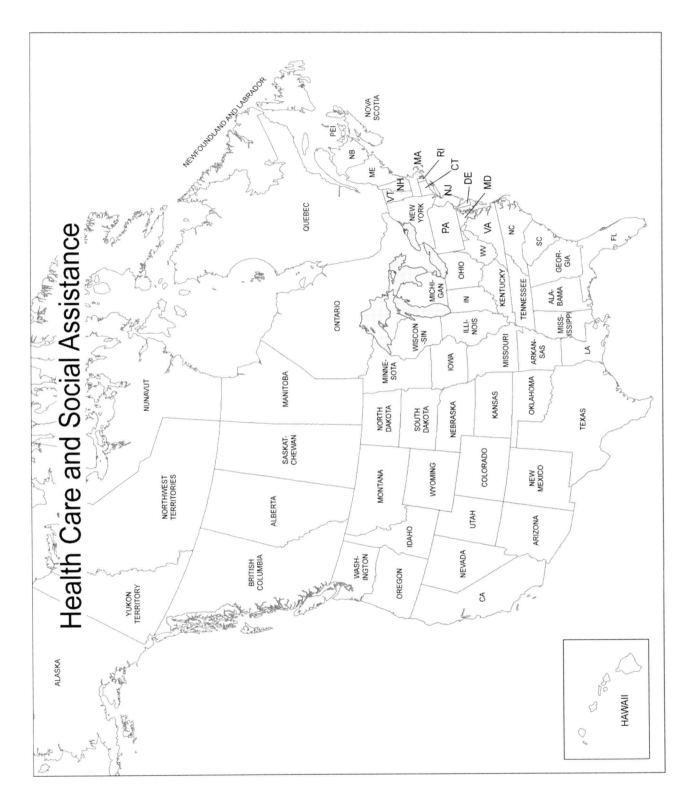

Figure 6.25 -- Location quotients for Health Care and Social Assistance.

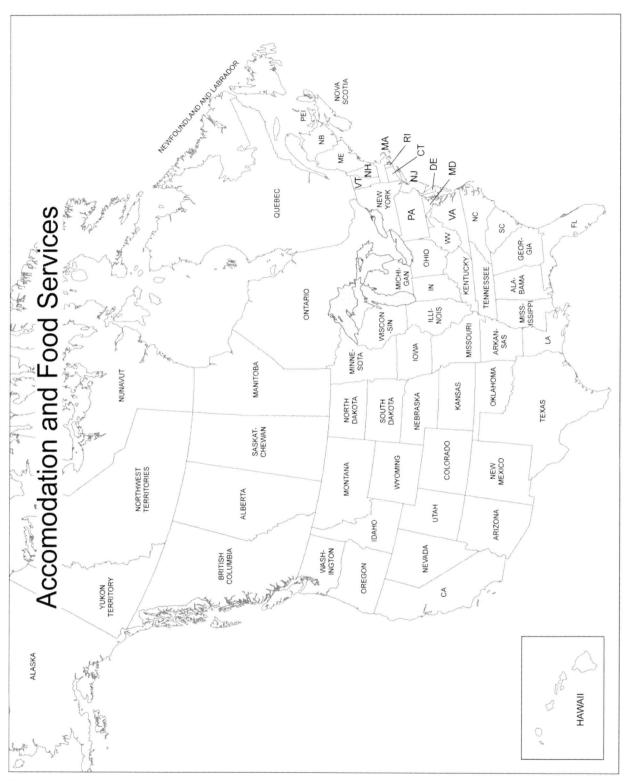

Figure 6.26 -- Location Quotients for Accommodation and Food Services.

GLOSSARY

absolute (specific) location – the exact location, usually given by coordinates of latitude and longitude, of a place.

aquifer – a subsurface layer of porous, permeable earth material through which ground water can move by the force of gravity and which is often associated with artesian wells in dry areas.

age-sex pyramid – a mirrored horizontal bar graph of five-year age groups with the males on the left and the females on the right with the youngest ages usually at the base.

agribusiness – the vertical integration of all business aspects related to farming, including producing fertilizer and other inputs, growing the farm products, and transporting and marketing the products.

air mass – a large body of air with similar temperature and humidity throughout.

air pollutant – a material introduced into the atmosphere which has a negative impact on life forms which depend on that air.

Alfisols – leached, humid soils of clay accumulations of iron and aluminum oxides formed under coniferous and deciduous forests in a variety of climates.

Appalachia – that region containing the Appalachian Mountains.

Aridisols – soils which developed under arid or semiarid conditions and are characterized by calcium and salt accumulations.

asthenosphere – the partially molten lower part of the upper mantle beneath the lithosphere on which "float" the solid plates and from where the magma rises to form the crust.

birth rate – the number of births in a year divided by the mid-year population.

bison – American buffalo.

bog soil – soils developed under locally poor drainage that have considerable accumulations of organic material.

caldera – a large depression usually caused by the collapse of a volcanic peak. Often the result of an eruption where large quantities of material are expelled from below creating a subterranean void into which the overlying volcano collapses.

calm – the lack of horizontal movement of air, but with a possible vertical movement of the air.

caribou – American reindeer.

cartogram – a map in which some thematic mapping variable – such as population or Gross National Product – is substituted for land area or distance. The geometry or space of the map is distorted in order to convey the information of this alternate variable.

cartography – the discipline dealing with the conception, production, dissemination and study of maps.

cavern – an opening underground formed by water percolating down to the ground water where it dissolved large amounts of weak limestone.

Chlorofluorocarbons (CFCs) – organic compounds that contain carbon, chlorine, and fluorine, produced as a volatile derivative of methane and ethane. They are emitted from a variety of synthetic chemicals and are believed to be leading to the depletion of the ozone layer in the stratosphere.

climatic region – an area of similar temperature and precipitation levels and/or regimes.

coniferous – cone-bearing, needleleaf evergreens, including pine, spruce and fir trees.

continental shelf – the gently sloping extension of the coastal margin that is submerged beneath the ocean (usually less than 600 feet, or 100 fathoms, deep).

convectional precipitation – precipitation caused by rising air currents usually associated with super heating of the earth's surface and frequently involving a thunderstorm.

convergence – the coming together of two lithospheric plates.

Counter urbanization – the 1970s trend in the U.S. when nonmetropolitan areas grew faster than metropolitan areas.

cultural poverty – that way of living generally associated with persons who have been in economic poverty for a long time.

cyclonic (frontal) precipitation – precipitation caused by the approach of a front so that the warmer, moist air rises over the cooler air causing condensation and the formation of a low pressure center of counterclockwise circulation.

death (mortality) rate – the number of deaths in a year divided by the mid-year population.

deciduous – trees that lose their leaves at the beginning of the cold or dry season.

delta – a fan-shaped deposit of alluvial sediment where a stream slows down as it enters a large body of water, such as a lake or sea.

Desert Climate – a region which usually has both an average of less than ten inches (25.4 cm) of precipitation annually and where evaporation exceeds precipitation; supports little vegetation;

differential erosion – erosion of softer rock material faster than harder rock.

divergence – the separating, or moving apart, of two lithospheric plates leading to the development of a mid-oceanic ridge or a rift valley.

Doppler radar – an advanced radar that can detect the development of a mesocyclone.

drift – any glacial deposit.

Dry Subtropical Climate – (See Mediterranean Climate.)

earthquake – the shaking of the ground caused by seismic waves from the sudden release of stored energy in rock within the earth.

economic poverty – the studied, though arbitrary, income level designated by the government as necessary for a person or family in order to have those necessities considered basic for a minimum standard of living in the U.S.

edge cities – See urban villages.

El Nino – warm water which periodically (every 3 to 10 years) spreads from the coast of Ecuador south to coastal Peru replacing colder upwelling water and which is thought by many meteorologists to account for abnormal weather conditions over North America and other parts of the world.

emigration – people leaving a country to go to another one.

end moraine – see terminal moraine.

Entisols – the youngest of all soils which are just beginning to develop and thus do not have layers; located mainly in relation to sand and volcanic ash deposits and bare rock.

epicenter – the point on the surface of the earth directly over the focus.

erratic – a large rock or bolder deposited by a glacier.

escarpment (scarp) – a cliff.

estuary – a drowned river valley that forms an embayment from the ocean.

extrusive – igneous material which solidifies and crystallizes above the surface of the earth.

eye – an area 10 to 15 miles (16-24 km) in diameter of calm rising warm, moist air at the center of a hurricane.

fault – a fracture and slippage of rock.

faulting – the sharp breaking and slippage of one mass of rock relative to the adjacent rock.

fiord – a submerged steep-sided deeply embayed glaciated valley along a coast.

focus – the point within the earth from where the energy and seismic waves of an earthquake are released.

folding – the bending of horizontal rock strata into folds as a result of great horizontal pressure beneath the surface.

footloose industries – industries which can locate anywhere and often produce a high value, low bulk product so that transportation costs are not of major importance in determining the location of the plant.

foreshock – an earthquake of lesser magnitude that precedes the main earthquake.

formal region – an area which has one or more characteristics being similar within and different from surrounding territories.

front – the leading edge of a mass of air different in temperature and moisture from the one being invaded, usually referred to as a warm front where warmer air is moving into an area of cooler air or a cold front where cooler air is moving into an area of warmer air.

functional region – an area unified by the spatial interaction (or flow) of one or more human activities, usually between a node and its surrounding hinterland.

geography – the study of the distribution of physical and cultural phenomena on the earth and of the spatial interrelationships among them so as to give a unique character to particular places; one of several possible definitions.

geosyncline – a broad downwarp of the surface or rock layers over a large region.

ghetto – a section of a city in which a certain racial, ethnic, or religious group is segregated either voluntarily or involuntarily.

glacier – a great mass of ice formed by the accumulation, compaction and recrystallization of snow and which moves across land because of the great pressure of its own weight.

Gondwanaland – the southern part of the supercontinent Pangea, including what is today Africa, South America, India, Australia, and Antarctica.

greenhouse effect – warming that results when solar radiation is trapped by the atmosphere; caused by atmospheric gases that allow sunshine to pass through but absorb heat that is radiated back from the warmed surface of the earth. Typically it refers to an increase in the warming of the lower atmosphere by the increased absorption of long wave energy radiated from the earth's surface by greater levels of CO_2 and other gases emitted by man.

groin – a concrete or wooden wall constructed at a right angle to the shore to catch drifting sand and thus maintain the beach.

ground moraine – a non-stratified or partially stratified layer of boulders, gravel, and sand deposited by a glacier where glacial melting exceeded forward movement of the ice.

hail – nearly round pieces of ice or clumps of spherical pieces with concentric layers formed by successive uplifts and freezing of water droplets around previously frozen ice. Formed in thunderstorms the hail "stones" are suspended aloft by air with strong upward motion until its weight overcomes the updraft and falls to the ground.

Hartshorne, Richard (1899-1992) – one of the most famous American geographers of the mid-20th century, in large part because of his book, *The Nature of Geography* (1939), which revived geography as an important discipline.

hectare(ha) – about 2.47 acres.

Highland (Mountain) Climate – a mountainous region of great variety of temperature and precipitation combinations depending on the elevation and whether on the windward or leeward side.

hinterland – the surrounding area which supports the core.

Hispanic – a person who claims Spanish as his main language, whether he is white, black, or of some other race.

Histosols – organic, or bog, soils with accumulations of organic material; located primarily in poorly drained lowlands of Canada and the western British Isles.

householder (previously head of household) – the person identified by the household as being the major wage earner/decision maker.

hurricane (cyclone, typhoon) – a large tropical storm with winds of 75-200 miles per hour (120-320 km/hr) and an average radius of 200 miles.

Humid Continental, Cool (Short) Summer Climate – a region of short, cool, wet summers (hottest month average below 71.6°F, or 22°C) and long, cold, snowy winters (coldest month average below 32°F, or 0°C); located in the interior and on the east coast of continents in the middle latitudes in the Northern Hemisphere only.

Humid Continental, Warm (Long) Summer Climate – a region of moderately, long, warm summers (hottest month average above 71.6°F, or 22°C) and long, cold, snowy winters (coldest month average below 32°F, or 0°C) with year-round precipitation; mainly located in the interior, but often extending to the east coasts, of continents in the middle latitudes of the Northern Hemisphere only.

Humid Subtropical Climate – a region of hot summers and mild winters (coldest month average above 32°F, or 0°C), year-round precipitation (convectional mainly in summer and cyclonic in winter); mainly located on the east coast of continents in the lower-middle latitudes

humus – decomposed organic matter found in the top layers of soil.

igneous – rock formed by the crystallization of molten earth material as it cools either below or above the surface.

immigrant – one who enters a country from another country.

impervious (impermeable) – material through which water will not move.

Inceptisols – slightly developed, young soils found largely in tundra, alluvial, and glaciated areas.

inertia cost of location – the cost of the investment in the present plant which would have to be lost when moving to a new location.

infant mortality rate – number of infant deaths per 1000 live births in a year.

internal migration – movement of people from one part of a country to another part of that same country.

international migration – movement of people from one country to another within the same continent.

intrusive – igneous material which solidifies and crystallizes beneath the surface of the earth.

inversion – an atmospheric condition which can result from one of several causes where the temperature near the surface becomes cooler than the layer of air above it causing air to be stable.

isohyte – a line connecting places of the same amount of precipitation.

isotherm – a line connecting places of the same temperature.

jet stream – a high-speed (75-200 or more miles per hour; 120-320 km/hr) wind in or near the tropopause, which moves generally west to east in the middle latitudes.

karst – topographic features formed by groundwater dissolving weak limestone material and including sinkholes, caverns, stalactites, and stalagmites.

lacustrine – glacial sediments deposited at the bottom of former glacial lakes.

lateral moraine – earth material and other debris that has fallen on the sides of the glacier from the valley walls <u>and</u> the hilly deposit of this debris left along side the valley wall when the glacier melted.

latitude – the angular distance from the equator.

Laurasia – the northern part of the supercontinent of Pangea, including what is today North America and Eurasia.

lava flow – an extrusive igneous feature formed by magma flowing onto the surface of the earth through fractures (cracks) in the rock.

leaching – the removal of minerals and organic material from the top layer of the soil by water moving downward through it.

leeward – the side of a mountain or landmass away from the direction from which the wind is blowing.

lithosphere – the solid outer portion of the earth, including the upper part of the upper mantle, as well as the crust.

loess – wind-borne deposits of fine material (silt) from dry areas.

long lots – French rural settlement pattern along the St. Lawrence and lower Mississippi Rivers in which property was elongated inland from the river.

longitude – the angular distance from the Prime Meridian.

magnitude – a measure of the amount of energy released in an earthquake.

maize – a grain native to the Western Hemisphere, popularly called corn in the U.S.

Marine West Coast Climate – a region of cool, wet summers and mild, wet winters; located on the west coasts of climates in the upper-middle latitudes.

maritime polar air masses – air masses which originate over oceans in upper latitudes and which are characterized by moist, cool conditions.

maritime tropical air masses – air masses which originate over oceans in lower latitudes and which are characterized by moist, warm conditions.

Mediterranean (Dry Subtropical) Climate – a region of hot, dry summers and mild, wet winters; usually located on the west coasts of continents in lower-middle latitudes.

meridian – a line around the earth from the North to the South Pole.

mesocyclone – an intense rotating wind near the bottom of a thunderstorm that indicates a developing tornado.

migration – the movement of a person across a county, state, or national boundary in order to change his residence.

Mollisols – dark soils which most often developed under prairie and tall steppe grasses, but occasionally under deciduous trees, with considerable activity by earthworms.

monadnock – a mountainous remnant of hard, resistant rock overlooking a peneplain.

mortality rate – (See death rate.)

natural hazard – unpredictable extreme fluctuations in atmospheric, geologic, hydrologic, or biological systems which put humans and their property in danger.

natural increase – the number of births minus the number of deaths in a year.

natural increase rate – the birth rate minus the death rate (divide by 10 to express it as a percent).

natural levee – an embankment paralleling a winding, wide river valley and which results from sediment being deposited when the river overflows its banks in flood stage.

nodal region – a functional region with one or more foci of flows of human activities.

nonrenewable resources – a natural resource that once used cannot be renewed or restored within a reasonable historic time period, and, thus, is considered to be of a limited amount.

orographic precipitation – precipitation which results from the cooling and condensation of warm, moist air rising up the slope of a hill or mountain.

Pangea III – the theoretical supercontinent that began to break apart over 200 million years ago.

per capita gross national product (GNP) – average production of all goods and services per individual.

permafrost – permanently frozen subsoil overlaid by an active layer that freezes and thaws seasonally; located in the Subarctic and Tundra Climates.

physiography – the study of the land formations on earth.

plate tectonics – the theory that the crust of the earth is composed of separate divisions, or "plates," which have been continually shifting, thus creating earthquakes, volcanoes, and mountains and moving the continents to various locations throughout geologic history.

pollutant – see air pollutant.

portage – the carrying of boats and goods over a low divide between two bodies of water.

poverty – See economic poverty and cultural poverty.

Prevailing Westerlies – winds of the middle latitudes which blow most of the year from a generally westerly direction.

primary sector – farming, fishing, forestry, and mining.

primary (p) wave – the fastest, and thus first to arrive, of the seismic waves travelling by compression and expansion from an earthquake's focus.

Prime Meridian – the meridian arbitrarily designated as being 0° of longitude.

pueblo – flat-roofed, adobe or stone houses, often multi-storied, found in the American southwest.

"pull" forces – factors at a migrant's potential destination which encourage him to move to that location.

"push" forces – factors at a migrant's origin which encourage him to move from that place.

quaternary sector – wholesale and retail trade, finance, insurance and real estate.

quinary sector – personal, professional, and business services.

rain shadow – a dry area on the leeward side of a mountain.

relative location – the location of a place with reference to its access to other places.

remote sensing – The gathering and recording of information about the earth's surface by methods which do not involve actual contact with the surface under consideration. Remote sensing techniques include photography, infra-red imagery, and radar from aircraft, satellites, and spacecraft.

renewable resource – a natural resource that can be used then renewed or restored within a relatively short period of time.

replacement level fertility – the average number of births women would need to have in order for the population to cease to grow in the long run. (It might have to remain at this level for 50 to 100 or more years before population actually stopped growing.)

Richter scale – the scale used to measure the amount of energy released during an earthquake.

rural – territory not considered urban.

Savanna Climate – a hot tropical region (average temperature each month above 64°F, or 18°C) with distinct wet and dry seasons and containing tall grasslands interspersed with short trees, especially along streams.

sea arch – an arch formed by two sea caves joining on opposite sides of a protruding steep coastline.

sea cave – a cavern formed by the sea hollowing out the base of a steep coastline.

sea wall – usually a concrete wall built at the dune line of the beach to prevent further horizontal encroachment of the sea.

secondary sector – manufacturing.

secondary (S) wave – the slower, and thus later arriving, of the seismic waves traveling at right angles (sideways) from the earthquake's focus.

sedimentary – rock formed from weathered pre-existing rock that has been transported, deposited, and lithified.

Seismic waves – waves of energy associated with an earthquake and resulting from faulting.

shield – a region of exposed Precambrian igneous and metamorphic rock, the oldest of all rock.

sink (sinkhole) – a depression in the surface caused by water dissolving weak limestone material. These often are depressions which collapse suddenly as the roofs of caverns below give way under the weight of the land above.

site – the location of the place in regard to its physical characteristics.

situation – the location of a place with reference to its surrounding hinterland.

specific location – see absolute location.

Spodosols – leached and weathered soils of coniferous forests in humid, less severe portions of the Subarctic Climate and adjacent parts of the Humid Continental, Cool Summer Climate, plus the Florida peninsula.

Steppe Climate – a region with usually 10 to 20 inches (25.4 - 50.8 cm) of precipitation; short grasslands.

storm surge – a wall of water which can reach 20 to 30 feet (6-9 m) above mean sea level accompanying the arrival of a hurricane and being the cause of most deaths from such a storm.

Subarctic Climate – a region of moist, short, cool summers (average temperature one to four months above $50°F$, or $10°C$), very long, severe winters and extreme annual ranges in temperature; coniferous trees; located in the upper-middle latitudes of continents in the Northern Hemisphere only.

subduction – the dipping along a zone of converging plates of one oceanic plate beneath another plate and into the molten mantle below.

surface wave – a seismic wave that travels along the surface of the earth and causes most of the damage to buildings.

taiga – coniferous (needleleaf evergreen) forest of Russia.

temperature inversion – see inversion.

terminal moraine – a nonstratified, hilly glacial deposit marking the farthest extent of a continental or a valley glacier and where glacial melting along the edge equalled the forward movement of the ice.

tertiary sector – transportation and public utilities.

threshold of poverty – the amount of income below which people are defined as living in poverty.

tornado – a short-lived, small, but extremely powerful, mid-latitude storm primarily associated with an advancing cold front in the spring.

tornado warning – an emergency bulletin that a funnel cloud has been sighted or that the development of a mesocyclone has been detected on Doppler radar.

tornado watch – a National Weather Service bulletin issued to alert people within an area of one or more counties of conditions being favorable for the development of tornadoes.

total fertility rate – the average number of children that women would have if the fertility rates for all ages remained the same during the next 30 to 35 years.

transform fault – a zone along which two lithospheric plates are moving past each other laterally.

transhumance – the seasonal movement of livestock to take advantage of seasonal changes in weather; commonly from lowlands to adjacent highland basins for grazing in the warmer months and back to the lowlands in the cooler months.

tree line – the extent of mature tree growth; often considered the 50°F isotherm for the coolest month.

tsunamis – high seismic sea waves which travel across the ocean and often reach great heights as they encounter the shoreline.

Tundra Climate – a region of very short, cool summers (warmest month average under 50°F, or 10°C), extremely long and severe winters; only elementary vegetation, such as mosses and lichens; located almost entirely on the northern margins and adjacent islands of continents poleward of 60° N. Latitude, except on the east coasts; also on the coastal margins of Greenland.

Ultisols – heavily leached and weathered soils with clay accumulations; located mainly in Humid Subtropical and wetter margins of Savannah Climates.

urban – in general, an incorporated place of 2,500 or more people and the surrounding closely settled territory, plus additional census designated places (CDPs).

"urban villages" ("edge cities") – U.S. suburban complexes dominated by office, retail, and hotel establishments.

Vertisols – soils in semi-arid to sub-humid areas which contain large quantities of clay and which expand and contract with the alternating wetting through precipitation and drying through evaporation.

volcanic eruption – an explosive volcanic extrusion spewing forth various forms of molten material and gases.

wave-cut cliff – a steep ocean-facing cliff formed by the erosive action of waves at its base and by mass wasting.

windward – the side or direction from which the wind is blowing.

xerophytic – drought resistant vegetation found in deserts.

zone of contact – the elongated area where the leading edge (front) of a warm, moist mass of air meets and rises over the leading edge (front) of a cool air mass leading to the formation of low pressure.

INDEX

A
accreted terrane 23, 54, 58
African American 125-126, 136, 138-141, 171, 178-181
age-sex pyramid 154-155
agribusiness 196
agricultural exports/imports 193-194
agricultural regions 197-203
air mass 81-84, 89
Alfisols 104-105, 197, 201
alluvium 104
Appalachia 177
aquifer 52
Aridisols 103, 106, 203
asthenosphere 21, 23
atmospheric hazards 84-96

B
Batholith 58
Bingham Canyon Copper Mine 24
biomes 104-105
birth rate 152
bison 104, 106, 115-117
bog 105
Boreal 105
British North American Act 130
Bryce Canyon National Park 20
bulk breaking point 207

C
caldera 59-60
Canadian Shield 65-66, 105
caribou 115-116
cartography 5-6, 11-12, 14
cattle production 200-201
cavern 44-45
center of gravity (population) 140-141
center pivot irrigation 192
central place theory 216-218
Cherokee 133-134
Chloroflourocarbons (CFCs) 96-97
choropleth 6

climate 81, 97-106
coniferous 104-105
continental shelf 34
corn belt 197, 200
craton 21
crust (see lithosphere)
cyclonic precipitation 83

D
dairy belt 200-201
death (mortality) rate 138, 153-154, 174, 180
deciduous 102, 104-105
Desert Climate 99, 106, 203
direction 14-15
distance 14-15
Doppler Radar 86, 89-90
Dow Jones Index 220
drift 47
drought
Dry Subtropical (Mediterranean) Climate 99-100
Dust Bowl 51-52

E
earthquake 26-30, 64
edge cities 166, 215
El Nino 94
energy supply 207, 210-211
Entisols 103, 105
epicenter 27-28, 64
escarpment 46, 49
esker 47
estuary 4, 121

F
farm ownership 195-196
farm size 195
fault 27, 63-64
faulting 27, 54, 57
federal debt 222-223

fertility 137-138, 140, 152-156, 165-166, 180
fiord 60, 65
fissures (lava) 57, 76
focus (earthquake) 27-28, 64
footloose industry 210
formal region 8
front 83-84, 89
Fujita tornado scale 89
functional region 8-9
fur trade 121, 123, 125, 129, 142

G
geologic hazards 26-31
geosyncline 44, 46
geyser 54, 57
glacial 37, 47, 49, 61-62, 66
glaciation 21, 47, 49, 60-62, 65
glacier 45-47, 54, 58-62, 65
global climate change 96-97
greenhouse effect 80, 94, 96
groin 88
ground moraine 47

H
hail 91-92
Hawaiian Islands 67
Highland Climate 99
hinterland 4, 142, 144, 164
Hispanic 151, 153, 167, 169-171, 178-180
Histosols 103, 105
Homestead Act 130
hot spot islands 67
Humid Continental, Cool Summer Climate 98-99, 105, 201
Humid Continental, Warm Summer Climate 98-99, 104, 197
Humid Subtropical Climate 98-100, 203
humus 106
hurricane 80, 84-89
    Andrew 86-87
    Dennis 80, 87
    Galveston 86-87
    Hazel 86-87
    Hugo 86-87
    Katrina 86-88
hydrophytes 104
hygrophytes 105

I
igneous 24, 41, 54
immigrant 135, 137-138, 149, 151, 153-159, 166-167, 169
immigration 132-138, 152-160, 170, 180
Inceptisols 103-105
indentured servants 125-126, 135
infant mortality rate 153-154, 174, 180, 182
Interior Lowlands 46-51
internal migration 159-162
Inuit 132, 142
isotherm 98

J
jet stream 81, 83, 94

K
karst 44-45

L
lacustrine 47
lateral moraine 61
latitude/longitude 3, 14-15, 18
lava 24, 30, 57, 67
leach 100, 104-105
leeward 81, 99
lithosphere 23
location
    absolute 3
    relative 4
location quotient 219
loess 28
long lots 121-122

M
magma 23-24, 30-31, 54, 67
magnitude 27, 30, 64
maize 115-118
manufacturing belt 208, 212-213
map- definition 6
map- oldest 5-6
Marine West Coast Climate 99-100, 105
market area 216-218
Mediterranean Climate 99-100, 105
Meech Lake Accord 143
mesophytes 104
metamorphic 41, 54
Mexican Cession 128
migrant trails 130-131
migration 115, 144, 151, 159-162, 165-166, 178
minerals 24-25, 45-46, 54
Missouri Coteau 49
Mollisols 103, 106
Moment Magnitude Scale 27, 64
monadnock 40-41
mortality rate (see death rate)

N
Native Americans 115-118
natural increase 152-153, 170
nodal 9
North American Free Trade Agreement (NAFTA) 224

O
Ogallala Aquifer 52, 93
Oregon Compromise 128-129
orographic 81, 99, 105
outwash 45-46
ozone 96-97

P
Pangea 21
panoramic map 114
Parti Quebecois 143
pedalfer 100, 104
pedocal 100, 106
permafrost 105
physiography 24
plate tectonics 21-23
pluton 58
pollution 210
poverty 164, 174-182
Prevailing Westerlies 81, 83-84, 99-100
prime interest rate 220-221
pueblo 117

Q
quaternary 191, 215
Quebec Act of 1774 130
quinary 191, 215

R
rain shadow 81
recessional moraine 47, 49
remote sensing 5, 7, 11
replacement level (fertility) 137, 153-154
research and development 213-214
Richter scale 27, 64

S
Saffir-Simpson Scale 84-85
Saguaro National Park 2
Savanna Climate 97
secondary employment (sector) 191
sediment 34, 37-39, 50
sedimentary 24, 43, 46, 49, 54
seismic wave 27, 64
sinkhole 44
site 4
situation 4
specialty industries 209
Spodosols 103, 201

Subarctic 98, 105-106
subduction 23

T
taiga 105
terminal moraine 47, 61
tertiary sector 191, 215
till 49, 61
time zones 18-19
tobacco 200, 203
tornado 89-91
total fertility rate 153, 156
trade balance 224-225
Trail of Tears 134
transform fault 63-64
transhumance 53, 99
tree line 98
tsunamis 28-29, 64
Tundra 98-99, 104-106

U
Ultisols 103, 104, 203
urban villages 215

V
Vertisols 103
volcanic 21, 26, 31, 48, 54, 57, 59-60, 67
volcano 24, 26, 30-31, 59, 67

W
wheat belt 200-201
Wheeling, WV 114
windward 81, 99
worker productivity 205-206

X
xerophytes 104, 106

Z
zone of contact 83